SEEING
AND BELIEVING

SEEING
AND BELIEVING

RELIGION,
DIGITAL VISUAL CULTURE,
AND SOCIAL JUSTICE

ELLEN T.
ARMOUR

Columbia University Press　*New York*

Columbia University Press

Publishers since 1893

New York, Chichester, West Sussex

cup.columbia.edu

Copyright © 2023 Columbia University Press

All rights reserved

Library of Congress Cataloging-in-Publication Data
Names: Armour, Ellen T., 1959– author.
Title: Seeing and believing : religion, digital visual culture,
and social justice / Ellen T. Armour.
Description: New York : Columbia University Press, [2023] |
Includes bibliographical references and index.
Identifiers: LCCN 2022050762 (print) | LCCN 2022050763 (ebook) |
ISBN 9780231209045 (hardback) | ISBN 9780231209052 (trade paperback) |
ISBN 9780231557764 (ebook)
Subjects: LCSH: Visual sociology. | Digital media—Social aspects. |
Photojournalism—Political aspects. | Photography—Psychological
aspects. | Journalism and social justice.
Classification: LCC HM500 .A76 2023 (print) | LCC HM500 (ebook) |
DDC 302.23/1—dc23/eng/20221222
LC record available at https://lccn.loc.gov/2022050762
LC ebook record available at https://lccn.loc.gov/2022050763

Cover design: Noah Arlow

This book is dedicated to my colleagues in the 2017–2018 Robert Penn Warren Center for the Humanities Faculty Fellows Program.

CONTENTS

ACKNOWLEDGMENTS

I have many people to thank for making *Seeing and Believing* possible. First, the students who took my course Theology, Visual Culture, and New Media in 2017 and in 2021. As is so often the case, I learned as much from them as they did from me, I'm certain—as later chapters will attest. I truly could not have written this book without the support of the doctoral students who served as my research assistants at different stages of this project: Zachary Settles, Htoi San Lu, and Debbie Brubaker. Zac and Htoi were particularly helpful in bringing new resources to my attention and Debbie in whipping the manuscript into shape for submission for review. Debbie also participated in both iterations of my course, first as a student in 2017 and then as my teaching assistant in 2021. Her thoughtful and generative partnership impacted what we all learned from the 2021 version in more ways than I can count. My thanks, as well, to former doctoral student Dr. Travis Ables for producing the index.

I am grateful, as well, to my editor and publisher at Columbia University Press, Wendy Lochner, and her colleagues for seeing this book through the review process all the way to publication. I owe the manuscript's anonymous reviewers many thanks for their feedback. *Seeing and Believing* is the better for it, as I hope they will agree.

I've had several opportunities to try out various aspects of the argument in *Seeing and Believing* at academic conferences and invited talks. My thanks to the organizers of the second annual Political Theology Network Conference sponsored by Union Theological Seminary and Columbia University in October 2017; of the Exploratory Session on Race, Coloniality, and the Philosophy of Religion held at the November 2017 Annual Meeting of the American Academy of Religion; and to the participants and attendees at the Scholar's Session held on my body of work as a whole (a tremendous honor in itself) at the October 2019 annual meeting of the Society for Phenomenology and Existential Philosophy. (My deep gratitude to Ladelle McWhorter and Lynne Huffer for all the time, effort, and profound insight that informed their generous assessments there of the scholarly work I've produced over the years.) I also benefited significantly from Shannon Winnubst's response to my previous book (which informs *Seeing and Believing*), initially at a session on it at the 2017 meeting of the Society for Phenomenology and Existential Philosophy, and subsequently in the online journal *Symposium* (cited later in this volume). Thanks as well to Mayra Rivera, Ron Hall and his colleague Melinda Hall, and Margaret McLaren for invitations to speak at Harvard Divinity School, Stetson University (my alma mater), and Rollins College, respectively. The talk I gave at Harvard gave me the opportunity to test out the fundamental framework of *Seeing and Believing*. The talks at Stetson and Rollins allowed me to experiment with applying that framework in ways that advanced my progress on *Seeing and Believing*.

I had the great honor of being selected to participate in the 2017–2018 Faculty Fellows Program, "Telling Stories, Stories

That Tell," sponsored by Vanderbilt University's Robert Penn Warren Center for the Humanities and led by my colleagues and now friends Dr. Laura Carpenter (sociology) and Dr. Catherine Molineux (history). The feedback provided by my fellow participants was invaluable to what *Seeing and Believing* became, and I will be forever grateful to all of them and to the center's staff members Mona Frederick (executive director, now retired), Terry Tripp, and Emma Furman. My deep gratitude as well to Vanderbilt University for its ongoing support of the center's vital work.

The Robert Penn Warren Faculty Fellowships included funding for the fellows to commission a work of art that would serve as a visual and tactile record of our collective work. We selected Britt Stadig, who created an amazing set of art books—one for each faculty member's project. My deepest thanks to Britt for rendering my vision for the project in such a powerful and moving way. The physical art books (including "Seeing Is Believing," which represents what became *Seeing and Believing)* reside in Vanderbilt University Library's Special Collections. Interested readers can see Amanda McCadams's photographs of all of them on the website created and maintained by the Library, http://tellingstoriesstoriesthattell.com/. Reproduced herein (and on the cover) are McCadams's excellent photographs of "Seeing Is Believing." My thanks to Amanda for sharing them with me for this purpose. Thanks as well to Special Collections staff members librarian Celia S. Walker and Special Curator Kathleen Smith (along with Laura Carpenter) for their assistance in securing them.

As always, I am grateful to my family—particularly my spouse, Barbee Majors—for their support. The year I participated in the Faculty Fellows Program was bookended by the death of my elderly mother in the fall, a beloved uncle a few weeks later, then of my father the following spring, and of a beloved aunt a few weeks after that. (That season of loss was followed a year later by the death of my advisor, the inimitable Sallie McFague, and another beloved aunt in August 2021.) Barbee has been there for me through it all and through all the other challenges that have come our way before and since—as I have tried to be for her. I am so fortunate to have such a wise, steadfast, loving, and resilient partner in the bumpy journey that is life.

I was not the only faculty fellow to reckon with the loss of family members over the course of our time together. But heartbreaking for all of us was the untimely death of our colleague John Janusak, also a faculty fellow. Going through loss together deepened the bond among us. I dedicate *Seeing and Believing* to my fellow faculty fellows James F. Brooks, Laura M. Carpenter, the late John Janusak, Shaul Kelner, Stan Link, Letizia Modena, Catherine Molineux, Jonathan Rattner, and Haerin Shin.

PREFACE

I f there was any question about the power of the conjunc-
tion of visual and social media to move people and propel
social or political change, two major events from 2020 to
2021 surely put that to rest. On May 25, 2020, a cell phone video
posted on social media showing Minneapolis police officer Derek
Chauvin casually and blatantly killing a Black man named
George Floyd by kneeling on his neck for over nine minutes led
to the largest protest—26 million people—in American history.[1]
Although particularly brutal, it was only the latest in a series of
videos of killings of people of color (men, women, trans folk, and
even children) by police (and self-appointed white vigilantes)—
with more to come. This proved to be a tipping point in multi-
racial, transgenerational, corporate, and international support for
the #BlackLivesMatter movement in the United States and in
many places around the globe.[2] Then, on January 6, 2021, supporters of soon-to-be-former president Donald J. Trump forced
their way into the U.S. Capitol in an ultimately unsuccessful
attempt to stop the U.S. Congress from certifying the election
of Joe Biden to replace him. Subsequent criminal inquiries—
aided by videos posted by the insurrectionists of the event

itself—found that many of them had organized themselves on social media.[3]

Photographs and videos generate, amplify, and accelerate what I call "photographic story lines." But photographic story lines can run in multiple directions. The #BlackLivesMatter movement began (on Twitter, note) in response to an event that went unphotographed but that is part of Floyd's photographic story line, the killing of Trayvon Martin by George Zimmerman.[4] But that event also generated another branch to this photographic story line that channels white supremacist violence, one that also continues to expand as I write.

In *Seeing and Believing: Religion, Digital Visual Culture, and Social Justice*, I inquire into the visual culture generated by the confluence of new technologies (digital photography, cell phones, the internet, and social media platforms, to be specific) and its impact on the ongoing struggle for social justice. As the story line I just mentioned indicates, while common parlance distinguishes between "virtual," or online, life and "real" life, the line between them is blurry at best. Indeed, that is true of photography itself—as a technology and as a social practice. *Seeing and Believing* extends the line of inquiry at the heart of my last book, *Signs and Wonders: Theology after Modernity*.[5] There, I offered an account of what I call "photographic subjection." Drawing on the work of Michel Foucault and scholarship on analogue photography and visual culture theory, I argued that photography (en)trains us in modern modes of seeing, knowing, doing, and being. When we pose for, shoot, or just glance at photographs—of ourselves or of others, whether we know them or not—we subject ourselves to bio-disciplinary power trained on us by the camera's lens. I traced and tracked the theological, philosophical, and political foundations and effects of these ways of knowing, doing, and being in and through four sets of photographs and the events they reference.[6] Those events all took place between 2003 and 2005. Much has changed about photography as a technology and a practice between then and now. A central question for *Seeing and Believing* is understanding the impact of these changes on our lives—individual and communal.

Signs and Wonders concluded with the observation that we need a new philosophy of life: a new ontology and a new ethos that face up to, rather than disavow, vulnerability and interconnection. Locating resources for a new ontology will have to wait for another time, but the questions I pursue in *Seeing and Believing* and the resolutions I offer embody the goal of sourcing a new ethos. The scholarship I engage herein demonstrates that the challenges and affordances offered by life online trade on both vulnerability and interconnection. I build organically on those insights from *Signs and Wonders* that remain particularly relevant to my concerns here by prioritizing recent scholarship by scholars whose earlier work was essential to that project.[7] This allows me to keep *Seeing and Believing* relatively brief and, I hope, more accessible to a wider audience—an important goal given the urgency of the immense challenges we face. That means, of course, that the perspective I offer is limited in some ways. For example, as I've noted, the photographic story line that anchors *Seeing and Believing* includes both videos and still photographs, but my focus continues to be the latter (as was the case in *Signs and Wonders*). This is due, first and foremost, to the specific opportunities that still photographs offer us, as will become clear later. I also think it's important not to conflate still photography with videography, a distinctive genre of visual media with its own body of scholarship. Giving that genre and that body of scholarship the focused attention it requires will have to wait for another time and place, especially given my primary goal for *Seeing and Believing*.[8] That goal also generates another limitation. Though it informs *Seeing and Believing*, the full scope of the deep dive I took in *Signs and Wonders* into the history of photography, visual culture studies, and other bodies of scholarship will be largely invisible here to readers unfamiliar with that book. I invite readers interested in those matters to read it as well.

My goal for *Seeing and Believing*, however, is what primarily distinguishes this project from its predecessor. If the focus of *Signs and Wonders* was on understanding photographic subjection, *Seeing and Believing* aims to promote its disruption, or what I'll call "photographic insurrection." Also, because it was imbricated in the systems and structures that promoted photographic subjection, religion—Christianity, specifically—was primarily part of the problem I analyzed in *Signs and Wonders*. Here, however, resources found in religion—specifically, in religious ways of seeing—are central to the strategies of intervention I propose. While those ways of seeing may be helpful when engaging videos, the kind of attention they call for is particularly well suited for engaging with still photographs, I will argue.

Though my turn to religion as a resource occurs in the final chapter, religion's pertinence to the topic at hand emerges much earlier—and not only (or even primarily) from direct engagement with work by religious studies scholars. It turns out that a certain metaphorical theo-logic widely associated with Christianity appears in scholarship on social media and its visual culture that has no explicit connection to the study of religion at all. That may be surprising to some readers but not to me. As I argued in the introduction to *Signs and Wonders*, thanks to its imbrication in colonialism and its successor, globalization, Christian theologics are in the (cultural) air we breathe and the (cultural) water we drink. As I document in subsequent chapters, scholars of social media see our new media ecosystem as godlike in the scope and power of its reach. Thus, they turn to traditional theological tropes like omniscience (God knows all) and omnipotence (God controls all) as metaphors to convey these insights—and quite effectively. This theo-logic persuasively illuminates this ecosystem's effect on us and on our world. However, I'll argue that it also risks overestimating its all-too-human limitations.[9]

Though I may be the first philosophical theologian to do so, I am hardly the first scholar of religion to analyze and try to respond to the challenges and affordances of our new media ecosystem. Nor am I the first to attend specifically to the role photography plays in this ecosystem and thus in our individual and social lives. Indeed, though there are important differences between them, my approach is similar to that of pastoral theologian Sonia Waters's 2017 essay written in the wake of the wave of protests prompted by the police killing of Michael Brown in Ferguson, Missouri.[10] My own attempt will be informed by some but by no means all of this growing body of scholarship.

Another aspect of my approach here differentiates *Seeing and Believing* from its predecessor. While *Signs and Wonders* focused on four specific sets of photographs of four different events, *Seeing and Believing* is anchored in the (still-expanding) photographic story line I limn above. While in many ways this story line is paradigmatic of the opportunities and challenges before us, it is hardly the only one for which the questions I'll raise are relevant, as I'll observe from time to time. For example, in the months following Floyd's killing, videos posted on social media documented Asians and Asian Americans being assaulted and even killed on the street after Trump dubbed COVID-19 the "China flu," rightly prompting calls for attention to the long but often neglected history of anti-Asian racism. But this story line provides a particularly rich context for my project for reasons that, I trust, will become clear as it unfolds.

Beginning with the visual image that precedes each chapter, I will invite readers to engage this story line and the analysis that it anchors through photographs of a visual artifact: an art book inspired by the then-nascent *Seeing and Believing* that was created by Nashville artist Britt Stadig.[11] (For more of the art book's origin story and the photographs that appear therein, please see the acknowledgments.) I cannot imagine a more powerful artistic representation of *Seeing and Believing*. The art book's combination of visual, tactile, and verbal elements, of the sacred and the mundane, presents the viewer with a sobering challenge that is both personal and social. It is my hope that the chapters that follow make good on the promise embodied in Stadig's amazing work.

Of course, I undertake this project not as an artist but as a scholar of religion—and a particular kind at that. First, a few words about the definition of "religion," itself a highly contested term, that I'll be working with herein. The word "religion" comes from the Latin *religio*, which is likely derived from *religare*, which means "to (re)bind." Religion, as I understand it, consists of multiple connections that bind religious practitioners to one another, to their world, and to what transcends it. Religious studies scholar Catherine Albanese provides a definition that lays out such an understanding of religion especially well. According to Albanese, religion is "a system of symbols (creed, code, cultus) by means of which people (a community) orient themselves in the world with reference to ordinary and extraordinary powers, meanings, and values."[12] This definition speaks to the multiple dimensions of religion—as a system of belief, yes, but primarily as a set of practices.[13] Creed gives the words that encode authoritative beliefs their due, but code, cultus, and community remind us that words alone are not enough. Religion also lives in rituals both communal and individual (cultus) and is lived out in how the community of adherents behave (code). We may commonly associate religion only with the extraordinary (deities or spirits, say), but Albanese reminds us that the extraordinary is always bound up in and with the ordinary—the brick and mortar of a church, temple, or mosque; the paintings, sculptures, or calligraphy that may adorn sacred spaces; the food that makes up sacred meals. And, of course, there are the quite ordinary human beings in all their complexity that make up religious communities in every tradition. Religion is, fundamentally, an embodied and enculturated phenomenon that interacts with other embodied and enculturated dimensions of our existence in all their complexity as well.

Scholarship in the study of religion is typically divided into descriptive and normative approaches, with theology (a term often confined to Christianity) consigned to the normative.[14] Based on its Greek etymology (*theos* = god; *logos* = word/reason), the discipline of theology is reasoned reflection on religious belief. Christian theologians like myself attempt not just to understand but to solve critical issues that confront our time and place. We do that critical and creative work in conversation with Christian traditions considered in light of the contemporary context. Doing that work well, of course, requires a "thick description" (in the words of sociologist Clifford Geertz) of the contemporary context and the issues at stake. To that end, theologians necessarily engage descriptive work not only in religious studies but well outside it. That is clearly the case for *Seeing and Believing*, as it has been with my previous work, including *Signs and Wonders*.

That I turn to Christian ways of seeing as resources for navigating the problems we face more productively and ethically may seem to meet expectations for a book by a theologian. However, that very turn disrupts those expectations in several ways. First of all, the particular visual repertoire on offer here (drawn from the work of the prominent scholar of visual culture and religion David Morgan in *The Embodied Eye*) may be grounded in Christianity, but Morgan also finds these ways of seeing present in other religious traditions.[15] Most importantly, given my goals for *Seeing and Believing*, these ways of seeing are built on ways of seeing exercised by all of us in our ordinary everyday interactions with what we see. Christian theologians typically address a primarily Christian audience. That has never been true of my work and it is not the case now. The challenges it identifies confront all of us in our time and place—whether we identify as Christian or not, as people of faith or not. If these ways of seeing did not "come naturally" to all of us, they would, in the end, be of little use.[16]

Having situated *Seeing and Believing*'s relationship to the study of religion and to theology in particular, let me now dig more deeply into its overall framework by saying more about the concepts embedded in its title and subtitle. Following many of the scholars of visual culture whose work I draw on here and in *Signs and Wonders*, I understand seeing as much more than the physiological impact of visual data registered by our brains through the visual organs we call our eyes. For one thing, seeing often occurs in concert with one or more of our other senses (hearing, smelling, touch, taste), including proprioception, which orients our bodies in space, and the vestibular sense, which maintains equilibrium and balance. But equally important, as Morgan writes in *The Sacred Gaze*, "Vision happens in and as culture, as the tools, artifacts, assumptions, learned behaviors, and unconscious promptings that are exerted in images. But seeing is about more than its product. . . . [It] is an operation that relies on an apparatus of assumptions and inclinations, habits and routines, historical associations and cultural practices."[17] That's true, he argues, for all ways of seeing, including religious seeing. All ways of seeing are embodied and enculturated practices—a claim that resonates well with photography's impact on us, as I argued in *Signs and Wonders* (and reprise later herein). What we see can "move" us—emotionally or to take action. Our responses to what we see run the gamut of emotions. Running across a photograph of a deceased loved one can prompt grief or consolation; encountering a famous painting, awe or disdain; watching a football game on TV, celebration, disappointment, or boredom; seeing a video that documents violence, disgust and outrage or nothing at all. How we respond to what we see is as much a product of culture as nature, of social as much as physical location.

The invention and adoption of new visual technologies also impacts not only *what* we see but *how* we see; that is, how we understand and experience seeing—and thus, I argue, on who and how we are in the world. As I observe in *Signs and Wonders*, scholars in the history of analogue photography Jonathan Crary and John Tagg document that technology's impact on those matters—including how we have come to experience and understand space and time—quite persuasively.[18] *Seeing and Believing* takes up that narrative with reference to digital photography. In many ways, this new technology simply expands and amplifies analogue photography's impact. But it also raises new issues for seeing and its import, issues exacerbated by other new technologies, including the cell phone camera, the internet, and social media. Tracing and tracking that confluence is central to *Seeing and Believing*.

Together, these new technologies have generated what I'm calling *digital visual culture*. Let me explain what I mean by that. The humanities and the social sciences are well known for giving birth to various interdisciplinary fields of study; what we now know as gender and sexuality studies or the currently unfairly maligned critical race theory are two examples. In recent years, a new interdisciplinary field called visual culture studies has also emerged, a phenomenon Morgan tracks in *The Sacred Gaze*. Visual culture studies recognizes that visual media are as important to human cultures as any form of expression and engagement. It calls attention to the role that what and how we see—informed by, and in turn informing, what and how we think and feel—plays in the construction, sustenance, and potential transformation of our worlds. Visual culture studies, Morgan argues, is therefore "a practice-centered discourse" attuned to how, when, and why we interact with visual images.[19] It seeks to understand "what images do when they are put to use."[20] The ways of seeing that constitute those practices are often embedded in or connected to other aspects of culture (religion, nationhood, sex/race/gender/ethnicity, etc.). Thus, Morgan opines that scholarship in visual culture can be produced by scholars in a variety of fields when they address visual media and ways of seeing.

Of course, as Morgan also makes clear, visual media are not really isolable from other forms of mediation. For the first one hundred–plus years of photography's existence, we often encountered photographs (still and moving) through what scholars now refer to as "legacy media": newspapers and magazines and, later, movies and television.[21] Still photographs that circulate in print serve primarily as illustrations whose meaning is supplemented, if not conveyed, by the accompanying words. Videos shown on TV or in movie theaters tell their stories via sight and sound (commentary and ambient noises, in the case of TV news coverage; words mouthed by the actors or written on screen and live musical accompaniment in the case of early silent movies; scripted dialogue and soundtracks along with ambient noises, as video technology advanced). Engaging with visual media, then, is often a multisensory experience. Indeed, W.J.T. Mitchell argues (rightly, in my view) that we need to redefine what we mean by "visual media" to reflect the multisensory nature of seeing and the multisensory nature of what we typically think we (merely) see.[22] Though I will continue to use the term "visual media" on occasion in what follows, it is always with the caveat that most, if not all, visual media involve at least one other sense: that of touch, our mode of access to them.

The new technologies at the center of *Seeing and Believing* inaugurated a dramatic shift not only in how photographs are made (whether by amateurs or professionals like photojournalists) but also in how we encounter and consume them. Though their numbers have declined substantially, legacy media still exist but have migrated online, which is where most of us consume what they produce. The same is true of the photographs and videos that we produce and consume in all their variety (e.g., souvenir photographs or selfies, memes or TikToks). Understanding digital visual culture, then, requires attention not only to the visual artifacts that populate it but also to the technologies that make them possible and the media platforms that house and circulate them. Only then can we really grapple with the perils and promise that this confluence creates. That said, as I'll make clear, digital visual culture is just as imbricated in and with embodiment and other aspects of culture as any analogue visual culture. Thus, *Seeing and Believing* will attend to those dimensions of it as well.

As this book's title promises, though, I also will be arguing that seeing is connected to believing. That connection is the linchpin of my turn to Morgan's scholarship on religious ways of seeing to address the challenges we face. Understanding how seeing connects to believing requires expanding what many of us assume belief to be, especially those of us steeped in Christian theology, my home discipline. As Morgan observes, theologians typically understand belief as conscious assent to a proposition. This understanding, he argues, reflects the long history of Christian theology's concern with orthodoxy (right thinking). (That this definition of belief is endemic in religious studies more broadly is one of many unfortunate consequences of Christianity's formative role in the field's genesis.) Understanding and appreciating belief's role in religious seeing, however, requires attention to what ordinary religious practitioners do—with conscious intent or not—rather than to what religious elites say (theology's primary concern, Morgan argues). He also observes that belief informs all aspects of religious doing: speaking (praying, reading, testifying), smelling (e.g., incense), how believers treat others. Like seeing, believing requires a body as well as a mind (which itself requires a very complicated body part—the brain—that is networked to the entire body). Like seeing, believing is an enculturated practice, one that interacts with other aspects of our social formation such as ethnicity, nationality, sexual/gender identity, and so on. Indeed, Morgan observes that belief isn't limited to religion but occurs in common parlance and behavior, another key insight for my project. "Belief may be an opinion, a fantasy, a groundless delusion, a conjecture, or an inference" about virtually anything.[23] We believe what certain people say but not others, for example; we believe we are driving in the right direction. And what we believe we see is often a reflection of how we've been formed. Belief is, in other words, mediated by embodiment and by culture, Morgan observes. Attending to the specific visual medium and the related artifacts that embody belief is critical not only to understanding religious seeing (Morgan's focus), I argue, but also to navigating the difficult challenges that confront all of us in this time and place. Which brings me, finally, to social justice. That we are caught up in fraught struggles for social justice is hardly a recent phenomenon either in the United States (my context and thus my primary focus here) or in many other countries around the globe. However, these struggles have also migrated online. That migration has come with all the complexities—positive and negative—that characterize digital visual culture. Ours has become a time and place characterized by division and polarization, by cultural conflict, by deep distrust of authorities and institutions large and small. This reality is both reflected in and exacerbated by digital visual culture. Whether we can believe what we see online is central to these dynamics, including the digital photographs and videos that we encounter there. And that is a matter of what I call in *Signs and Wonders* both photographic truth—whether we can trust that what a given photograph purports to show is real—and photographic affect, or how photographs "move" us, emotionally and sometimes to take action. No photograph or video—analogue or digital—moves all of us in the same way, as the photographic story line that anchors *Seeing and Believing* illustrates.

It is my intent to bring insights from the study of religion to bear on this challenge in particular. Thus, to be clear, while I certainly hope to contribute to these interdisciplines, I do not intend this book to be a full-fledged treatise on religion and visual culture or theology and visual culture. Readers more familiar than I am with those bodies of scholarship will, no doubt, find relevant issues and insights left unattended in *Seeing and Believing*—likely more of them than I could possibly address. I hope that *Seeing and Believing* will inspire others to take up these matters in their own work.

CHAPTER OUTLINE

Chapter 1 sets the stage for *Seeing and Believing* first by situating the project in relationship to the tectonic technological and cultural shifts generated by the convergence of new digital technologies with the new media ecosystem they've helped create. Photographs and videos play a particularly prominent role in the real-life social and political impact of that convergence. Understanding the similarities and differences between our contemporary (mostly digital) photographic lives and our previous (mostly analogue) ones will help us better navigate our current situation. Thus, this chapter also offers a summary of the approach I take in *Signs and Wonders* and its central arguments on its way toward describing the new ground that *Seeing and Believing* stakes out.

Chapters 2 and 3 focus on the role of social media in this tectonic shift. I track how our virtual world is (re)making time and space (chapter 2) and (re)making us (chapter 3) in the process. I say "*(re)*making" because scholarship shows that this tectonic shift we're experiencing is in many respects an expansion and acceleration of aspects of our reality that I tracked and traced in *Signs and Wonders*. The 24/7 connectivity that social media provides (courtesy of our smart phones, especially) provides instantaneous and potentially global access to others. But it also creates a sense of obligation to be "on" 24/7. This risks erasing the lines not only between the so-called virtual world and the real one but also between worktime and downtime, workspace and domestic space (something the COVID-19 pandemic has only exacerbated). The fact that we call social media platforms our new public square speaks to their remaking of public spaces as well. Though we inhabit this new public square via flat screens of various sizes, it creates new virtual spaces for gathering that intersect with gathering IRL (in real life) in various ways. Not only are we able to stay connected with geographically distant friends old and new, but our new public square also makes possible a level and form of social or political organizing that wasn't possible before. However, scholars of social media make clear that these opportunities come with costs and benefits, challenges and affordances. How can we make the most of the benefits and affordances while minimizing the costs and successfully navigating the challenges?

Chapter 3 digs more deeply into how online life is impacting what we see and thus what we (think we) know, what we do, effectively (re)making who we are. The visual images we interact with online are stored and accessed through digital information systems like the databases that Google and Facebook collect, house, and use. According to philosopher Colin Koopman, these digital information systems essentially "fasten" us to our data, thus determining who we are online, which both reflects and impacts who we are offline. Yet, he reminds us, they are not the first information technologies to do so. The (analogue) birth certificate, the driver's license, and the passport and the information systems in which they are embedded determine who we are, especially in the eyes of the state and its various agencies. These documents affect how easily we move through the world and give or deny us access to certain goods and services (public schools, the social safety net, etc.).[24]

Digital information systems and their analogue predecessors all too often channel biases embedded in the social systems that give rise to them—and with real-world effects. Driver's licenses, birth certificates, and passports classify us according to a mostly binary system of identity markers set up by those systems without regard for the complexities of how we identify. For example, the ability of trans folk to move quickly and easily through airport security is hampered if a gatekeeper's visual perception of them is at odds with their gender as documented on their passport. What we see online can also be impacted by social biases. We may think that, as essentially mathematical equations, the algorithms that determine what we see online (including visual images) are free of social biases, but they often encode and reinforce those biases, it turns out. Safiya Umoja Noble aptly dubs this "digital redlining," a reference to analogue redlining, the real estate assessment practices that produced color-coded maps of neighborhoods that guided racist lending practices.[25] (By the way, analogue redlining, one of the information systems that Koopman analyzes, demonstrably increased segregation and racial wealth disparities that persist to this day, as I note in chapter 3.)

Similarly, recent scholarship on digital photography and its impact (chapter 4) shows how it accelerates and amplifies certain features of analogue photography (as a technology and a practice) that I traced in *Signs and Wonders* even as it inaugurates others. Questions of seeing and believing are not new to photography, but socially mediated digital photography has made them, if anything, more critical. Exploring those questions—especially given the prominent role photographs and videos play in our new public square—is vital to both our virtual and our real lives. By "believe," I mean not only whether we trust what a given photograph purports to show (photographic truth) but also how photographs move us—emotionally and to take action (photographic affect). Like their analogue predecessors, digital photographs move us in different ways. Sadly, our default ways of seeing are all too often complicit with cultural biases like racism, sexism, ableism, and trans- and homophobia. This isn't necessarily intentional but reflects our own formation by the systems that gave rise to these biases. However, every now and then, a photograph or video—especially when posted on social media—breaks through normative and normalized ways of seeing and prompts us to see differently. That experience can set us down the path toward doing, knowing, and ultimately being differently. Seeing the videos of Black men being killed at the hands of police officers—especially the horrific video of Floyd's murder—has proven to be such an experience for many. How can we cultivate ways of seeing that open us up more deeply and more regularly to such opportunities? What might religious ways of seeing contribute to that goal?

This is the central challenge that drives *Seeing and Believing*. Responding to that challenge is, appropriately, the focus of its fifth and final chapter. I begin that chapter by laying out the need for a diverse visual repertoire of gazes setting criteria for them along the away, criteria that Morgan's gazes meet. It may surprise readers that I turn to these religious gazes as resources for photographic insurrection given that none of them directly address any of the social biases present in normative gazing. However, individually and together, they disrupt a central feature of biased normative seeing (evident, for example, in what philosopher George Yancy, whose work I also draw on here, calls "white gazes"): the hierarchical relationship of seer over seen. As evidence that these gazes can prompt nonnormative seeing, I describe the results of an assignment I gave students in my Theology, New Media, and Visual Culture class in the fall of 2021. My students' reflections on using this visual repertoire augur its promise. Finally, in the epilogue to *Seeing and Believing*, I maintain that photographic insurrection is not a panacea for all that ails us. However, cultivating it can potentially jump-start the deeper dive necessary to change the ways our current social and economic systems perpetuate long-standing inequities and injustices. The epilogue offers some final reflections on what *Seeing and Believing* has (I hope) achieved and my goals for what it can contribute to the struggle for social justice.

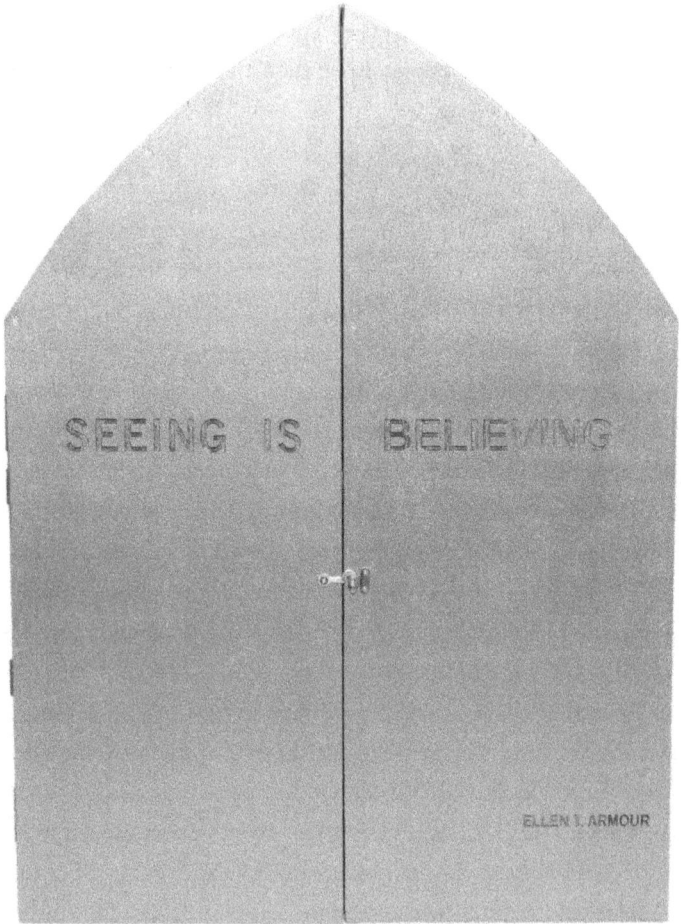

FIGURE 1.1 *Seeing Is Believing*, art book cover.
Artist: Britt Stadig. Photographer: Amanda McCadams.
Printed with the permission of Vanderbilt University.

1

SETTING THE STAGE

Human beings live in a world that is simultaneously real and
virtual, material and symbolic, sensate and mediated.

—Robert Hariman and John Louis Lucaites, *The Public Image*

Photographs . . . trade simultaneously on the prestige of art and
the magic of the real. They are clouds of fantasy and pellets of
information.

—Susan Sontag, *On Photography*

E arly in March 2020, the global pandemic of COVID-19
hit the United States and everything changed. Schools of
all kinds and at all levels pivoted from in-person to online
teaching, a wrenching change for everyone involved. Faith communities, too, shifted from in-person to online worship. Thanks
largely to the federal government's incompetence, what could have
been a relatively controlled outbreak was anything but—except in
states or cities with competent leadership (that is, leadership that
crafted policy based on the advice of public health experts). The
economic consequences were dire, with approximately 10 percent

of Americans suddenly unemployed and 25 percent anticipating losing their jobs within the next twelve months.[1] Those of us who could went into virtual quarantine at home, leaving "essential workers" (e.g., medical personnel, grocery store workers, agricultural laborers, and meatpacking plant employees) on the job and risking their lives as a result. The pandemic put in stark relief the dire consequences of decades-long policies that have eroded the social safety net, access to health care, and created economic inequality like the United States hasn't seen since the Gilded Age. Thanks to systemic racism, the consequences fell particularly hard on people of color.[2]

Then on May 25, two cell phone videos "went viral," as we say, on social media. One was the video of Minneapolis police officer Derek Chauvin kneeling on George Floyd's neck for nearly nine minutes, causing his death. The second, taken by Christian Cooper, a Black gay man, featured a cisgender (or cis) white woman, Amy Cooper (no relation), whom he encountered while birdwatching in Central Park. Mr. Cooper had asked Ms. Cooper to leash her dog, as required by law. Rather than complying, she called the police, claiming "a Black man" was threatening her and her dog. This time it was Ms. Cooper who paid the price for playing the race card, as she was fired from her prestigious job, had her dog taken from her for a while because she appeared to be choking the animal, and was later charged by the police with filing a false report.[3]

Coming on the heels of police killings of Tamir Rice, Sandra Bland, Michael Brown, and (just a few months earlier in 2020) Breonna Taylor, we found ourselves in a moment of racial reckoning manifest in a variety of ways. In addition to joining protests, white Americans formed reading groups centered on the work of public intellectuals like Ibram X. Kendi's *How to Be an Anti-Racist* and Robin DiAngelo's *White Fragility*.[4] Within two months, Confederate monuments in many southern states had been taken down, and the Confederate flag was removed from the Mississippi state flag and banned from NASCAR events.[5] All the major sports leagues—including the National Football League, which had been spectacularly tone-deaf (to put it mildly) to prior player protests inspired by these earlier events—endorsed and enabled forms of protest and expressions of solidarity and committed themselves to working for social change.

But these movements for change were met with resistance in various corners. Calls to "Defund the Police"—to provide resources for mental health professionals as first responders, where appropriate—were denounced as promoting anarchy. Individuals and groups motivated by white supremacism or white nationalism infiltrated #BlackLivesMatter (#BLM) protests stoking violence and destroying property. Then-president Trump refused to acknowledge their role, blaming the violence and destruction instead—without evidence—on antifa, a loosely affiliated group of self-identified antifascist resisters.[6] During a presidential debate, moderator Chris Wallace of Fox News asked Trump if he would denounce the white supremacist group the Proud Boys. Trump's response, in which he told the Proud Boys to "stand back and stand by," was heard by this organization not as a denunciation but as an endorsement, which they featured on Proud Boys' merchandise.[7] And then, during a #BLM protest in Washington, D.C., peaceful protesters were tear-gassed, allegedly to enable Trump to walk a few blocks from the White House and pose for a photo op outside St. John's Episcopal Church—traditionally, the president's church—holding up a Bible.[8]

It turned out that there was worse to come. On January 6, 2021, Congress had convened to certify the election of President-elect Joe Biden and Vice President–elect Kamala Harris when, incited by President Trump, rioters (including members of the

Proud Boys[9]) who had organized on social media descended upon the Capitol determined to "Stop the [nonexistent and fraudulent] Steal" by violent means. The lives of both Vice President Mike Pence and Speaker Nancy Pelosi were explicitly threatened, and they, along with Congress, were whisked away to safety as the insurrectionist mob was literally breaking down the doors to the congressional chambers.[10] At least five people died from the day's violence, including a Capitol Police officer beaten with a fire extinguisher and one protester shot by another officer as the break-in occurred.[11] The insurrection prompted a much-needed reckoning by many social media platforms and companies whose infrastructure provided access to them. Twitter and Facebook, for example, removed a significant number of groups and individuals from its platforms—including President Trump (Twitter permanently, Facebook and Instagram temporarily).[12] Google and Apple removed Parler, a lesser-known social media platform that had become home to far-right extremists, from their app stores. Amazon removed it from their servers, which had hosted Parler, causing it to go completely dark.[13]

These photographic story lines provide a point of entrée into the problem that *Seeing and Believing* aims to address. They limn some of the ways that our flesh-and-blood lives—individual and communal; social, political, and religious—intertwine with our virtual ones; that is, the lives we lead online, including our photographic lives. The benefits and drawbacks of our new media ecosystem and the new technologies that enable it are on prominent display in all of these photographic story lines. On the one hand, without these new technologies, teaching, worship, and social gatherings would have ground to a complete halt. But relying solely on these technologies made users all too aware of the limits to the connectivity they enable. Schools had to wrestle with the reality of unequal access to reliable access to the internet, especially in rural areas and in poorer urban areas (traditionally underserved in all kinds of ways). Even with the best service, the platforms themselves can still be glitchy and annoying. And while they are certainly better than sheer isolation, Zoom and its ilk are a pale substitute for human contact in many respects. Seeing someone else's face in a small two-dimensional box on a screen and hearing their voice even through state-of-the-art headphones or earbuds cannot substitute for the full sensory experience of sharing physical (rather than virtual) space with others.

These costs and benefits pale in significance to the political impact and import of life on our new media landscape. Social media and the technologies that feed them mobilize, accelerate, and expand political movements not only online but also in real life—to peaceful *and* violent ends. How can we harness their benefits while mitigating the serious harms they can do?

These story lines call attention to the literal life-giving or death-dealing impact of our so-called virtual world on the "real" one, but the relationship runs both ways. Moreover, the virtual is every bit as real—that is, physical—as our actual flesh and blood. Though it won't be my focus here, it's important to remember that our virtual lives would not exist without the hardware and hardwire that constitute the World Wide Web, a global network of physical computers connected by a physical network of cables and fueled by various energy sources. Many of us store what we produce on our personal devices in "the cloud," a euphemism for networks of massive computers called "servers" housed in climate-controlled giant warehouses often hidden from view. Those computers and cables and the microchips and other devices embedded in them that actually do the computing are engineered, encoded, installed, laid, monitored, and cared for by specially trained human beings. They are, moreover, produced from metals, plastics, and other materials mined or manufactured by other human beings—sometimes at great cost to their health and to the environment. To say that the World Wide Web and all it makes possible impacts every dimension of our lives is no exaggeration.[14]

My reference to our "new media landscape" or "new media ecosystem" is intentionally multilayered, intentionally literal and metaphorical. It would not exist without the infrastructure I just described, an infrastructure that impacts our physical landscapes and our ecosystem. But it has also impacted the production and consumption of the more metaphorical media landscape and ecosystem in ways that are more than physical. Before the advent of the internet, so-called legacy media served as the gatekeepers of our access to information. Newspapers, magazines, radio, and television outlets paid journalists to cover local, national, and global events and employed editors to decide which ones we needed to know about. While such outlets and gatekeepers still exist, they now must compete for our attention on a new virtual landscape. The social media platforms that constitute it were originally created to enable social connections, but they have become for many of us our primary sources of access to information about what is going on in our world. While some of that information still comes from traditional media outlets (either through purchased placements or as readers/viewers share it), it can now come directly from those impacted by or participating in events. Moreover, social media platforms allow us to share directly and immediately with our virtual networks not only what we see or hear but also what we think or feel about it. Thanks to "smart phones"—that is, cellular phones that are powerful little computers—we can engage in those activities anytime and (almost) anywhere. And because our smart phones are equipped with digital cameras, photographs and videos constitute much of that content, rendering this new landscape visually saturated.

Whether we can believe what we see online is a very real and existential question. In December 2016 a man armed with an assault rifle fired two shots into a Washington, D.C., pizza restaurant that, thanks to conspiracy theorists on 4chan, he believed was the site of a child sex trafficking operation run by Hillary Clinton and John Podesta.[15] In 2019 a video of Speaker of the House Nancy Pelosi (D-CA) that had been edited to seem as though she were slurring her words circulated widely online (thanks in part to President Trump).[16] And alarm bells started sounding well in advance of the 2020 election about so-called deepfakes.[17] These are photographs (still or moving) in which the original photographed subject's face has been replaced with someone else's, effectively substituting someone who wasn't present for the person who was. Whether one could believe what one saw in a photograph—analogue or digital—has always been a question, as photographs, following the epigraph above by Susan Sontag, have always been both "clouds of fancy" and "pellets of information," but the combination of new technology and new media puts concerns about seeing and believing on steroids. While analogue photographs are certainly vulnerable to manipulation (during and after their production), it requires a degree of skill possessed by a relative few. Our smart phones come with rudimentary editing capacity built in. Apps that allow for more elaborate editing are readily available too. More to the point, as we'll see later, while analogue photographs require the presence of a visual object in front of the lens, digital photographs can be generated ex nihilo.

But seeing and believing isn't just about whether we can trust what we see; it also pertains to how we respond to what we see. We believe so strongly in what we see in certain photographs that we are "moved"—emotionally and to take action. But a given photograph doesn't move all of us in the same way or in the same direction. For some, a photograph of a young Black teenage boy in a gray hoodie arouses fear and distrust—not in whether the photograph accurately represents a real person but due to what they assume about and thus expect from a *real* young Black teenage boy in a gray hoodie.

As I noted in the preface, *Seeing and Believing* builds on my previous book, *Signs and Wonders: Theology after Modernity*. *Signs and Wonders* centered on photography's role in crucial challenges—national and global, theological and philosophical, social and political—that we face as we live into modernity's anticipated end.[18] These challenges are the effects of the outworking of two forms of power that philosopher Michel Foucault identifies as distinctively modern: biopower and disciplinary power ("bio-disciplinary power," for short).[19] Disciplinary power is a system of carrots and sticks that runs through modern institutions like prisons, clinics, and asylums (as well as the modern school, workplace, and family). It uses those carrots and sticks to mold human beings into docile subjects: avowed delinquents, compliant patients, obedient workers, good boys and girls. Biopower harnesses disciplinary power to serve its goal of nurturing human life by eliminating social and biological abnormality. Following Ladelle McWhorter, I argue that bio-disciplinary power is both positively and negatively—productively (for white people) and destructively (for everyone else)—racist.[20] While so-called abnormalities are to be found throughout the human race, they have an uncanny knack for allegedly taking root in minoritized populations. Thus, these populations suffer bio-disciplinary power's most virulent and violent effects.

Though Foucault doesn't make this claim, I see in his work evidence that bio-disciplinary power is channeled through what

I call a "fourfold" made up of modern "man," his raced and sexed others, his divine other, and his animal other. Man's others are essentially a network of mirrors centered on man. Seeing himself thus reflected secures man's boundaries and sense of mastery—over himself and, not coincidentally, over those who embody otherness and the world they inhabit together.[21] As bio-disciplinary power's conduit, the fourfold affects how those subjected to that power (that is, thanks to colonialism and its heir, globalization, all of us) become, live, and die. Individually and collectively, consciously and unconsciously, we live out our lives by conforming to or resisting bio-disciplinary power's normative demands. To live as, say, a straight white woman or a gay Black man is to take up one's place in the taxonomy of identities proffered us by bio-disciplinary power as gendered, sexed, raced, or ethnicized and sexual subjects. Depending on where we fit (or fail to) within this asymmetrical system, we reap its benefits or suffer its harmful effects.

Photography played a foundational role in the establishment and institutionalization of bio-disciplinary power, I argue in *Signs and Wonders*. Though we now take what I call "photographic truth" as a given, photography's claim to simply represent the photographed object (what I call, riffing off Roland Barthes, its "that-there-then"[22]) was established by photography's use as an instrument of bio-disciplinary power channeled through the fourfold. In turn, photography was essential to realizing bio-disciplinary power's drive toward normalization—manifest in and as the establishment of modern man's mastery over himself and his (animal, raced, and sexed) others. Both casual snapshots (family and souvenir photographs) and professional photographs (by photojournalists, for example) continue to circulate bio-disciplinary power. Subjecting oneself to the camera—willingly or unwillingly, as its viewed object or viewing subject—(en)trains

us in the modes of seeing / being seen that are integral to modernity as a way of knowing, doing, and therefore being. Colonialism
and racism, anchored by modern understandings of sexuality,
were and are critical players here.[23]

But photography's role in the circulation of bio-disciplinary
power—and our ongoing subjection to it—involves more than
a given photograph's that-there-then (or what photographs
"index"). It also involves photographic *signifiance* (a term I get
from Julia Kristeva via Roland Barthes); that is, what photographs open up and onto.[24] We've come to speak of certain photographs as "iconic," as able to stand in for the events they reference
because they capture what's at stake in those events with remarkable pathos and power. In *No Caption Needed: Iconic Photographs,
Public Culture, and Liberal Democracy*, Robert Hariman and John
Louis Lucaites position iconic photographs as circuits of political affect that arise out of situations of social conflict or crisis.
By "concentrat[ing] and direct[ing] emotions," they serve as "aesthetic resources for performative mediation of conflicts."[25] And
yet, as I noted above, the same photograph can "move" us to
feel or to act in very different ways, a dynamic I call "photographic ambivalence."

FROM *SIGNS AND WONDERS* TO *SEEING AND BELIEVING*

In *Signs and Wonders*, I used this framework to analyze four sets
of photographs, the events they index, and what they open up
and open onto: photographs of Rev. Gene Robinson's consecration as the first openly gay bishop in the Anglican communion, photos of the mistreatment (if not outright torture) of
detainees at Abu Ghraib, video stills of the late Terri Schiavo,

and photographs from Hurricane Katrina. All of the photos reference events that took place between 2003 and 2005. A lot has changed in our photographic lives in the years since, thanks to the invention (2002) and widespread adoption of the (now ubiquitous and video-capable) cell phone camera and the advent and spread of social media. These developments have changed the production and public circulation of photography in multiple ways. Three of the most popular social media platforms are specifically photographic: Instagram (founded in 2010), Snapchat (founded in 2011), and the Chinese video sharing platform Tik-Tok, which landed in the United States in 2018. Even those platforms that are primarily text based (e.g., Facebook and Twitter) circulate visual images. Virtually every post in my feed on Facebook (founded in 2004 and now the owner of Instagram) is headlined by some kind of visual image—often a photograph taken with and uploaded via someone's cell phone.

The new media landscape has further democratized the making and circulating of photographs (already a widely available technology in analogue form), thus somewhat leveling the playing field between amateur and professional media producers and curators. Indeed, all of the photographic story lines I cited at the outset illustrate in different ways the interdependence of new media and legacy media in our photographic lives. Social media platforms enable story lines like these to extend and expand across time and space—including into or alongside legacy media—giving photography an ever more prominent role in our real lives as well as our virtual ones. And let's not forget that long before the pandemic, religion had migrated online—including institutional and para-institutional forms of Christianity. Not only had many brick-and-mortar churches created social media pages, but at least two denominations (the Metropolitan Community Church and the Anglican communion) started virtual congregations on the online multimedia platform Second Life.[26] Thus, photography and other forms of visual representation are as important to virtual religion—perhaps especially (at least, pre-pandemic) its para-institutional forms (think Christian "influencers," for example[27])—as to other aspects of our intertwined virtual and real lives.

We call social media the new public square. Navigating photography's place in that public square and its impact on us requires understanding social media's role in both. Scholars of new media are divided about their social costs and benefits. Some (e.g., Clay Shirky) see social media as empowering communal action.[28] Others (e.g., Sherry Turkle) argue that our reliance on technology to connect us is diminishing embodied capacities (empathy and emotional resilience) that are vital to living well together.[29] The same ambivalence appears in scholarship on virtual religion.[30] When designed and managed well, there is compelling evidence that virtual religion can foster greater engagement between religious leaders and faith community members, but the jury is out on how fully it can substitute for religion IRL.[31]

Scholarship on photography's role on the new media landscape exhibits a similar ambivalence.[32] That ambivalence is reflected in popular perceptions of the relationship between our virtual lives, our photographic lives, and our real lives and their impact on one another. We live (virtually) in "filter bubbles" that tend to reinforce what we already believe, it seems, and what we already believe shapes what we see.[33] The inaugural event that launched the photographic story line that anchors *Seeing and Believing* was not caught on camera. On February 6, 2012, Trayvon Martin (age seventeen) was walking through a mostly white neighborhood in Sanford, Florida, in his gray hoodie when George Zimmerman confronted and killed him. Zimmerman later successfully used Florida's "Stand Your Ground" law in his defense against murder charges. Trayvon Martin's murder launched the #BlackLivesMatter movement, and a black-and-white photograph—a selfie—of Martin in a gray hoodie became the visual center of its pursuit of justice for Martin.[34] However, googling for more information about the killing eventually led to the online radicalization of a young white man, Dylann Roof, who tried to start a "race war" by killing eight members of Mother Emmanuel A.M.E. Church in Charleston, South Carolina, on June 17, 2015.[35] Roof's actions, in turn, helped inspire a twenty-eight-year-old white Australian man to murder more than fifty worshippers at mosques in Christchurch, New Zealand, on March 15, 2019.[36] And that, in turn, inspired the mass murder in Buffalo, New York, in 2022, at the Tops grocery store (in a predominantly Black neighborhood).[37] Clearly, then, photographic truth, *signifiance*, and ambivalence remain deeply relevant to how we navigate our new public square.

FROM PHOTOGRAPHIC SUBJECTION TO PHOTOGRAPHIC INSURRECTION

If my focus in *Signs and Wonders* was on photographic subjection, my interest in *Seeing and Believing* is in photographic insurrection—something we will need if we hope to live well in this mediated world. I am particularly interested in mobilizing those wooed into photographic subjection by bio-discipline's carrots.[38] The wave of unrest we saw in March 2020 stood out because of the wide spectrum of folks of all races and backgrounds who came out in support of #BLM—including record-setting numbers of white people. No doubt, many of them were really and truly "woke," as we say; that is, they truly understood systemic racism and wanted to change it. They have done the

hard work—intellectual and affective, individual and communal, personal and political—that has made them credible to people of color as true allies. And as the plethora of book clubs
committed to reading such crucial texts as Kendi's and DiAngelo's demonstrate, others started down the path of doing the
work. How far they've gotten—or will get—is of course an open
question, especially given the virulent reaction from the far right
and the recent deliberate misrepresentation and demonization of
critical race theory by Republican strategists for political gain
that has followed.[39] Central to this process of re-formation (and
it truly *is* a process) is wrestling with the desire to be a *good* white
person. You want to do, think, and say the right things and be
on the right side, but you aren't always sure what those things
are or where that "right side" is. And you are desperately afraid
you'll do or say the wrong thing and be judged harshly for it.
Your focus, in other words, is on yourself and how people of color
perceive you rather than on those you want to support. True ally-
ship requires much more from "good white people" than this,[40]
but it is, in my experience, the default position from which the
journey begins. That said, it does not have to be where it ends.

"Good white people" are particularly vulnerable to liberal
sentimentality, limned in Saidiya Hartman's work as liberal
humanism in affective mode. This affective repertoire includes
outrage and empathy, shame and pleasure (among other feelings).
I read Hartman's analysis as illuminating liberal sentimentality
as (white) mastery in affective form.[41] Mastery manifests not only
as domination *over* others but as moral goodness *to* others that
makes "us" feel like good people but maintains the hierarchy of
"us" (whites) over "them" (people of color).

Joining a book club, attending a protest, and organizing to
change the public policies responsible for these problems in the
first place are laudable actions—especially when one's ostensible

self-interest would align otherwise. Liberal sentimentality can be the spark that lights the flame of activism on behalf of others, but it can also become a barrier to genuine solidarity with those others—and it seems unlikely to sustain the steady burn required to work for change in the face of recalcitrant resistance. And yet, we have evidence of the promise (even if limited) of photographic insurrection; that is, of a potential response to what we see that disrupts our docile compliance with bio-disciplined seeing. What can we do to nurture and cultivate that promise—especially in our new media landscape? Might photographic insurrection prompt us to cultivate the ability to see through bio-disciplined (photographic) normativity and what it would have us believe about ourselves, others, and the world we share?

That I turn to religion as a resource for *Seeing and Believing* may surprise some readers. But wrestling with the promise and limits of media and mediation is arguably intrinsic to many religious traditions, including Christianity. Anthropologist Birgit Meyer asserts that religions are forms of mediation in two senses. They claim to mediate the transcendent, and they do so in and through the media available to them.[42] Many of those are visual media (paintings, sculpture, or architecture; ordinary writing or calligraphy; the scroll, the book, the tract; film or television; Facebook or Second Life).[43] Likely because they seek to mediate transcendence, religions are extremely sensitive to visual mediation's complex relationship to seeing and believing—in one common idiom, for example, to the power of iconography and the danger of idolatry.

Historian and scholar of religious visual culture David Morgan brings these insights to bear on Christianity in ways I find particularly productive. Citing written gospels, visual icons, and cathedral architecture as examples before focusing in on the British Evangelical tract, Morgan demonstrates that Christianity has been a mediated religion for virtually its entire history.[44] Indeed, navigating the relationship between seeing and believing has meant negotiating with one media revolution after another (e.g., the printing press, television, and now online social media) and the visual cultures in which they are embedded. And Christianity's status as a global lingua franca (itself a reflection of its imperial and colonialist legacy) has impacted those visual cultures as well.[45] The religious rhetoric (iconicity and iconoclasm, photographic literalism) repurposed so productively by the scholarly and popular discourse on photography I have sketched in brief here is but one example. As we'll see, scholarly discourse on social media also resorts to a metaphorical theo-logic commonly associated with Christianity to alert us to the power that the multinational corporations who own our new public square hold over us. The presence of such theo-logics, I argue, calls for engagement by scholars of religion, especially theologians.

But there is yet more. *Seeing and Believing* extends and expands what I called in *Signs and Wonders* photographic askesis, an approach to looking at photographs that attends to their formative effects on us. My reference to askesis (rooted in Foucault's use of it, by the way) exploits a convergence of the religious and the philosophical. Of Greek provenance, askesis refers to practices of deliberate self-(re)formation undertaken under the aegis of philosophy (Stoicism, for example) or religion (including Christianity). Those practices were directed toward realizing the human being's proper end (*telos*): *eudaimonia* for Stoic ascetics, union with God for Christian ascetics. In both cases, the practices engaged require looking both outward and inward for the effects of de-formation and resources for re-formation. In *Signs and Wonders,* I described photographic askesis as a contemplative exercise of sorts, one that asks viewers to slow down and pay careful attention to the photographs that anchored that book and what they open up and open onto—particularly the effects of bio-disciplinary power. As we'll see, that approach remains critical to photographic insurrection.

Like *Signs and Wonders*, *Seeing and Believing* invites readers to practice photographic askesis, but in a slightly different vein. It seeks out resources that can support a more intentional approach to *how* we look. My ultimate goal is to curate a visual repertoire—a repertoire of ways of looking that is crafted with the benefits and challenges of our new media landscape in mind, a visual repertoire that, if cultivated, can promote photographic insurrection. As a result, *Seeing and Believing* also takes a different stance toward Christianity. In *Signs and Wonders*, Christianity was primarily part of the problem because of its collusion with bio-disciplinary power. In *Seeing and Believing*, however, I turn to ways of seeing found in Christianity (and, crucially, other religions) as a vital resource for photographic insurrection. Like other religions, Christianity has been wrestling with the relationship between seeing and believing for eons now. (Indeed, its founding moment is arguably a crisis of seeing and believing: what to make of the sight of an empty tomb intended to house the body of the colonized Jew believed by his followers to be *messiah* but crucified by imperial Roman forces as a dangerous rebel.) The fact that Christianity has been so deeply interwoven with bio-disciplinary power, however, only enhances the importance of locating resources for photographic insurrection in Christian ways of seeing.

That we speak of "iconic" photographs at all references another important element of the history of religious visual images, a history characterized by conflicts over the relationship between seeing and believing. In Christianity the controversy over icons divided the Western church from the Eastern church long before the Reformation divided Catholicism from Protestantism. Were visual images of Christ and of Christian saints windows onto the divine (and thus worthy of veneration), or were they idolatrous representations? Concerns about seeing and believing also carried over into the Protestant movement. Reformers stripped churches and cathedrals of visual media deemed idolatrous and thus dangerous to true belief and right practice. And yet Protestantism can hardly be accused of jettisoning seeing as an aid to believing. Morgan notes that John Calvin exhorted Christians to look instead at nature, where they would encounter the glory of God.[46] As Morgan has shown, modern Protestantism—both conservative and evangelical—went on to invest significantly in visual resources especially with the advent of modes of their mechanical reproduction.[47]

As I noted in the preface, foregrounding the visual risks treating vision as though it were isolable from the other senses—and indeed from embodiment itself. Similarly, it also courts ableism by ignoring a significant portion of our population: those with visual impairments. Capitulating to either or both would also leave unchallenged bio-disciplinary power's understanding of vision and policing of normalization. It would also ignore crucial (if sometimes clumsy) affordances made available by the very same new technologies on which social media rely. Smart phones, tablets, and computers open access to people with disabilities (though not always perfectly, to be sure), including those with visual impairments. For example, providing a written description of a still photograph posted online allows someone who is visually impaired to "see" the photograph in narrative form—read to them by Apple's Siri, say. But it's also the case that ablebodied and -minded people interact with photographs online through multiple senses. Though we touch screens now to do so, we have always accessed photographs via touch, as I discuss at some length in *Signs and Wonders*. And watching a video is both a visual and an aural experience. Notably, the videos present in the photographic story lines I have referenced move us as much because of what we hear as what we see. When photographs move us—emotionally or to take action—that movement extends into and mobilizes our bodies. Emotion is both experienced and expressed bodily, whatever form that experience or expression takes. Thus, only ways of looking that are explicitly grounded in the fullness of embodiment will truly be capable of aiding and abetting photographic insurrection. As we'll also see in some detail, how we "look" and thus what we "see" in the visual media that we encounter reflects and refracts our social formation. I place "look" and "see" in scare quotes to let readers know that when I speak of looking and seeing in the pages that follow, I intend to reference their full sensory and embodied context. While we (visual) normates enter that context primarily through our eyes, the differently abled among us enter through other sensory organs and capacities. Only a visual repertoire that offers options that situate seeing in this multidimensional context will do. And they must be multiple options; one size will not fit all.

I am not the first to turn to Christianity in search of resources for navigating the challenges posed by our new media landscape and the technological innovations that support it. Indeed, my account of photographic insurrection builds on the work of Christian ethicist Kate Ott. If my colleague pastoral theologian Jaco Hamman focuses on the challenges the digital world poses to healthy subject formation, Ott attends to the challenges that world poses to ethically sound subject formation.[48] While their focus is on the individual, both remain ever mindful of the communal context of subject formation. For all three of us, turning to Christianity for these resources is neither implicitly nor explicitly an assertion of its superiority to other religious or spiritual traditions or a claim that only religious resources offer us what we need. I start there, in particular, because well before photographs were embodied in silicon and binary code, Christianity—understood as a discourse and a visual practice—was navigating the complicated relationships between the "real and [the] virtual," the "material and [the] symbolic," the "sensate and [the] mediated," as not simply "clouds of fancy" or "pellets of information" but routes to self (de- and re-)formation. To complicated and sometimes conflicting ends, of course, but with lessons to teach us as we do the same in our (not-so?) newly mediated world.

FIGURE 2.1 *Seeing Is Believing*, Layer 1 (no mirror).
Artist: Britt Stadig. Photographer: Amanda McCadams.
Printed with the permission of Vanderbilt University.

2

LIFE ON THE NEW
PUBLIC SQUARE

*In our culture of simulation, the notion of authenticity is for us
what sex was for the Victorians—threat and obsession, taboo
and fascination.*

—Sherry Turkle, *Alone Together*

*The second industrial revolution, unlike the first, does not pres-
ent us with such crushing images as rolling mills and molten
steel, but with "bits" in a flow of information traveling along
circuits in the form of electronic impulses. The iron machines still
exist, but they obey the orders of weightless bits.*

—Italo Calvino, "Lightness," *Six Memos for the Next Millennium*

*If you can honestly love a cat, which can't give you directions to
a stranger's house, why can't you love the web?*

—Kevin Kelly (quoted by Sherry Turkle)

I t is ironic, to say the least, that I embarked on this new book
project just in time for the 2016 election season. Donald
Trump's surprise victory in the presidential race made many

of us newly aware of the power of social media—Facebook and Twitter, in particular—to amplify (for good or for ill) what we see, say, (think we) know, and do. The dire and unsettling consequences of that power became dramatically visible—and in real time—in the last days of his presidency, as I noted earlier. What counts as "news" on our social media pages includes not only the products of legitimate media outlets that abide by journalistic standards but also "fake news"—not Trump's version (any news story he doesn't like), but actual fake news: fiction dressed up to look like news, pastiches of real news repackaged in inflammatory dress to draw and incite readers (so-called click-bait), and so on.[1] It includes updates from our friends and family as well as ads for certain products. And it includes our responses to what we encounter expressed sometimes in words but often via emoticons, "like" buttons, or actual comments. Collectively, these become the equivalent of a personalized news digest, available 24/7, ever changing as new content shows up. It's personalized but not exactly curated or edited—not, at least, in the way that professional journalism is. Rather, what we see is a product of the combined actions of ourselves and our online networks, for-profit companies and nonprofit organizations, and, notably, algorithms. We ourselves and our networks post, "friend," and share—sometimes self-produced content, sometimes content produced by others in our network or by professionals. Facebook's algorithms take whom we friend, what we post and share, and determine the order in which we see things *and* suggest new content (including ads) based on what it determines are our interests. We decide what's truly worthy of our attention—first by who we friend but mostly by what we look at—or don't. Some of this is conscious and deliberate, some not. What catches my eye and stops my scrolling may be something that challenges or reinforces what I already think or feel. Much of this is affectively driven. We stop on what attracts or repels us, our attention captured by something that makes us smile or, these days, terrifies us. Frequently, whether we stop or move on is a matter of how we respond to the visual image—a photograph or video, a meme, a cartoon—embedded in the post.

Facebook calls that virtual space our "feed" (formerly "news feed"). According to *Merriam-Webster*, "feed" means "to satisfy, gratify, support, encourage, channel, supply, or route" Something A to Something B.[2] Something A can be essential to Something B's development or sustenance; it can be the "food" that sustains an organism or the signal that sustains a circuit. The degree to which our Facebook feeds actually nourish us is questionable, I'd say, though it may depend these days on your political preferences. My feed is typically full of "news"—much of it quite legit (from legacy media), much of it questionable insofar as it comes from "alternative" news outlets, some of it apparently "fake," as we've learned. But very little of it is actually *news*—that is, accounts of what has happened or is happening. More of it consists of (often dire) predictions about what *will* happen or is *likely* to happen—or opinion about that. And I also get lots of requests to sign petitions, to support this or that good cause, or this or that political candidate, etc.

So just what is Facebook feeding me? More to the point, *is* Facebook feeding me? Is it offering me sustenance or satisfaction? Is it offering me what I need? These days I would say it's offering me very little of either. If Facebook used to be a respite from the stress and strain of a day's work, it's become for me primarily a source of stress and strain. My stomach tightens and I stop breathing for a moment every time I click on that little blue icon, terrified of what I'll find. (And, just to clarify, this is not because I'm being trolled. I don't typically engage much on Facebook. I repost things I consider newsworthy from time to time, but I rarely comment on them or on anything.) Of course, the same thing used to happen every hour on the hour when the local classical station (affiliated with National Public Radio, or NPR) I keep on in the background as I work played NPR's hourly news update. Mercifully, early in 2020 they stopped including the news updates and my life is much improved!

Yet, every now and again, something uplifting pops up. And it's not just a cat video or hilarious meme. Often, it's evidence of resistance to the racist, sexist, homophobic, and xenophobic vitriol that takes up so much oxygen in our world today. In the immediate wake of the 2016 election, I was moved to tears by news of spontaneous acts of friendship, hospitality, and support toward Muslims in Texas, on New York subways, and in Memphis, Tennessee, where I used to live. I witnessed the online empathy extended to folks seeking in virtual space the sense of belonging and understanding that has been denied them in real space. I was astounded by corporate acts of goodness like Delta Air Lines' imposition of a lifelong ban on a belligerent Trump supporter accompanied by the offer to refund tickets of all—yes, all—passengers on the flight where he behaved so badly.[3] And like Starbucks' circulation of a short film about the welcome extended by a Memphis Christian congregation to the Muslim mosque that opened across the street from it.[4] And an Amazon ad that featured the friendship of an imam and a Catholic priest (both elderly).[5] More to the point, I found advice on concrete actions I could take. In those first weeks and months, especially, I made it a regular practice to call someone in Congress—whether my representative, or my senators, or a relevant committee chair—to share my perspective (calmly, rationally, respectfully). I donated money to organizations and causes that were doing work I wanted to support.

And then early on the morning of September 3, 2017, my mother died. I shared the news on Facebook by reposting what my brother, Steve (a screenwriter), had posted on his Facebook page: a photograph (taken with his iPhone) of the sun rising over the beach outside the room where my mother died coupled with perfectly crafted words describing our last hours with her and anticipating the seismic shift we were experiencing. In that virtual space, I found great comfort in the responses that poured in over the subsequent hours and days (an experience repeated six months later when my father died).

This snapshot of my experience on Facebook is, I suspect, fairly typical. The ambivalence I described is mirrored not only in what I hear from friends and family but also what I read in the scholarly literature on the subject. Scholars of new media— including those in the theological disciplines and religious studies more broadly—agree that this new media landscape has profoundly impacted our social fabric for both good and ill. In doing so, it has also profoundly reshaped who we are and how we are at virtually every level. All agree that the critical task before us is discerning and cultivating practices of engaging online that mine the promise inherent in this new media landscape while avoiding its peril.

WHAT'S NEW ABOUT NEW MEDIA?
IS IT . . . TECHNOLOGY?

Sherry Turkle, a professor at the Massachusetts Institute of Technology trained in both psychoanalytic theory and ethnography, has been researching the social impact and import of technology for decades now. In *Alone Together* (2011), she focuses on then-dominant mobile devices (iPhones and Blackberries) and on then-ascendant social media platforms (Second Life, Facebook, and MySpace). While she acknowledges their benefits, they also concern her—primarily because of their impact on how we relate to one another. That 24/7 connectivity has blurred the line between work and home is a commonplace observation. We are both overwhelmed by this level of connection and drawn in by it. Turkle primarily analyzes the effect it has on the relationships between parents and children, on how teenagers engage with one another, and thus on how they experience adolescence. She cites a study that provides evidence of the loss in millennial college students of the value of empathy, a loss that the authors of the study attribute to the time spent on social media and online gaming rather than in-person socializing.

Many other insights from Turkle's analysis are, by now, familiar (the pressures of constantly curating your Facebook profile, knowing that it will quite likely outlive you, for example). The changes that she tracks are spatial and temporal as well as relational. The promise of 24/7 instantaneous connection makes us worry when we can't establish that connection with someone we love. That said, our devices—especially our smart phones—also give us multiple options for connecting and allow us to choose which to use and when. A clear hierarchy has developed, Turkle claims, that ranks the forms of connection (text, email, phone call—in that order) by the level of intimacy and time required.

Given the prominence of smart phones and the forms of connectivity they enable (and disable), we are increasingly alone together. Even when families are physically in the same room, each person is often focused on their own screen with its own content. Turkle worries that we may come to prefer that state of being. Virtual life seems to offer us at least some of the pleasure of relationships without at least some of the pain. Indeed, one of her research subjects, a teenager, describes her relief at learning of a friend's death via text message rather than in person. In person, she'd have been emotionally overwhelmed in public; the

LIFE ON THE NEW PUBLIC SQUARE   29

text message allowed her to have that experience in private. And yet the lure of life online causes pain, too. Turkle's research also shows that children suffer when their parents can't disengage from their own devices long enough to truly engage with them. In the end, Turkle's research suggests that life online is but what Jean Baudrillard would likely call a "simulacrum" of relationality.[6] In settling for the simulacrum, we risk shortchanging ourselves and stunt the emotional capacity necessary for the real thing. Moreover, "if convenience and control continue to be our priorities,"[7] we're likely to cede the real—with all its complexity—to the technological simulacra to come: robotic pets and caretakers, for example, currently in development, that Turkle also researches.[8] This is a loss we'll likely fail to notice (much less grieve) as we live into it. But this isn't the only alternative. We don't *need* to give ourselves over to technology hook, line, and sinker: "Needs imply that we must have something. To move forward together—as generations together—we are called upon to embrace the complexity of our situation. We have invented inspiring and enhancing technologies, and yet we have allowed them to diminish us."[9] The solution, Turkle argues, isn't going off the grid or rejecting these new technologies; it is, rather, what she calls *realteknik*: taking (self-reflective) control over what are still, as I write, very young technologies.

Of course, this is hardly the first technology-driven media revolution that humanity has experienced—all with anticipated or actual ambivalent effect. In ancient times, Plato famously deemed writing a *pharmakon*—cure and poison—for forgetting. Although the printing press is rightly credited with democratizing access to knowledge and information, the effects of the print culture to which it gave rise were ambivalent. For example, it enabled the creation and codification of a racialized classification system for human cultures.[10] Some feared that television would replace community with isolation, interpersonal engagement with narcissistic enthrallment. Its advent immersed us in what Guy DeBord famously dubbed in the 1960s a "society of the spectacle," a form of capitalism in which the image replaced the thing itself as the object of our desire.[11] And so it goes.

While our new "attention economy" (more about that later) resembles its predecessor, the differences are notable. The contrast between social media and legacy media is particularly striking. Before the internet, broadcast television and radio along with professionally produced newspapers and magazines were the primary media through which we got our news. That news was mediated in another sense too: it was produced by journalists (including photojournalists) and curated by their editors, who decided what was worthy of our attention. Our current "information age" has displaced not only the physical medium that relays news and other information but also the mediators who determine what information gets relayed. Everybody, Clay Shirky says, in the aptly titled *Here Comes Everybody*, now not only consumes but also produces and edits (through sharing it, if nothing else) what we encounter online.[12]

Information technology has enabled a new media ecosystem, one that links producers (professional or amateur, legacy media or social media) and consumers (readers/viewers) in new ways. In the good old days, communication via media was unidirectional: from the broadcaster to the (passive) consumer. But now communication—and broadcasting—goes both ways. What's newsworthy used to be determined by the professionals. We wouldn't even know what they left out. But now what's newsworthy is often a response to stories posted by non-journalists that legacy media then pick up. We are indeed all "prosumers"— that is, producers and consumers.[13] And if the ethos of the old ecosystem was "why publish?" (i.e., is this newsworthy?), the ethos of this new ecosystem is "why *not* publish?" (let's see if my friends care about it), says Shirky.

Shirky provides evidence of the gains for social organizing that come with this new tech-driven (or enabled) ecosystem. If legacy media primarily did big things for money, social media enables us to "do big things for love," he writes.[14] Online connectivity has lowered the transactional costs of social organizing and changed the trajectory of social organizing. If "gather, then share" was the MO of analogue social connectivity, digital connectivity runs in the opposite direction: "share [online], then gather [Meetup]."[15]

Sociologists distinguish between three levels of social interaction, Shirky writes. Sharing requires the lowest effort or the lowest "cost." Next up is cooperation, then collective action. Cooperation requires knowing who you're connected to (and it creates that knowledge). Collective action requires collaborative decision making, which in turn requires knowing that others know you know others. Our electronic networks are making possible the creation of networks of all three types that are "larger and more distributed than at any time in history," Shirky observes.[16] And this is having major impacts not just online but in real life. Shirky offers numerous examples of virtual social organizing that effected social change (the Catholic sex abuse scandal, the Arab Spring, etc.). But online connectivity also mutes the role social approbation has in limiting community formation. Members of affinity groups marginalized by society can now find each other online and form virtual—and sometimes real—communities. His example is Pro-Ana (online groups sharing advice on how to be anorexic); more recent examples would be white supremacists and neo-Nazis, including those involved in the U.S. Capitol insurrection on January 6, 2021.[17] How do societies, governments, etc., work with that reality?

The power and limitations of this new public square are laid out with particular clarity and import by Zeynep Tufekci in *Twitter and Tear Gas: The Power and Fragility of Networked Protest*.[18] A sociologist and former computer programmer, Tufekci brings that expertise together with her own experience in political organizing to create a rich and complex portrait of the socially mediated protest movements of 2011–2016 with particular attention to the Arab Spring and Occupy Wall Street. She documents the critical role that social media—Twitter and Facebook, in particular—played not only in mobilizing and organizing people to participate in street protests but in generating material help from supporters spread around the world as well. Yet, those who would describe the revolts of the Arab Spring as, say, "Twitter revolutions" or "Facebook uprisings" are overlooking the role of flesh-and-blood organizers on the ground.

"Networked protest" refers to the intermingling of real and virtual life in protest movements of the twenty-first century (the so-called digital age). Truly understanding the impact of social media requires avoiding "technodeterminism"—the idea that technology determines the reality it interacts with—and focusing instead on their "affordances," meaning what they make possible and the limitations of same.[19] Digital technologies and social networks (Twitter and Facebook, in particular) afford quick and widespread connectivity, which enables large crowds to gather in protest at a moment's notice, hence the power of networked protest. (Consider, by contrast, the effort required to launch the 1955–1956 Montgomery bus boycott. One teacher stayed up all night mimeographing a pamphlet announcing and justifying the boycott, which was then delivered by hand to every Black household in the city within two days *by a previously existing group*. Consider, in addition, all the labor that went into organizing transportation for the workers boycotting the buses, etc.). Unlike flesh-and-blood connections, social media connections are not limited by geographical proximity, thus enabling what Tufekci calls "globalization from below."[20] And, thanks to global transportation and delivery networks, supporters of the protests can take actions from far away that help IRL. A chief example cited by Tufekci is the supporters of the January 2011 protests located outside Egypt who organized the collection and delivery of medical supplies to Tahrir Square from wherever they were. However, sustaining protest movements—and using them to produce real change—still requires good old-fashioned person-to-person organizing. While digital technologies and social media help keep folks in touch, they're no substitute for IRL connections, hence the fragility of networked protest. The modern civil rights movement's success may seem inevitable in hindsight, she observes, but it was anything but at the time. And it had to adapt its strategies over and over in response to those in authority. Furthermore (indeed, most important), as students of the movement know, it relied on any number of organizations and networks some of which preexisted it, others of which came into existence in response to specific needs and desires. And that means serious labor from thousands upon thousands of people behind the scenes of its most spectacular successes (like the 1963 March on Washington). And by "labor" I mean not just recruiting folks to participate but the hard work of navigating disagreements about strategy, tactics, and goals as well as personal conflicts. It's that work that builds the resilience and trust necessary to success over the long term. It requires what sociologists call strong ties (versus weak ties). Digital connectivity can certainly be helpful in connecting people's strong and weak networks and in sustaining them, but they are an effective supplement to—not a substitute for—face-to-face work.

Digital connectivity can not only generate new and unexpected IRL connections but also extend and expand preexisting ones. Both are evident in Tufekci's account of the protests she studies. I was unaware of the degree to which those protests built on social networks of activists from around the world who had gotten to know one another at previous international forums—particularly, in the case of the Arab Spring, one organized by the Zapatistas in the late 1990s, which Tufekci attended. She reports running into folks from all over the world whom she met there at Gezi Park, for example, and that's not coincidental. These activists reached out to each other via social media asking for support.

Networked protests also bring together folks who wouldn't have met otherwise and who might not seem compatible. Tufekci describes, for example, the moving encounter she observed in 2013 between a Turkish trans woman activist and a very traditional Kurdish cis woman at the Gezi Park protest who had journeyed there from northern Turkey after seeing the protest on social media. They talked for quite a while about what brought them to the protest, about their larger life experiences and other topics. Their encounter concluded with the two crying and embracing each other in a remarkable show of mutual understanding.

Moving to the face-to-face, though, also exhibits the fragility of networked protests. The "affordances" of social media are the ease with which it connects us to one another, no matter how "strong" or "weak" our connections are, as sociologists say. That is, absent special effort on my part, my Facebook feed does not distinguish between the latest posting from my best friend and the one from someone I barely know IRL. Yet successful protest movements must navigate all kinds of challenges, both internal and external. Conflict over strategy is an inevitable aspect of working for political change, as is negotiating with governments or other institutions one is trying to change. That requires levels of trust and knowledge of one another that can only be built

face-to-face, Tufekci argues. The Montgomery bus boycott succeeded in part because of preexisting strong networks that connected potential boycotters to one another socially and politically
(including, but not limited to, of course, the city's Black churches).

REMAKING SPACE, REMAKING TIME

Religious studies scholar S. Brent Plate credits film with changing the way we experienced space and time in the early twenty-
first century compared to the early twentieth.[21] Scholarship on
social media suggests that this media revolution is having a similar impact on us. Tufekci's research into how political activists
use social media illuminates how social media remake space, in
particular. She observes that for political organizers, social media
platforms are analogous to coffee shops and living rooms, to
underground newspapers and telephones. Like coffee shops and
living rooms, they provide (online) space to connect, socialize,
and plan. Like newspapers and telephones, they serve as outlets
for communication, one-to-one, one-to-many, many-to-many.
One advantage the digital public square has over its analogue
counterparts is its global reach. Globalization from below enables
like-minded folks from all over the world to find each other and
connect. As we've seen, this can be a powerful tool in political
organizing. The fact that Facebook is so deeply integrated into
people's ordinary lives discourages even authoritarian regimes
from cutting off access to it, she observes. But its algorithms and
policies sometimes inhibit organizers' ability to get their mes-
sages out. A major Facebook page for the Egyptian protests that
ousted Hosni Mubarak, "We Are All Khaled Said," was run by
an Egyptian who used a pseudonym in part to protect himself
and his family. Because Facebook requires people to use their

real, legal names, the company deleted the page. It eventually put the page back up (after massive protests from the international human rights community and some of its own employees), but only when an Egyptian ex-pat agreed to let the site go back up under her name as organizer, thus risking permanent exile for herself and potential harm to family members still in Egypt. That Facebook relies on "community policing" to enforce this policy creates yet another degree of vulnerability and exposure for activists. The policy is enforced only when another member of the Facebook community alerts their (extremely small, relative to their user base) staff to a violation. Organizers are much more likely to attract such alerts than others, given the nature of their work and thus the nature of what they post. This can put organizers—especially those subject to authoritarian regimes—in real danger.

The Ferguson, Missouri, protests in 2014–2015 illustrate another limitation to this public square. Initially, at least, the protests failed to get the kind of traction on Facebook that the famous "ice-bucket challenge," which supported a charity fighting ALS (Lou Gehrig's Disease), received. This wasn't because people weren't sharing the protests and what they thought about them, nor was it due to any intentional decision by Facebook to keep Ferguson out of view. It was rather the effect of the digital culture created and enforced by the algorithms that govern this particular public square and that decide what populates it. Posts "go viral," as we say, when they generate sufficient "likes" and "shares" to catch algorithmic attention. While responding to videos of people dumping buckets of ice water on themselves with a "thumbs-up" seems perfectly appropriate, the same reaction hardly does justice to a photo of police in riot gear with dogs and guns at the ready. (Eventually, the Ferguson protests went viral on Twitter, prompting legacy media to take notice of them.)

We must remember, however, that globalization from below is made possible by globalization from above. Our digital public square is constituted by social media platforms owned and operated by just a few for-profit corporations mostly based in the United States but with a global reach. Recall that the gatekeepers of legacy media are editors who decide what is newsworthy and what's not. The internet may be populated by prosumers, but that doesn't mean it's without gatekeepers. The gatekeepers are—for now, at least—the global corporations that own the platforms that constitute the public square. They write the algorithms (or pay those who do) and set and enforce the policies that determine what we see on these public squares—and both come with built-in limitations. For one thing, distinguishing between problematic and unproblematic content often takes nuanced human insight; something algorithmic moderation lacks. Relying primarily on online community policing for that insight also has its limits. And the relatively few paid staff charged with making decisions about that content often lack the experience or knowledge (including contextual knowledge) needed to make good decisions, Tufekci warns. Yes, a policy that prohibits posting naked pictures of children, for example, will help cut down on child pornography, but it could also eliminate a reposting of *Accidental Napalm*, the iconic image from the Vietnam War informally known as *Napalm Girl*.[22] And removing content is a perpetual game of Whack-a-Mole. Enforcers may remove it from this particular platform or from this particular feed, but odds are that copies of it will live on somewhere else (on someone's hard drive, for example, or on the "dark web"). It may not circulate as widely as it once did, but eliminating it entirely is all but impossible and requires constant surveillance.

While Tufekci and Shirky track the (mostly) positive effects of our virtual political lives on our real ones, other scholars have raised serious concerns about longer-term and deeper effects of this ecosystem given that its economic engine runs on "big data." Shoshana Zuboff has coined the term "surveillance capitalism" to describe the economy that drives this ecosystem.[23] The connective devices we carry, wear, listen to, and talk into are the nexus of the network of data production and capture that generates their profits. They may tout their idealistic goals (Google's original slogan, "Don't be evil," and Facebook's more recent one, "Be Connected. Be Discovered. Be on Facebook"[24]), but the corporations that run these platforms are in business to make money. Like their mass media predecessors, their income comes primarily from advertising—directly (in the form of ads that we see) and indirectly (in the form of aggregated data sold off as raw material). These companies are incentivized to collect as much data on their users as they can, which can then be sold to other corporations that seek to sell us their goods and services.

Surveillance capitalism, Zuboff argues, is the "author" of the latest chapter in "the long saga of capitalism's evolution."[25] Like its predecessor, industrial capitalism, surveillance capitalism perpetuates "the economic and social contests of the twentieth century" and the divisions that result.[26] Also like its predecessor, it has launched revolutionary changes that impact both our economic system and society writ large. Zuboff describes surveillance capitalism as a form of rendition: we (sur)render unto this Caesar—Google, Facebook, Twitter, etc.—our virtual lives, which its technologies render into data like fat into oil. Everything from who we call, what we do, where we go, what we talk about when we get there; from who we know, what we look at, and what we buy to our sleeping habits, our heart rate and temperature, etc. is trackable. Though they are not the only devices involved now (smart speakers and other "smart home" devices—including, potentially, Roombas—collect data too[27]), our smart phones—and the cameras built into them—play a central role in surveillance capitalism. Indeed, Zuboff observes that "smart is a euphemism for rendition."[28]

If this seems like a violation of your privacy, that's understandable. Indeed, that's a chief concern of Zuboff's. Currently, these companies mine the data they collect from us with our (legal) consent. When we sign up for Facebook, say, we sign onto a (legal) contract that governs how Facebook will use our data. Because we give our legal consent by clicking "I agree," these contracts have been dubbed "click-wrap." Few if any of us read those contracts and thus know what we are signing onto and signing away, including our privacy.[29]

Since our data can live forever online, we will remain "wrapped" up in these contracts long after we are dead. In 2014 a lawsuit against Google filed by ninety Spaniards established in European Union law the "right to be forgotten"—that is, the right to erase one's virtual life (or episodes from it)—though subsequent court decisions limited it somewhat.[30] As of this writing, the United States has yet to recognize such a right—even a limited one. As Jeffrey Chester, the executive director of the Center for Digital Democracy, recently observed, the United States has "the opposite of that. We have the First Amendment."[31] Of course, unlike the government, private corporations aren't bound by that constitutional provision, but as recent allegations that social media companies like Facebook are biased against conservative voices indicate, that value is top of mind when it comes to our new public square.

That said, the Constitution (supposedly) guarantees a right to privacy as well, so perhaps that value will become more prominent in these discussions over time.[32] The unfolding of a series of scandals in recent years (Edward Snowden's revelations of National Security Agency [NSA] data collection practices,

Cambridge Analytica's alleged misuse of Facebook data on behalf of Donald Trump's presidential campaign, etc.) raised the average layperson's awareness of the downsides of this new media ecosystem.[33] While Facebook remained popular, over 70 percent of respondents to surveys done by *Consumer Reports* in 2018 and 2019 reported changing the way they use the website, including taking what actions they could to limit data sharing and location tracking because of rising concerns about privacy; an example of *realteknik*.[34] But a *New York Times* investigation, undertaken with the aid of a digital file belonging to a location data company leaked to its Privacy Project in 2019, showed that tracking data can be easily de-anonymized to (literally) connect the dots that trace a given individual's movement.[35] In the wake of the January 6, 2021, insurrection at the U.S. Capitol, the *Times* used another dataset (specifically of certain Trump supporters who traveled to Washington, D.C., to attend rallies that day) to identify and track the movements of individuals present at and allegedly involved in the insurrection.[36] While many will celebrate the ease with which these perpetrators of violence were identified, the authors alert readers to a deeper cause for concern. Absent new laws and regulations, we are all vulnerable to being tracked and traced not only by the giants of surveillance capitalism but by anyone who gains access to the data they collect—and for whatever reason—including nefarious ones.[37]

Yet, as Turkle recognized in 2011, fully detaching from this system is very difficult to do. We submit to it because of the affordances it offers us: connections to friends and family and, as Roberto Simanowski observes in *Data Love*, access to things we want and (think we) need. Those things range from safety, security, and health to the latest shiny object. Multinational corporations aren't alone in loving data; we love it too. Not only do we submit to data tracking; we also track ourselves: our workout habits, our food intake, our sleep time and wake time, even (ironically) our screen time! Many of us (especially we "good white people") tell ourselves that we have no reason to fear and nothing to hide from becoming essentially transparent subjects,[38] but how can we know what the future holds? Many employers routinely do Google searches on job candidates, rejecting some whose digital past contains relics deemed unsavory. In *Algorithms of Oppression*, Noble cites examples of schoolteachers and principals (women, of course) being demoted or fired when evidence of sexually explicit activity from their past (sometimes shared online without their permission) comes to the attention of employers.[39] In the spring of 2020, we saw multiple examples of employers firing employees caught on viral videos exhibiting racist behavior; most famously, as in one of the photographic story lines I discuss in chapter 1, Amy Cooper, the woman who called the New York Police Department when a Black, gay male birdwatcher asked her to comply with the law and leash her dog. Laptops and other digital devices are subject to confiscation by Customs and Border Patrol agents in many countries (including the United States, which, in recent years, has hardly been a model of openness to others).[40] I doubt that my university is alone in recommending that faculty members do their best to leave their digital selves behind when they travel internationally— particularly to certain countries. While deleting apps may allow you to ditch some of your digital selves from your smart phone, surveillance capitalism makes it all but impossible to escape big data's reach regardless of what devices we own. Indeed, as we'll see later, we have (according to philosopher Colin Koopman) become our data.[41] This has implications not only for our present but for our future too. As predictive analytics increasingly become the engine that drives surveillance capitalism, the very notion of the future as radically open seems to be disappearing—especially when predictions are deployed to lure us in a certain direction, Zuboff observes.

Clearly, then, this new media landscape isn't just remaking space; it is remaking time as well. Not only does it expand our connectivity geographically; it also accelerates it temporally. No doubt, Shirky and Tufekci offer compelling evidence of its upside: the speed with which we can organize online and IRL responses to unfolding events. But Zuboff and Tufekci also alert us to the ways that surveillance capitalism and globalization from above can slow down those very same responses—intentionally and unintentionally. And Turkle alerts us to a deeper challenge yet: succumbing to the allure of the virtual may cause to atrophy the very capacities we need in order to navigate those challenges successfully.

SEEING IN THE NEW PUBLIC SQUARE

The social, ethical, and political challenges and opportunities afforded us by social media and digital technologies, then, are beginning to emerge. But one aspect of life on the new public square—one that is central to *Seeing and Believing*—still needs attention: the role of the visual in the virtual. That role is absolutely central, as visual images are arguably the lifeblood of this new ecosystem. Across the platforms that make up our new public square, visual images are the bait that attracts and holds our attention, fixing our eyes (and ears and fingers) to our devices. As I noted previously, three of the most popular social media platforms feature visual images (Instagram, Snapchat, and Tik-Tok). The platforms that began as text based (e.g., Twitter, Facebook) also circulate visual images: photographs, videos, memes, and more. Attending to the role of vision and the visual is critical, then, for understanding the relationship between our virtual and our real lives.

Jonathan Crary and Dominic Pettman are among the prominent scholars of visual culture who are paying attention. Their work focuses on the challenges and opportunities that the intersection of the virtual, the real, and the visual present to us in ways that reinforce and challenge the insights discussed above. In his book *24/7*, Crary puts a visual spin on concerns raised by Turkle and Zuboff.[42] This new media ecosystem has changed our experience of time and space, he argues. In this always-on world, consumption and production enclose us in a never-ending cycle, "a time without time" (29). Because we now inhabit "a switched-on universe for which no off switch exists," our experience of time is flattening (30). Among the casualties of this new ecosystem is the erosion of the everyday as a sphere of unmediated (and unsurveilled) living. The Industrial Revolution may have launched everyday life's devaluation, but at least it allowed it to exist, Crary argues. However limited, time at home was (mostly) downtime; leisure time, free time—ours to do with what we wanted. Until the advent of television, that is. That new technology encroached on the everyday by luring us into joining thousands or even millions of others in passively watching what corporations and media networks had determined would entertain us. The content may have been free, but that was because corporations bought airtime to show advertisements to entice us to buy their products. In (freely) giving over our free time to watching, we (freely) gave ourselves over to its particular combination of consumption and production. Still, the line between work and leisure, work time and downtime, remained in place. That is no longer the case, Crary argues.

Like Zuboff, Crary places the blame not on our always-on digital devices themselves but on the larger socioeconomic system in which they are embedded. Digital technologies may be new, but they are simply the latest versions of what Karl Marx identified as a perpetual revolution "of forms of production, circulation, communication, and image making" aimed at coaxing us—mostly successfully—into our proper roles as cogs in the consumption/production machine (37–38). The real matters only insofar as it translates into the digital. As the virtual replaces the fleshly as the site of value, what of the fleshly refuses translation (very little, Crary argues) declines in value. As a result, our ability to navigate the real atrophies. "Docility and separation are not indirect byproducts" of this new global digital economy, but "are among its primary aims" (42–43). This new ecosystem has finally succeeded in merging without remainder "management of economic behavior" with the "formation and perpetuation of malleable and assenting individuals" (42–43). And seeing is absolutely central to this goal and result.

Crary urges us to attend to "how the rhythms, speeds and formats of accelerated and intensified consumption are reshaping experience and perception" (39). In the service of extending monetized productivity to 24/7/365, companies spend billions of dollars every year studying how we look not only to figure out how to *get* us to look but also how to "reduce decision-making time, how to eliminate the useless time of reflection and contemplation" (40). Yes, immersing ourselves in this never-ending stream of "ephemeral [and] interchangeable" images renders us nodes in a "network of permanent observation" (47). But *how* we look is changing too. Viewing is no longer the steady state of looking. As we click from one image to another, attention is fragmented "into repetitive operations and responses" as we choose between the various "options of simultaneous and interruptive actions, choices, and feedback" that constitute digital viewing (52). The "processes of homogenization, redundancy, and acceleration" that characterize the "infinite cafeteria" of visual enticements have cost us our ability to "join visual discriminations with social and ethical valuations" (33).

How we look has consequences for how and who we are—individually and collectively. Building on Crary's insights, Dominic Pettman helpfully contrasts the impact of mass media with social media. By offering content that drew us en masse to the same content at the same time, mass media synchronized us. Social media, on the other hand, subject us to "staggered distraction." The algorithms individuate not only what we see online but when we encounter it.[43] Our individual attention is fragmented, and so is our collective attention. While we may see some of the same things (cat videos, memes, whatever goes viral), we don't see them at the same time. Not only do we each occupy "fabricated microworlds of affects and symbols,"[44] but "we never feel the same way at the same time."[45] We are individually hypermodulated: "Our nipples tweaked, our noses turned, our eyeballs twisted. We are being played like a giant keyboard."[46]

Of particular import for *Seeing and Believing* are the concerns that Crary and Pettman raise about the impact of the virtual and the visual on our flesh-and-blood collective life. Like Pettman, Crary is deeply skeptical of "clicktivism." Recirculating videos, memes, or petitions may make us feel good, for the moment, but it just distracts us from the deeper conditions that underlie the realities they reflect, leaving them unchanged. "Any social turbulence whose primary sources are in the use of social media will inevitably be historically ephemeral and inconsequential," Crary writes in *24/7* (121). Political activists who "kettle themselves in cyberspace" are all too easily tracked, manipulated, and even sabotaged—playing right into the hands of the very state powers they want to challenge (121). Those of us who place our confidence in clicktivism are settling for the image of collective action rather than actual collective action. Clicktivism squanders the power of the visual to create community and connection: "If one's goal is radical social transformation," the tools of our new media landscape must be put to use "in the service of already existing relationships forged out of shared experience and proximity" (121). Otherwise, they will simply "reproduce and reinforce the separations, the opacity, the dissimulations, and the self-interestedness inherent in their use" (121).

On the one hand, much in these critiques resonates with what we've heard previously. Without doubt, our 24/7 world has, for so many of us, eroded the line between work and leisure, the everyday and the workday, though in different ways (and for different reasons—not all of them connected to technological "disruption"). Those of us in the professional class feel obligated to respond to work emails or texts wherever we are and whenever we see them. This new ecosystem has also produced new (precarious) ways of earning a living (or trying to). In the new gig economy, it's not just musicians and actors whose income depends on the occasional; it's drivers, repair workers, or dog walkers summoned by apps on their smart phones. "Influencers" make money through curating an online self whose characteristics (chief among them "authenticity") inspire others to buy the products they endorse (and whose manufacturers pay the influencers). Whether it's our source of income or not, all of us are incentivized by this attention economy to self-curate our online profiles so that we appear productive, creative, and, above all, happy.

Similarly, thanks to algorithms that curate what each of us sees, we often find ourselves increasingly alone together—spatially, temporally, and affectively. That said, Pettman and Crary risk overlooking the opportunities for connection that this new public square offers—particularly when it comes to political organizing. Ironically, given more recent developments, Pettman's example of failed virtual protest is the collective videos that circulated on social media of Black men killed by police that gave rise to the #BlackLivesMatter movement.[47] While it was certainly the case that it took the video of George Floyd's brutal murder to prompt many "good white people" to do the necessary deeper dive Pettman calls for, that was most emphatically never the case for the #BlackLivesMatter movement. Much more than just a hashtag, the hard, on-the-ground work done by those activists and their allies—including here in Nashville, where I live—meant they were ready to try to take advantage of the tipping point that arrived in the spring of 2020. Of course, one could say the same for the organizers of the Capitol insurrection and related events.

CONCLUDING THOUGHTS

So what have we learned? Well, first and foremost, we have learned that life on the new public square brings both promise and peril, costs and benefits—and not just to our virtual lives. Our virtual lives are inextricably intertwined with our flesh-and-blood lives—at every level and in every aspect: individual and collective, social and political, affective and economic. And seeing—and being seen—is really the linchpin of this ecosystem. We are drawn onto the public square by what we see. In turn, what we see becomes the economic driver of the economic system that runs the public square. While the visual "raw material" of that economic system can come from anyone, anywhere, anytime (assuming they have access to the necessary technology), it's the algorithms created by the multinational corporations that own the platforms that make up the public square that determine what we see. And what we look at (and for how long) in turn becomes data that feeds the economic system we call surveillance capitalism.

The promise and peril, costs and benefits of living on this new public square show up in the ways they are remaking our experience of space and time (virtually and IRL). As Tufekci claims, globalization from above makes possible globalization from below. That is, the platforms owned and managed by global companies have created a global public square, one that enables us to generate, join, or expand global networks of connection. While virtual networks are no substitute for IRL networks, they provide soil and nutrients that allow them to grow. And they can dramatically reduce the time it takes to mobilize those networks into effective action IRL. On the other hand, if our old public squares were places where we gathered together—at the same time, in the same place—we are never quite together—at the same time, in the same (virtual) place—on this new one. Because the algorithms curate our experience on this new public square to each of us individually, we occupy it alone together. Thus, the affordances it offers to collective organizing are potentially undercut by the threats it poses to the very capacities that we need to live well together.

Figuring out strategies for maximizing the promise and minimizing the perils of life on our new public square is the critical challenge before us. And given how central seeing is to life on this new public square, identifying practices of looking that meet that challenge will be particularly important. But before we get to that, we need to understand more deeply the specific challenges that confront seeing on this new public square. Some of those challenges are anything but new, I argue, and even those that *seem* new are often, as we've seen with the new public square, updated versions of challenges that have been with us for quite a while. That will prove particularly true when it comes to the challenges related to seeing and believing.

FIGURE 3.1 *Seeing Is Believing*, Layer 1 (mirror).
Artist: Britt Stadig. Photographer: Amanda McCadams.
Printed with the permission of Vanderbilt University.

3

(RE)MAKING US

Science Finds—Industry Applies—Man Conforms
—Motto of the 1933 Chicago World's Fair

*"I post, therefore I am": Those who do not create a data trace do
not exist.*
—Roberto Simanowski, *Data Love*

If Google isn't responsible for its algorithm, then who is?
—Safiya Umoja Noble, *Algorithms of Oppression*

As I observed in the previous chapter, our incorporation
into and by this new ecosystem comes with both costs
and benefits, to what we know, and to who and how
we are—individually and collectively. At least in some ways we
are being remade—individually and collectively—by life on this
new public square. As we've already seen, the new public square
mines (by exploiting or nurturing) various aspects of our humanity, especially our desire to know and be known, see and be

seen. It taps into all aspects of our lives—social, political, economic, emotional, intellectual—and we register its impact in all of those ways as well. As much as the new ecosystem may be changing who and how we are, it is also clearly reinforcing who and how we have long been. The mechanisms of surveillance capitalism and the engines that drive it are human creations, so it is not surprising that they reflect the best and worst of humanity. That includes structural inequities and biases that are baked into our flesh-and-blood socioeconomic system.

In *Algorithms of Oppression,* Safiya Umoja Noble brings expertise in critical information studies engaged through a "Black feminist lens" to expose examples of what she calls "technological redlining": the encoding (intentional or not) of racial and gender bias into online search results.[1] The term riffs off real estate redlining, the practice begun in the 1930s of mapping mortgage risk via color-coded maps (about which more later). It is a particularly apt metaphor given that both forms of redlining encode racism with significant real-world impacts. Neighborhoods deemed the riskiest (often because they were populated by people of color, especially Black people) would be outlined in red. Those trying to buy houses in such neighborhoods paid higher interest rates—if they were able to get mortgages at all. Although redlining was outlawed in the 1970s, its role in creating the enormous wealth disparity between Black families and white families that exists today is indisputable. Indeed, in an influential article in *The Atlantic,* Ta-Nehisi Coates builds his case for reparations in large part on that reality.[2]

Photographs figure prominently in many of the case studies that anchor *Algorithms of Oppression.* Noble undertook the book project in response to the jarring results she got one afternoon in 2010 when, looking for ways to entertain her stepdaughter and nieces who were coming to visit, she did a Google search for

"Black girls." She was horrified by what showed up at the top of the results: images from the website HotBlackPussy.com. (So much for filter bubbles showing you what you *want* to see, she observes.) Another of Noble's examples may be familiar to some readers. A public controversy erupted in 2016 when a young Black Twitter user posted a video showing him googling "three Black teenagers" and reacting to the results: three mug shots of young Black men.

What googling yields by way of search results is a complex product of a cyborgian ecosystem created where the computational and the human meet (which, as we've seen already, is basically everywhere). Coders paid by Google create algorithms (proprietary, thus kept secret, of course) that feed on the search data provided by prosumers to create a ranked list of websites that contain the search terms we've selected. The information available on those websites is produced or curated by all kinds of organizations or individuals whose motives range from making money to promoting critical thinking, from spreading conspiracy theories to fighting them. Notably, Noble begins one chapter with the story of Dylann Roof's online radicalization. In his online manifesto, which Noble quotes at length, Roof described going online to search "Black on White crime."[3] His descent into a deep rabbit hole of hate that ultimately led to the massacre at Mother Emmanuel Church started with the first website he encountered, one curated by the Council of Concerned Citizens (CCC, classified by the Southern Poverty Law Center as a hate group). The CCC is one of several white supremacist organizations that run what another scholar, Jessie Daniels, calls "cloaked websites" made to look and read like legitimate journalism.[4]

It doesn't help that, as Noble observes, Silicon Valley's workforce—especially in the high-tech jobs—is hardly a model of diversity. According to Google's own statistics from 2016, just

2 percent of its employees were African American and 3 percent Latinx, she reports.[5] By 2022 the percentages had risen to 9.4 percent and 9 percent, which puts them slightly ahead of the field in general, according to a 2021 study by the Pew Research Center.[6] On those occasions when Noble has had future computer engineers in her classes at UCLA, they have been stunned to learn that racial stereotyping is as deeply encoded in our virtual lives as in our real ones. Noble argues (rightly) that Silicon Valley needs to recognize the value of expertise in critical race studies, gender and sexuality studies, religious studies, and other inter-disciplines to their work and seek to hire employees trained in those fields as well.

No surprise, then, that searches for "Black girls" or "Black teen-agers" yielded results that only reinforced long-standing racist and misogynistic associations of Black women with sexual promiscuity and Black men with criminality. The results may not be surprising, but that doesn't excuse them. Because algorithms are human creations, they can be reconfigured to correct such biases. By the time of *Algorithms'* publication, these searches were yielding markedly different results—evidence, Noble observes, that Google's coders altered their algorithms (putting the lie to Google's initial attempt to deflect responsibility for the search results by blaming larger social dynamics). Googling "Black girls" now yields wholesome images that connect Blackness with beauty and links to positive, helpful, and legitimate sources of information, support, and inspiration—including, notably, the website for Black Girls Code, a training initiative aimed at equipping Black girls for tech careers. Googling "three Black teenagers" takes you first to three news articles about the controversy (all from reputable news outlets). Similarly, googling "Black on white crime" now takes you to legitimate news articles debunking racist disinformation and websites that track actual data on crime statistics and race.[7]

In January 2020, Google announced the creation of a team of two thousand "Inclusion Champions" headed by a Haitian American woman, Annie Jean Baptiste, charged with testing new products for bias. Significantly, photography played a central role in Google's decision to launch this new initiative. An email from a Google engineer alerted upper management that the camera embedded in Google's Pixel phone wasn't sufficiently sensitive to the full variety of nonwhite skin tones. No one had thought to test the phone's digital camera on a wide array of skin tones before it was offered to the public. It is not clear whether the team responsible for this oversight included coders, but the article mentioned that, since becoming aware of the Pixel problem, Google had trained twelve thousand "technical engineers" in "inclusive design and how to bring it into their goals."[8] However, Google continues to struggle with encoded bias. In December 2020 and February 2021, the company fired two of its most prominent Black female scientists over alleged policy violations. One, Dr. Timnit Gehru, had coauthored an important study of facial recognition bias in artificial intelligence (AI).[9] She was fired allegedly because she did not retract a more recent scholarly article critical of racist bias embedded in AI linguistic software.[10]

What we see on the web reflects and refracts the larger system we have all inherited and been shaped by, a system shaped by the social hierarchies that constitute our flesh-and-blood world. We should not be surprised to find, then, that the virtual world mirrors these real-world dynamics—and, in some instances, magnifies and amplifies them. As Noble writes, "Knowledge management reflects the same social biases that exist in society because human beings are at the epicenter of information curation."[11]

Ultimately, then, the source of the problem—and thus of the solution to the problem—is us. And by "us" I don't mean just those who work in the tech industry; I mean *all* of us who produce and consume what the engines of surveillance capitalism render from us and to us. Taking on that responsibility in an effective way will certainly require media literacy; that is, attending carefully to the sources of what we see and hear online and off. But we also need to grapple not just with *what* we see and where it came from but *how* we see; in other words, what we believe we are seeing. Grappling with what seeing opens up and opens onto will require a deeper literacy: an understanding of the historical roots of the larger systems that encode and enforce bias—racism, sexism, cisgenderism, homophobia, ableism, etc.—in what and how we see online and in real life. Only if we understand the impact and import of these systems on us—on who we are, what we (think we) know and see, what we do, and why we (think we) do it—will we be able to resist some of their most maleficent effects. Only then can we begin to identify and cultivate alternative ways of knowing and doing that actively work against how we've been schooled.

> *Big data is neither a sociopolitical nor a simple technological problem but a historical and philosophical one.*
> —Roberto Simanowski, *Data Love*

In many ways, the dynamics that shape what we encounter online are modernity on steroids. Google searches are hardly the first form of information technology to incorporate socioeconomic inequities such as racism and sexism into their structures. Google's founders originally based the search strategies that would guide their search engines on the analogue systems that libraries use, systems (including the Library of Congress Subject Headings system and the Dewey Decimal System) that have historically had their own problems with encoded oppression (the topic of an entire chapter of *Algorithms of Oppression*).[12] Moreover, Simanowski argues that the pursuit of big data simply extends and expands (into digital form) "the Enlightenment impulse for mapping and measuring."[13] While our digital ecosystem has certainly accelerated and expanded this trend, the roots of what Simanowski calls the "quantified self" lie in what philosopher Colin Koopman calls "the informational person," a form of personhood birthed in the early decades of the twentieth century.[14] The informational person is a product of what he calls "infopower," a tripartite process of gathering, analyzing, and disseminating data into sanctioned and standardized forms.

Infopower "fastens" us to our data in two senses, Koopman argues. Formatting information about us into documents (analogue or digital) attaches us to our data, which is channeled into the various containers ("users, accounts, records") that constitute us as informational persons. Attaching us to our data determines who we are—at least in the eyes of certain authorities and systems. Confirming those records—showing our passport, providing our Social Security number—gives us access to the goods and services on offer from those authorities and systems. Take the birth certificate, one of the earliest (and most quickly and universally adopted) examples of infopower Koopman investigates. It gathers data (your name, date, place, time of birth, your parents' names) onto a carefully designed form. A state-sanctioned signature at the bottom makes it the official record of who you are. Presenting your birth certificate allows you to enroll in public school and to get a Social Security number, which, in turn, allows you to work legally and pay taxes. And on it goes. The presence or absence of such documents can also constrain us (to our gender assigned at birth, for example) and slow down or prohibit altogether our access to certain goods and services. Being "undocumented" subjects one to the risk of deportation, for example, and limits one's access to certain jobs, etc. Thus, the documents and the informational person they represent are rightly understood as products and channels of power.

Of particular pertinence is Koopman's work on what he calls the "informatics of race"; that is, the way analogue information technologies (predesigned forms with check boxes, for example) "datafied" race. Significantly, given Noble's work, Koopman devotes a chapter to analogue redlining.[15] Redlining was inaugurated by two organizations created by the New Deal: the Federal Housing Authority (FHA) and the Home Owners' Loan Corporation (HOLC). Neighborhoods deemed the riskiest (most often populated by people of color, especially Black people) were outlined in red. The practice might seem to simply encode the results of racism manifest in segregated neighborhoods and so-called ghettos, with high concentrations of poor people of color. However, real estate appraisal practices developed in the 1920s and solidified in the 1930s aided and abetted segregation and ghettoization. Studies show that segregation in urban areas became materially and measurably worse in the period between 1910 and 1940, peaking around 1950. In 1910 only 38.8 percent of residents of a given city in the United States would have had to move for each neighborhood's population to mirror the percentages of Black and white people in that city's total population. By 1940 achieving the same goal would have required 81 percent of the population to move.[16] What happened?

In the north, increased segregation was a response to the Great Migration of the early to mid-twentieth century, when 6 million Black people moved northward and westward to escape the horrors of the Jim Crow south and seek economic opportunity. This growing influx of people of color prompted more than a little racial anxiety among the white majority in these areas. Evolving real estate practices codified that anxiety, which materialized as residential segregation. One such practice was the creation of restricted covenants, in which (white) property owners agreed not to sell (or rent) homes within a particular neighborhood to people of color.

The practice of segregated home selling was codified into the professionalization of real estate brokerage. In 1924 the National Association of Real Estate Boards (NAREB) adopted a Code of Ethics that encouraged agents not to engage in real estate sales that would alter the racial composition of a neighborhood. The rationale was explicitly economic, not attitudinal. When people of color moved into white neighborhoods, property values went down. Thus, preserving property values required preserving a neighborhood's racial character. The fact that this was due to attitudinal racism was simply ignored or deemed unfortunate.

Racially restrictive covenants and such codes of ethics were ultimately deemed illegal, but another technique connected to them, the real estate appraisal (which was formalized during this period), perpetuated the datafication of racism and accelerated residential segregation. Two organizations, the American Institute of Real Estate Appraisers (AIREA) and the Federal Housing Authority (FHA) played critical roles here. Following NAREB's lead, the AIREA encoded racial diversification into the analogue algorithm that it recommended its members use to calculate property values. In the systematized multipage form published in the 1937 edition of the official manual, the presence of "racial and foreign neighbors" ranks second on the "table of common deductions" (following "noise and dirt"). Each deduction is quantified as a flexible percentage of the algorithm: up to 25 percent for noise and dirt, but up to 60 percent for "racial and foreign neighbors."[17] The FHA incorporated such standards for appraisal into the standardized appraisal forms that its loan application and approval processes relied upon. The HOLC produced the color-coded maps that delineated economic risk: red for those deemed "hazardous," green for the least risky, yellow and blue for those in between.

The effects of these analogue information technologies are with us to this day. A 2018 study conducted by the National Community Reinvestment Coalition found that 65 percent of today's "'majority minority' communities" are neighborhoods originally redlined by the HOLC, while 91 percent of neighborhoods greenlined by the HOLC are almost entirely white. Given that home ownership is a primary source of wealth to American families, the economic impact is dramatic, as "the typical Black family has just 8 cents of wealth (bank savings, investment holdings or home equity) for every dollar of wealth held by white families."[18] But as with digital technological redlining, the effects of analogue redlining and the techniques of datafication that aided and abetted it impact who lives and who dies. Take Minneapolis, Minnesota, for example, where George Floyd's murder took place. According to the interactive map of Minneapolis created by the Mapping Prejudice project housed at the University of Minnesota, approximately twenty-two thousand restrictive covenants were put in place in that city between 1910 and 1954, a year after the state legislature made the practice illegal.[19] The impact of those covenants extends into the present, Kirsten Delegard, founder of the Mapping Prejudice project, observes. Neighborhoods that adopted those now-defunct covenants remain "the whitest part of the city today," she reports, as Black residents ended up "sorted into just a handful of very, very small neighborhoods."[20] In turn, those neighborhoods were subject to much more intensive and often abusive policing than white neighborhoods, especially at their borders. Floyd, whose killing set off massive protests around the country and the world, was killed at one such former border.[21]

Vision [is] a mutable faculty . . ."embedded in a pattern of adaptability to new technological relations, social configurations, and economic imperatives."
—Liz Wells, *Photography: A Critical Introduction*, citing Jonathan Crary, *Suspensions of Perception*

As is the case with our new media landscape, technological racism—in both its analogue and digital forms—literally incorporates seeing. The effects of both forms of datafication extend into real, flesh-and-blood life. Analogue redlining's color-coded maps visually datafied attitudinal racism, enabling it to materialize and metastasize as residential segregation. The digital algorithms that selected the photographs for the searches Noble describes similarly encoded and thus metastasized systemic and attitudinal racism. The success—or failure, for that matter—of both forms of visual datafication relies on the connection between seeing and believing. For them to work, we must believe that the visual data they yield are the result of purely mechanical processes.

That infopower bends seeing and believing to its needs in these ways reflects the larger context of infopower's origins—a context shaped, as we're beginning to see, by systemic racism and all of the other systemic "isms" woven into our social fabric along with it (sexism and heterosexism, ableism, classism, cisgenderism, etc.). Understanding that context, the particular shape many of those "isms" take within it, and the role of seeing therein, is central to *Signs and Wonders*. And as I noted earlier, key to my understanding of those issues is the work of the French philosopher and cultural theorist Michel Foucault—a figure also central to Koopman's account of infopower. Both *Signs and Wonders* and *How We Became Our Data* expand and extend, supplement and correct Foucault's account of modernity. All three understand modernity as *episteme* and *ethos*; that is, as constituted by certain ways of knowing and doing that incarnate a distinctive regime of power.[22] Foucault calls what we typically think of as power—domination, essentially—sovereign power. Two new forms of power, dubbed by Foucault "disciplinary power" and "biopower," emerge in modernity.

Whereas sovereign power is embodied ultimately in the sovereign's right to kill his (or her) subjects, disciplinary power and biopower work in more subtle and diffuse ways. Disciplinary power seeks to form people into docile subjects who will go along (with normative identities and behaviors) to get along. Virtually every institution that constitutes our world—from schools and hospitals to prisons and factories—train us in those norms. Biopower was built off a shift in our understanding of nature. Whereas the natural world in all its variety had previously been deemed the manifestation of a singular, infinite teleology determined by a singular and infinite God, each form of life—from plants to animals to humans—was now understood to have its own internally generated and finite teleology. Where human beings were concerned, biopower's goal of nurturing human life by eliminating abnormality aligned closely with disciplinary power. I use the term "bio-disciplinary power" to signal that these two distinctive forms of power usually work in tandem.

Although Foucault himself arguably fails to fully recognize it, bio-disciplinary power is both positively and negatively racist; that is, biopower's (positive) aim of nurturing human life (aka the human race) has asymmetrical effects on those populations deemed especially prone to abnormality. Though they potentially afflict every human, defects and deficiencies—illness (mental and physical), sexual deviancy, criminality, and disability (physical or intellectual)—are believed to show up in greater numbers in minoritized populations. Thus, these populations find themselves subject to bio-disciplinary power's most punitive and violent sticks. Those deemed less vulnerable to abnormality (e.g., white people) are lured into docility primarily by bio-disciplinary power's carrots: the "goods" that came with being (perceived as) normal.

To Foucault's triad of sovereign power, disciplinary power, and biopower, Koopman adds infopower. Though it deploys "its own tactical operations, meticulous techniques, enlisted subjects, and correlative rationality of data," infopower bears the marks of its birth "within biopolitical and anatomopolitical [sic] contexts."[23] Those marks are visible in analogue redlining, which implicitly, if not explicitly, reinforces the attribution of increased deviance to minority populations. The same is true, I argue, for digital redlining. That a Google search for "Black girls" yielded photographs posted on pornographic websites reinforces the association of Black femininity with sexual deviancy, an association that has justified sexual exploitation—by white men, primarily—of Black girls and women since slavery. That a Google search for "three Black teenagers" yielded mug shots of males reinforces the association of Black masculinity with another form of deviance, criminality.

But where seeing and believing is concerned, this is just the tip of the iceberg. Seeing and believing are both essential to the installation, consolidation, and exercise of bio-disciplinary power that I laid out in *Signs and Wonders*. Joining Koopman's and Noble's work to elements of the analysis I offered there offers important insights into both the promise and peril of our new media ecosystem. First and foremost, the origins of surveillance capitalism lie not only in modern economic transformations but in modern visual transformations as well. Seeing as surveillance is central to Foucault's account of disciplinary power, found in his analysis of the modern prison system (known to Anglophone readers as *Discipline and Punish* but titled in French *Surveiller et punir* [surveil and punish]). Adapting to carceral existence required becoming what Foucault calls a "docile body,"[24] submitting oneself to prison discipline, including its processes of interrogation and confession, and taking up a new identity—that of a delinquent—on the way to reform.

Along with punishment, surveillance—embodied in the panopticon, a round tower surrounded by expanding rings of cells, that nineteenth-century prison reform advocate (and philosopher) Jeremy Bentham infamously articulated as the ideal architecture for a prison—served this system's goal. Its name, Greek for "all seeing," bespoke its purpose. Housing those judged to be criminals in such a structure would allow guards unimpeded round-the-clock visual access to the prisoners. That literal oversight was essential to the effectiveness of the other disciplinary practices (enforcing a set schedule of sleeping, waking and eating, interrogation and confession, work and other edifying activities) undertaken in pursuit of reforming self-avowed delinquents.

If surveillance is disciplinary power's signal contribution to modern seeing, a new visual subject, whom Jonathan Crary dubs "the observer," is biopower's.[25] In their quest to support and extend human life, scientists sought to understand how the human body worked. Physiologists divided it up into multiple isolable mechanical systems, including those connected to each of the senses, such as seeing. The human body came to be understood as vision's space-time container rendering vision autonomous, singular, and perspectival: what is seen is specific to *this* observer's body at *this* site. Various technologies (the stereoscope and the camera chief among them) were designed to exploit and extend modern vision to various ends. Photography as a technology and a practice came to be essential to "that modern play over bodies, gestures and behavior" that bio-disciplinary power embodies, writes historian John Tagg.[26]

PHOTOGRAPHIC SUBJECTION AND INFOPOWER

In *Signs and Wonders* I offer an account of what I call "photographic subjection." As conduits of bio-disciplinary power, I argue, photographs entrain us in its ways of seeing and believing. Those ways of seeing and believing refract what I call there a "fourfold"—of man and his others (raced and sexed, divine, and animal)—that channels bio-disciplinary power. Simultaneously subject and object of the modern *episteme* and *ethos*, man stands at the center of the fourfold. His "others" surround him like a network of mirrors reflecting man back to himself, thus establishing his claim on mastery (over himself, his "others," and the world they co-inhabit).

By channeling bio-disciplinary power, the fourfold affects how all of us become, live, and die. This is largely thanks to the role colonialism and its heir, globalization, played in institutionalizing and spreading bio-disciplinary power, I claim in *Signs and Wonders*. As a result, we all live out our lives—individually and collectively—by conforming to or resisting bio-disciplinary power's normative demands, issued as carrots or sticks. And photographs not only document but also transmit, and thus consolidate, bio-disciplinary power.

Significantly, given its role in *Algorithms*, the analogue mug shot exemplifies photographic subjection as an installation of bio-disciplinary power. While we may think of it as anything but a studied photographic practice, a good mug shot is no accident. Tagg mines police archives to chart the evolution of standards for it and the establishment of practices that will yield it. A cadre of professional police photographers were trained in how to use the camera to deliver "the [delinquent] body made object; divided and studied, enclosed in a cellular structure of space whose architecture is the file-index; made docile and forced to yield up its truth; separated and individuated, subjected and made subject."[27]

The mug shot encapsulates photographic subjection in a way that, we can now see, links bio-disciplinary power and infopower. The mug shot essentially dissects and thus diagnoses alleged criminality and fits it into a specified format, creating a form of infopower. Successful visual datafication of alleged delinquency involves massaging the perspectival nature of modern seeing. Achieving the appearance of objectivity and neutrality requires precisely calibrated production values. Too lavish or too spare and the photograph's evidentiary value suffers. Applying those techniques requires, first, training the photographers to see in a certain way so they can get viewers to see that way, too. What we see in a given mug shot, though, isn't just a reflection of its production values. It also reflects our own formation by bio-disciplinary power, including its racisms for and against.

This modern power regime incorporates not just alleged criminals but all of us. This is also true for what I call "photographic (bio-disciplinary) infopower." Bio-disciplinary power and infopower come together not only in mug shots but also in seemingly benign versions of visual datafication: the passport photo, the driver's license photo, and so on. These, too, impose certain conventions on the accompanying photograph that render it legitimate. In all of these cases, the photograph fastens us to data points on these official documents: our name, age, and place of residence, etc., yes, but also to our place in the distinctively modern taxonomies of identity that are themselves products of bio-disciplinary power. Based on infopower's visual datafication mechanisms, we are either Black or white, male or female (and presumptively cisgendered and heterosexual) regardless of whatever biological, historical, or autobiographical complexities inform who we understand ourselves to be. How well a specific mug shot or driver's license photograph—or any photograph, for that matter—succeeds in reinforcing these taxonomies, particularly in cases where the photograph may blur the lines between categories, is an open question. In the aggregate, however, as Noble's work demonstrates, photographs can and do reinforce those taxonomies and any associations with deviance (or presumptive normativity). We've all seen, in recent years, just how critical driver's licenses, passports, and birth certificates are to reinforcing normative identities as trans folk have pushed for policy changes that allow them to change the information such documents contain to reflect who they understand themselves to be.

ADD SURVEILLANCE CAPITALISM AND STIR?

The mere presence of mug shots on the World Wide Web is one example of the various ways that, as Koopman observed, infopower has migrated into our virtual world—and with it, biopower and disciplinary power. Noble's excavation of digital redlining calls attention to the impact of that migration on our real lives as well as our virtual ones—thanks to the engines of surveillance capitalism. Infopower has always been what we might call a public-private partnership—in the case of analogue redlining, between government agencies, private banks, real estate agents and appraisers, and, ultimately, us (new home buyers and their neighbors). But the private, multinational corporations that own the new public square do more than simply provide digitalized infopower with a new searchable storage facility. Surveillance capitalism effectively renders our virtual lives into monetizable information creating giant reservoirs we call big data. The corporate owners of those reservoirs fasten us to our data in ambivalent and sometimes ambiguous but impactful ways—and to a variety of ends and effects. This rendition is eroding the boundaries between public and private as well as between our real and our virtual lives. Digital infopower is, in other words, remaking us—individually and collectively—for good or for ill. It is no coincidence that virtually all of Noble's examples of digital redlining involve photographs. Seeing and being seen are pivotal to that remaking, with photographs playing a particularly central role.

Surveillance capitalism does more than simply trade in digitalized versions of analogue photographic infopower like mug shots. The larger photographic databases that Google's algorithms mine contain photographs that come from multiple sources, are taken for any number of reasons, and follow (or flaunt) different conventions associated with very different photographic genres. They may be formal (portraiture or landscape photography) or informal (family photos, souvenir photos, the now-ubiquitous selfie), produced by professionals (photojournalists, say) or amateurs. But regardless of its source or its genre, once a photograph is posted online, it becomes a data point for, and thus a conduit of, this new form of infopower. And this reality is remaking not only *what* we see but *how* we see.

While prior technological innovations (the camera, the x-ray machine, etc.) subjected the analogue observer to being seen on occasion, our current devices double down on visual subjection of the digital observer. Not only does the ubiquitous cell phone camera make us potentially observable at any time and without our knowledge, but surveillance capitalism tracks us 24/7 via our various devices, thus subjecting us to perpetual observation. It tracks both where we go and what we look at—not only on our screens but also what catches our eye when we shop in certain stores—with the goal, ultimately, of attracting our "eyeballs" more often. And viewing is no longer the steady state of looking. Facebook and Instagram invite us to "like" and "share" what catches our eye in the never-ending stream of visual imagery they offer up to us—and then move on. As we click from one image to another, our attention is fragmented "into repetitive operations and responses" as we choose between the various "options of simultaneous and interruptive actions, choices, and feedback" that constitute digital viewing.[28] Because what we see is more or less unique to each of us individually, digital viewing takes us into "fabricated microworlds of affects and symbols."[29] As a result, the digital observer is, if anything, more singular than its analogue predecessor.

Analogue vision was already finite and perspectival but at least presumptively autonomous and agential (for the seer, that is). Add in the economic incentives that drive this digital visual system, and the consequences for who we are become clear. Surveillance capitalism has succeeded in merging without remainder "management of economic behavior" with the "formation and perpetuation of malleable and assenting individuals . . . Docility and separation are not indirect byproducts" of this new digiglobal economy but "are among its primary aims," Crary writes.[30]

The use to which observations of digital subjects are put—
"unendingly solicited . . . into information that will . . . enhance
technologies of control" and be marketable[31]—if anything, tips
the balance further away from presumptive autonomy and agency.

THE THEO-LOGIC OF OUR
NEW MEDIA LANDSCAPE

You have searched me, LORD, and you know me.
—Psalm 139; quoted by Roberto Simanowski, *Data Love*

Given digital infopower's impact on us, it is perhaps no surprise
that several of the scholars discussed herein turn to a metaphorical theo-logic to describe the seismic shifts that have occurred as
we've transitioned to this new media ecosystem. They do so
because they find in this lexicon apt descriptors for the power that
surveillance capitalism holds over those subjected to it. Tracing
and tracking—and, in some cases, modifying that metaphorical
theo-logic in light of the account of modern power presented in
this chapter, though, adds complexity and reveals additional
dimensions of those power dynamics.

Seeing (and, I argue, believing)—first and foremost as
surveillance—features prominently in this metaphorical theo-
logic. Following sociologist Zygmunt Bauman, Simanowski
describes digital surveillance as post-panoptical. Like "snails
carry their homes," we all carry our own "mobile, portable single-
person mini-panopticon," the ubiquitous cell phone.[32] The all-
seeing eye of the single watchman has been replaced by all-seeing
algorithms (which Noble describes as "object[s] of faith" that
"freely provide, it seems, a sorting of the wheat from the chaff,
and answer our most profound and most trivial questions)."[33]

Simanowski dubs Google the "all-seeing eye of God."[34] The algorithm and the watchman embody godlike omniscience deployed (via our mini-panopticons) toward (customer) care rather than (prisoner) discipline. In claiming to use all that knowledge to better care for us (that is, provide us with what we [think we] need), Google renders its users "the new chosen people."[35]

Zuboff and Crary each turn to a similar theo-logic to describe the hold of the multinational corporations that embody surveillance capitalism over us. The goal of these corporations is basically omniscience, Zuboff observes. They seek to know not only everything about the present moment but, given their investments in predictive analytics, also about the future. She dubs those who serve this goal as a (secretive) "data priesthood" that mostly hides its work from us.[36] Both describe our relationship to our new sovereigns in terms of a new (and highly problematic) social contract. In Crary's view, the social contract in which subjects gave themselves over to monarchical rule in exchange for monarchical protection has been nullified. Per the terms of the click-wrap contracts that Zuboff argues we effectively sign when we use Facebook or Google, we (sur)render to these sovereigns of surveillance capitalism our virtual lives and, with them, our privacy and our right to a self-determined future. Absent the right to be forgotten, we will remain bound to these contracts eternally, for all practical purposes, given how long data lives online.

A metaphorical theo-logic focused on the traditional attributes of God—omniscience, eternity, and omnipotence—certainly bespeaks worrisome aspects of the dynamics of surveillance capitalism, but it also risks oversimplifying them. That further risks obscuring the ways that surveillance capitalism—a new form of infopower, I'm arguing—continues to circulate bio-disciplinary power, if in slightly modified form. Reviewing the relationship between this theo-logic and bio-disciplinary power will open up a more nuanced (metaphorical) theo-logic that better fits surveillance capitalism. Those moves will, in turn, address both problems and expose another geological layer to bio-disciplinary power.

Central to my account of photographic subjection in *Signs and Wonders* is Foucault's observation in *The Order of Things* that, in modernity, man displaced God as knower. However, to displace is not to replace, I argue. Whereas God both knows all and sees all, man's knowledge—of himself and the world around him—is finite and his vision perspectival. Moreover, man (unlike God) is simultaneously the subject and object of modern knowing. Under surveillance capitalism, man (as knower and known) has been doubly displaced: now by the algorithms that generate big data and the multinational corporations that create those algorithms and own the data they collect, mine, and circulate. Once again, to displace is not to replace. These corporations (technically, persons under U.S. law) may aspire to omniscience, but they have not yet achieved it—and it's not clear they ever will. Their servers may store every bit of data that exists on the internet, but storing per se isn't knowing. It is only when particular bits of data catch the "eye" of a particular algorithm that that bit of data becomes "known." Of course, algorithms "know" far more than any individual human about whatever the algorithm seeks out, but, as Noble's work demonstrates, algorithmic knowing is perspectival, as is human knowing. Of course, like human knowing, algorithmic knowing can always learn to know better and to know more (or not). But even outsourcing algorithmic generation and modification to AI will not entirely bypass the limitations of human knowing. For one thing, AI will remain, at bottom, a human creation even as it "outgrows" what its "parents" have taught it. For another, the data that surveillance capitalism mines—what we do, what we want, what we look at—is still, at bottom, mostly human data. However small it may be, a gap remains between our flesh-and-blood lives and our virtual ones—and, equally importantly, between and among our various virtual ones. What Google knows about me may overlap with what Facebook knows about me, but the two virtual me's, if you will, are not identical. In addition, if I leave my phone behind (as I do when I swim laps or go on my workout walk outdoors), neither Facebook nor Google—nor any other app that tracks me—will ever know about those activities. And even if I do take my phone on my workout walk, they will never know what I thought about on that walk unless I verbalize it.

Another dimension of the gap between our flesh-and-blood lives and our virtual ones becomes apparent when we consider what surveillance capitalists (think they) know. We have all had the experience of conversing with friends about a consumer good in the presence of our phones ("Where did you get those new glasses?") only to have an ad for the object pop up in our Facebook feed or on a Google search. Google and Facebook know that the optical shop See was mentioned in my (phone's) presence, but they don't know *why*. They don't "know" whether I commented on my friend's new glasses because I liked them or because I was just making conversation. Nor do they really care, of course, as all they want to do is lure me into buying something (or at least looking at the ad long enough to make See's purchase of said ad worthwhile).

Fully grasping the actual (metaphorical) theo-logic embedded in surveillance capitalism, though, requires a deeper dive into Bauman's concept of the post-panoptical. Though the term first appears in *Liquid Modernity* (2000), it gets its fullest treatment in *Liquid Surveillance* (2013), a book-length exchange (originally conducted by email, it turns out) between Bauman and fellow sociologist and surveillance theorist David Lyon.[37] At first glance, Bauman and Lyon's observations seem to reinforce the metaphorical theo-logic that we traced above, thus further oversimplifying the relationship between liquid surveillance and modern (bio-disciplinary info)power. That Bauman repeats in *Liquid Surveillance* his claim from *Liquid Modernity* that the panopticon is Foucault's central metaphor for modern power is particularly problematic. Remember that the panopticon, with its flesh-and-blood (singular) watchman, embodied analogue surveillance. Their physical presence would ensure that the surveilled stayed confined to the circumscribed space of the prison cell and the time of its imposed routine. The analogue panopticon— and, by extension, modern power (as Foucault understood it)—would seem to be, on Bauman's read, all about control: visual and ultimately behavioral. That risks oversimplifying Foucault's understanding of modern power, first by conflating disciplinary power with sovereign power.[38] Disciplinary power (only one form of modern power) does not run simply from the top of the tower down, nor does it manifest only as the watchman's control over prisoners. Analogue surveillance and externally imposed discipline were designed to provoke and promote the self-discipline required to produce docile (delinquent, in this case) bodies. The panoptical prison was designed not just to contain and control those deemed criminal, but to re-form them. It achieved that goal by "encouraging" prisoners to adopt a new identity (that of the delinquent) and then by "encouraging" them to normalize. True, the prison uses more sticks than carrots, but it is not the only institution to channel (bio-)disciplinary power. The ratio of carrots to sticks used in schools and factories, clinics and families will be different from prisons and will vary depending on the perceived potential for docility in the particular human beings subjected to them.

That said, the analysis of post-panoptical surveillance that Bauman and Lyon provide helpfully complicates—even undercuts—the metaphorical theo-logic that I'm critiquing here in several respects. The solid and singular panopticon has been replaced by our pocket panopticons, the singular watchman by the multinational corporations that track us via those same panopticons. Thanks to these digital technologies and the institutions that source and resource them, surveillance has become post-panoptical—and liquified—in all respects. The distribution of labor for surveillance and management has shifted as well, Bauman argues. Formerly the province of managers, now the managed are increasingly expected to manage themselves—and, as we've seen, we generally comply. Moreover, the panopticon (where the few watched the many) has become what Thomas Mathiesen dubs a synopticon (where the many watch the few).[39] Post-panoptical surveillance, then, is dispersed through the network of diffuse and diverse connections—mechanical, technological, virtual, and fleshly—that constitute and connect our real and our virtual lives.

That post-panoptical surveillance works via a network, however, does not distinguish it from its panoptical predecessor. True, digital post-panoptical networks themselves are much larger, more complex, and more cyborgian than their analogue predecessors (which they incorporate) by several orders of magnitude. Bauman's liquidity thesis purports that they also move more quickly—not to mention more fluidly—than their analogue predecessors. And as we've seen, they are, if anything, *more* difficult to escape—even for a moment. It's their seemingly totalizing spatial and temporal reach/grasp that motivates this turn to a metaphorical theo-logic of omniscience (and omnipotence) in the first place. But that particular theo-logic needs modification if it is to aid our understanding of the relationship between surveillance—liquid or solid—and modern power (and knowledge). The giants of surveillance capitalism may indeed aspire to godlike omniscience and omnipotence, but that aspiration is actually a human (all-too-human) one—indeed, a modern (all-too-modern) one.[40] It is, metaphorically speaking, the lifeblood of modern (bio-disciplinary and info)power. While the institutions that channel modern power may have liquified only recently, I argue that modern (Foucauldian) power per se has always been liquid.

This theo-logical course correction is critical to *Seeing and Believing* for two major reasons. First, recall that my central concern is with resourcing resistance to how we're being (re)made by surveillance capitalism. Were the metaphorical theo-logic of omniscience and omnipotence to stand, resistance to that (re)making would seem to be either impossible or futile. Yet, as we've seen, globalization from above makes possible globalization from below. It is possible to use our pocket panopticons to resist. That possibility exists because and despite the fact that we are embedded in the network that is modern (bio-disciplinary info)power. That network incorporates both our virtual and our real lives, but gaps between our virtual and our real lives remain. It's not only surveillance that's gone liquid but also the modern institutions that gave solidity to our larger world—and with them the ties that bind us to them and, most importantly, to one another. Those institutions include, notably, analogue social networks, the territories to which they are often bound (whether nation-states or neighborhoods), and the agencies (governmental or non-) that set and secured those boundaries. Marshalling effective resistance will require labor on all of these different levels; clicktivism alone will not suffice. It will also require cultivating an awareness of our conformity to docility and strategic attention to the opportunities for resistance.

Like its predecessor, post-panoptical surveillance channels bio-disciplinary and infopower. Thus, like its predecessor, it serves bio-disciplinary power's imbrication in systemic racism. Here, Bauman and Lyon are particularly helpful as they call attention to the asymmetrical effects of liquid surveillance on different populations. Those with sufficient cultural and financial capital can become global citizens free to travel for business or pleasure wherever they want (what we might call a "cosmopolite").[41] For refugees and asylum seekers, on the other hand, the post-panopticon is essentially what Didier Bigo dubs a "banopticon."[42] Governments use liquid surveillance (sometimes aided and abetted by surveillance capitalism, intentionally or not) to search out undesirables in order to keep them out—if necessary, I'd add, by confining them to camps located in the middle of (sometimes literal, always metaphorical) nowhere. The same is true for those deemed of little or no worth to surveillance capitalism, those with little or no money to spend and thus little to offer by way of desirable data, according to Bauman and Lyon.[43] Meanwhile, those who make self-management possible (e.g., coders) and those who actually "hold the levers" of this new form of infopower recede from view.[44] Like the Wizard of Oz, they disappear behind the curtain of the global, multinational network they have created.

That said, allowing *any* theo-logic to stand—even the modified one I'm suggesting here as a more apt metaphor for surveillance capitalism—might call into question my plan to turn to religious ways of seeing to resource resistance, but the opposite is actually true. Just as our resistance to its formative effects is made possible because of our imbrication in modern power, so too with religion—Christianity, in particular. Its (metaphorical) presence, if you will, as one of the geological layers of modern power that (in)forms surveillance capitalism not only justifies turning there for resources; it arguably requires it.

SEEING, BELIEVING, AND RELIGIOUS RESISTANCE

Here again, Bauman and Lyon are helpful. Seeing and believing make a brief appearance together in *Liquid Surveillance*—notably, when the two authors take up the issue of cultivating an ethical response to the asymmetries embedded therein. They agree that a central ethical challenge is learning to see through those asymmetries: to see refugees not as threats, but as deserving of refuge, to see correcting surveillance capitalism's inequities as an ethical obligation. Lyon (a Christian, it turns out) puts forward a theo-logic that speaks to that challenge: the biblical ethic of obligation to the other. That theo-logic is central to both the Hebrew Bible and the New Testament and thus to Judaism and to at least some versions of Christianity (including the version of the latter that Lyon and I both claim as our own). It is also central to the work of the Jewish philosopher Emmanuel Levinas that Lyon also references—prompting Bauman to observe that Levinas, like Lyon, was "a believer."[45] Bauman acknowledges Lyon's point, but with caveats: this demand was issued, he says, to "the saints,"[46] those who "made those words flesh," as he puts it, by their ethical practices. More power to them, he seems to say, but we're not all saints. And more to the point, while Levinas and Lyon may be, we're not all believers—particularly not in the divine origin of such an obligation. Divine provenance cannot be the premise for an ethical response if it is to be effective.

I certainly agree, but I don't think that requires putting religious resources like these off the table. As I've said from the outset, for such to be of use, they cannot be available only to those who identify with the specific tradition in question (or any other religious tradition, for that matter). The high regard in which Levinas's work is held by continental philosophers who not only don't share his religious affiliation but also know little to nothing about Judaism in the first place is exemplary here. But this chapter has shown us that more is also required in this case. Theological resources beholden to the notion of an omniscient, omnipotent, and all-seeing God risk reinforcing that theo-logic's alleged resurrection in surveillance capitalism and failing to engage with how bio-disciplinary power continues to infuse surveillance capitalism.

That doesn't mean belief is off the table; in fact, quite the contrary. As we've already seen, belief is hardly confined to the sphere of religious faith. What we believe (about other people, other places, about the provenance of a given photograph, even about photography itself) informs how we see. And all of those beliefs are informed by bio-disciplinary power. Nor is belief confined to the irrational or a-rational; indeed, quite the contrary. Recall that, for Foucault, modern power is also knowledge. As my brief reprise of biopower and infopower reminds us, rationality too has been conscripted to serve the modern power regime. Indeed, when I say we "believe" what we see, I mean we have confidence in it, a confidence that often rests on and refracts our formation by bio-disciplinary power/knowledge.

All of this raises the stakes where seeing and believing are concerned. Seeing has always been more than a mere sensory response to visual data; it is as much a matter of the social as the physiological whether it takes place online or in real life. What we believe we see when we encounter, say, a tall Black teenage boy wearing a gray hoodie—whether in person or in a photograph, online or in real life—is shaped by such factors as attitudinal and systemic racism and our relationship to them. As the murder of Trayvon Martin and the photographic story line that unfolded from it demonstrates, what we believe we see can determine whether someone lives or dies—Martin himself, the good Christian folk at Mother Emmanuel that Dylann Roof massacred, the pious Muslims murdered in New Zealand, the security guard and customers killed and wounded at Tops grocery store, and on and on. How might we—especially those of us who benefit from bio-disciplinary power—cultivate ways of seeing that will amplify resistance to the (literally) death-dealing dynamics at play in our time and place?

Surveillance capitalism provides us with fodder for resistance. And much of that fodder consists of photographs and videos. Of course, the sociopolitical impact of online photography can and will run the full spectrum of our real-life social and political perspectives. While our default might be to capitulate to photographic subjection, many of us are moved by what we see to resist and refuse, to align otherwise. That was the case with every set of photographs I discussed in *Signs and Wonders*, and it's also the case with the photographic story lines I reference herein. My interest, in *Seeing and Believing*, is in resourcing and supporting photographic insurrection; that is, engagement with the photographs that populate our new public square in ways that prompt deeper reflection, personal re-formation, and social realignment. Achieving that goal will require remaining mindful of both the affordances and the barriers, the promise and the peril, that our virtual lives offer to our flesh-and-blood ones uncovered so far in these pages. It will also require specific attention to how digital photography plays into the larger media landscape that constitutes our new public square in both positive and negative ways. What distinguishes digital photography—as a technology and a practice—from its analogue predecessor? What remains the same? How does digital photography interact with our new media landscape and its affordances and barriers and with surveillance capitalism?

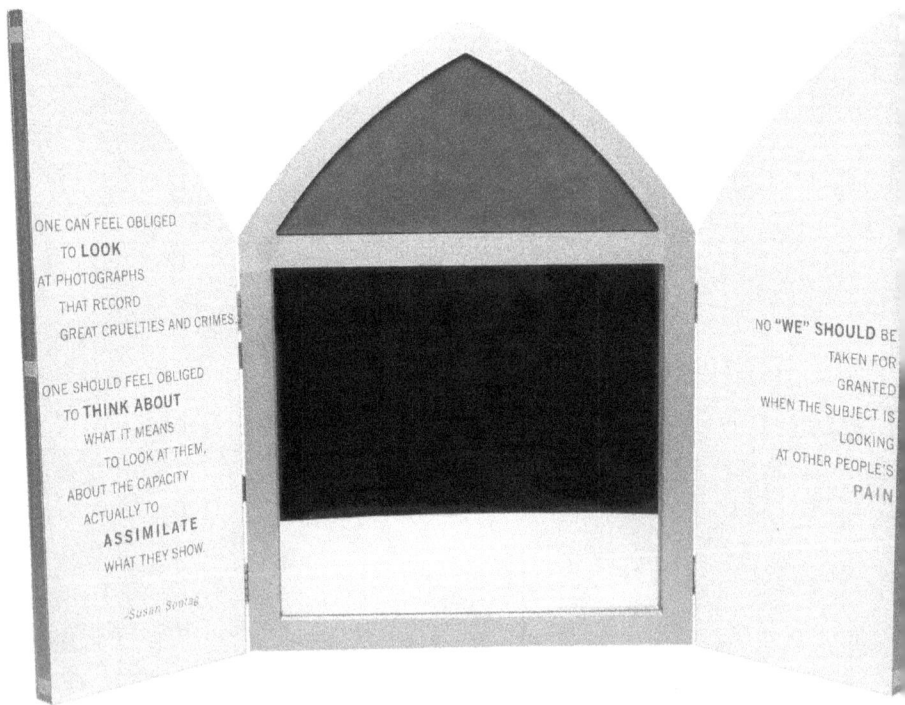

ONE CAN FEEL OBLIGED
TO **LOOK**
AT PHOTOGRAPHS
THAT RECORD
GREAT CRUELTIES AND CRIMES.

ONE SHOULD FEEL OBLIGED
TO **THINK ABOUT**
WHAT IT MEANS
TO LOOK AT THEM,
ABOUT THE CAPACITY
ACTUALLY TO
ASSIMILATE
WHAT THEY SHOW.

Susan Sontag

NO **"WE" SHOULD** BE
TAKEN FOR
GRANTED
WHEN THE SUBJECT IS
LOOKING
AT OTHER PEOPLE'S
PAIN

FIGURE 4.1 *Seeing Is Believing*, Layer 2.
Artist: Britt Stadig. Photographer: Amanda McCadams.
Printed with the permission of Vanderbilt University.

4

REFRAMING PHOTOGRAPHY

The age of digital replication is superseding the age of mechanical reproduction.

—William J. Mitchell, *The Reconfigured Eye*

The social photo is not just a reflection of yourself and your world but . . . equally the creation of yourself and your world. It is a primary way we now learn to recognize ourselves as selves, our reality as reality.

—Nathan Jurgenson, *The Social Photograph*

The convergence of the digital camera, the internet, and social media has significantly altered photography as a technology and a practice in several respects. As we saw in the previous chapter, analogue infopower—under the aegis of governmental agencies, primarily—often annexed analogue photography to its documentary and evidentiary practices by attaching photographs to them. As we've noted, certain kinds of photographic infopower have migrated online (mug shots, for example) alongside the vast majority of digital photographs, which, regardless of genre or provenance, now live online. We store them in "the cloud," share them on social media, and search for them using Google or one of its competitors. Photos posted on Snapchat may be programmed to disappear, but most of the multinational corporations that embody surveillance capitalism retain potentially permanent access to a significant portion of our collective photographic archive. We give our photographs over to them because they make sharing and storing them so easy, of course. But in addition to making photographs accessible to prosumers, those corporations also essentially render them into data—bits of information, in other words, that they use to various ends. Thus, digital photographs themselves have become essentially a new kind of photographic infopower. Digital photographic infopower is harnessed not primarily to governmental agencies and aims but to private corporations who use it to capture our attention, sell ads, develop facial recognition software, predictive analytics, and so on. Like analogue photographic infopower, digital photographic infopower is both distinct from and connected to bio-disciplinary power, though in somewhat different ways and for different reasons. Certainly, as we saw in the previous chapter, those ends often channel (intentionally or not) bio-disciplinary power and its racisms for and against, for example. I am particularly concerned here with what we can do—individually and collectively—to respond thoughtfully and ethically to photographic infopower as a channel of bio-disciplinary power. Algorithms may be all-too-human creations, but humans are not algorithms. We respond to the photographs we encounter online as photographs, not simply as bits of data. And our responses to what we (believe we) see in the photographs we encounter online refract the full complexity of our individual and collective formation as embodied, social, rational, and emotional beings, formations shaped by bio-disciplinary power. To know, to do, to be, to see is to take up—or to refuse or resist—one's place in the social order that it has produced.

As the previous chapter showed, bio-disciplinary power has had a formative impact on photography too—as a visual technology and a social practice—from its inception. As I argued with reference to analogue photography in *Signs and Wonders*, we subject ourselves to bio-disciplinary power by shooting, posing for, or viewing photographs. That is as true of digital photographs—regardless of genre or provenance—as it was of analogue photographs. That said, there are significant differences between digital and analogue photography, many of which track with the dynamics of our new media ecosystem. Like the shifts in our media landscape, the changes in photography are cultural and technological, evolutionary and revolutionary. Some of those changes accelerate and amplify characteristics of analogue photography while others represent innovative departures from it. Understanding these dynamics is critical to navigating the complicated relationship between seeing and believing in our virtual and our real lives—especially given the prominent place that visual media occupy in our virtual world. Back in 2015, Facebook reported that videos on its platforms received up to four billion views per day. Approximately half of its active users watched at least one video every day.[1] A 2018 update reported that adult users spent more time on their mobile devices than they did watching TV. The time they spent watching digital videos had also increased dramatically in the interim: from 4 percent to 28 percent of the time they spent online. Those trends coincided with a dramatic increase in video content. The number of short-form videos (then called "Stories," now "Reels") present on Facebook, for example, doubled in just one year, resulting in 1.5 billion active users interacting with at least one Story every day.[2]

FROM ANALOGUE TO DIGITAL:
CULTURAL CONTINUITIES,
TECHNOLOGICAL DIFFERENCES

According to Abigail Solomon-Godeau, "All of the problems posed by image culture, spectacle, and simulation in the globalized network of late capitalism"—including "questions about reception, spectatorship, regimes of viewing, subject formation, and processes of signification"—that digital photography raises originated with analogue photography.[3] The advent and spread of digital photography has not created a "'post-photographic' condition," in other words, but constitutes "an intensification and proliferation" of what the "industrialization" of analogue photography set in motion.[4]

William J. Mitchell's masterful inquiry into digital photography, *The Reconfigured Eye*, largely backs up that claim.[5] The groundwork for modern digital surveillance capitalism, for example, was laid with the invention of stereography, the first photographic technology. As early as 1859, Oliver Wendell Holmes imagined its use to produce a massive archive of all the riches of the known world—cultural and natural. Stereographers, Holmes argued, will "hunt all curious, beautiful, grand objects, as they hunt the cattle in South America, for their skins and leave the carcasses of little worth."[6] Stereographs of such monumental human achievements as the Colosseum in Rome or wonders of nature like Niagara Falls would become a "universal currency of bank notes . . . which the sun has engraved for the great Bank of Nature,"[7] available both for private consumption and circulation (think coffee table books) and public display. Emergent digital technology took Holmes's vision of a "great Bank of Nature" to a new level, Mitchell observes, one torqued to a different purpose thanks to the United States Geological Survey. Digital photography started out as form of governmental infopower. Invented in the 1950s, it was deployed by NASA as early as 1964.[8] In 1972 its Earth Resources Observation and Science (EROS) Data Center began to create an archive of satellite images of the earth—one that now lives online—ultimately rendering "the entire surface of the earth . . . a continuously unfolding spectacle and an object of unending fine-grained surveillance."[9] In the 1990–1991 Gulf War, digital imaging technologies and visual tracking software (GPS, facial recognition, etc.) embedded in weapons systems rendered "slaughter...a video game" as "death imitated art,"[10] Mitchell writes. In the decades since, digital photographic infopower's reach has only expanded, both in its governmental forms (think drone warfare) and its nongovernmental ones as well.

Well before digital photography became widely available, Susan Sontag anticipated these effects of (analogue) photography's conscription and expansion, Mitchell notes. She sounded the alarm in 1977 about (in his words) "panoptic photographic production" as "a potentially sinister ally of the late-capitalist state."[11] As a source of entertainment, photography functions as an opiate for the masses that "anesthetize[s] the injuries of class, race, and sex."[12] It also acts as a financial stimulus—directly, insofar as images inspire consumers to buy things, and indirectly, insofar as photographic technologies are used to identify natural resources for exploitation, help wage war, and keep order. Sontag further envisioned photography as the tool of a new dystopian social order, one that would replace genuine freedom with the mere freedom to consume (both the images themselves and what images lead us to desire), a vision come to fruition in the digital visual culture we now inhabit.

FROM ANALOGUE TO DIGITAL: REFRAMING PHOTOGRAPHIC TRUTH

Whether digital or analogue, photography's usefulness to any of the systems of power that trade in it rests on viewers' belief in its evidentiary value. As my reference in chapter 1 to "deepfakes" noted, the ease with which digital photographs can be altered has raised serious questions about its evidentiary value—and the stakes therein. But whether we can, in fact, believe what we see in a given photograph was a question from photography's inception. We largely take for granted that photographs give us nothing more—and nothing less—than what I call (riffing off of Roland Barthes) the "that-there-then" that prompted the photographer to click the shutter in the first place. But photographic truth is more than mere correspondence of image to referent—what it indexes, in other words. It is a matter of what we (believe we) see in what it frames, which is, in turn, shaped by what we believe about our world and our place in it, including what we believe about photography. All of that has been shaped by modern bio-disciplinary power. As I argue in *Signs and Wonders*, photography was one of the managerial and disciplinary techniques and technologies annexed by bio-disciplinary power. It served as an essential tool in the production of the modern human taxonomies it generated and perpetuated and in our subjection to them.[13] But photography does not simply reflect bio-disciplinary power; it was definitively shaped by it. The attribution of direct referentiality to analogue photography was neither automatic nor immediate; rather, it had to be established—and learned. The "evidential force" of photography is an archival creation accrued and consolidated by and through its use in the material operations of bio-disciplinary power.[14] In turn, looking at photographs trained their viewers in how to see each other and what to look for in each other. Mug shots are a clear example, as we've seen, but even casual snapshots like family photographs generally reinforced the proper roles of mothers and fathers, sons and daughters as defined by bio-disciplinary normalization.[15]

While photographic content has not changed much as we've moved from analogue to digital, the relationship between digital photographs and their "that-there-then" differs significantly from analogue photography, thanks to technological innovation. As Liz Wells aptly puts it, if analogue photography "transcribed" people, places, and things into images, digital photography is a process of "conversion" of the visual into computer code.[16] In *The Reconfigured Eye*, Mitchell details the technological differences and tracks their import in detail. The analogue camera was heralded by Henry Fox Talbot as a "light pencil" that promised objectivity without the interference of the human agency required for painting. The photographer's role was simply to direct the light pencil—to decide what's worth recording and then let the camera do its thing. This rendered the analogue camera a "supereye—a perceptual prosthesis that can stop action better than the human eye, resolve finer detail, remorselessly attend to the subtlest distinction of intensity, and not leave unregistered anything in the field of its gaze."[17]

The analogue photograph is arguably more faithful to its "that-there-then" than its digital counterpart. For one thing, it contains far more than it reveals at first glance. Enlarge it and more and more detail of a photograph's that-there-then appears, detail that was likely invisible to the photographer. Enlarge a digital photograph, on the other hand, and whatever details it has captured start to erode. Make it big enough and the image eventually dissolves into a pixelated grid. That's because the digital camera converts what it sees by bending it to fit what's called the "raster grid," a preset two-dimensional grid of pixels (cells that encode color, shade, and intensity).

Both digital and analogue photography enable the production of multiple copies of a given photograph, but the two technologies differentiate the relationship between copy and original (and copy to copy) in significant ways. Transcription via the interaction of light with chemicals, film, and photographic paper results in physical artifacts: first the negative and then the printed analogue photograph. Producing multiple copies of an analogue photograph from the negative causes details like gradations of light and shadow to slowly erode from copy to copy. This process of erosion enables knowledgeable viewers to distinguish not only copy from original but copy from copy (hence the practice in art photography of limiting the number of reproductions and identifying each one by number and series). Because code is code is code is code, a digital photograph can be reproduced infinitely without any degradation. But because there is no real digital analogue to the photographic negative (beyond a time/date stamp, which can be altered), it is impossible to discern digital copy from digital original, much less digital copy from digital copy.[18]

Clearly, then, "the stored array of integers has none of the fragility and recalcitrance of the photograph's emulsion-coated surface,"[19] which yields important differences in the relationships between digital and analogue photographs to their that-there-then. But the most significant difference between digital and analogue photography is the *role* of the external referent: an actual "that-there-then." Analogue photographs require one; digital photographs do not. Digital photographs are not only easier to alter but also can be created out of whole (digital) cloth. The capacity to create new digital images out of newly generated code either by itself or in combination with preexisting cyber-objects (other digital photographs, say) is built into digital photography's DNA, binary code embodied in the pixel. (Should we even call such images "photographs"—"light writing"—at all?) Analogue photographs "seem to bond image to referent with superglue,"[20] but "the referent has come unstuck" from the digital photograph, Mitchell astutely observes.[21] "We have entered the age of electrobricollage [sic]."[22]

The consequences for how we see and what we see are profound but not unmanageable. If analogue photography was emblematic of modernity's confidence in (photographic) truth as correspondence (in this case, between image and referent), digital photography has given us instead "indeterminacy . . . process and performance."[23] Yet Mitchell also insists that whether digital or analogue, presumptive photographic truth and the challenges to it are as much a matter of convention as of a click of the shutter, of culture as of technology. In this respect, the shift from analogue to digital is as much cultural evolution as technological revolution.

Photography celebrated its 150th anniversary in 1989, and digital manipulation was already on the rise. By 1991 the genie was completely out of the bottle. Just as the Brownie camera (coupled with Kodak's capacity to develop and print) had democratized analogue photography decades earlier, new digital cameras (coupled with storage devices like CDs and computers for viewing) were democratizing digital photography. The means to take, alter, or create digital photographs was well on its way to becoming available to anybody and everybody. Photojournalists were the first to have to wrestle with this new reality. The *Wall Street Journal* estimated in 1989 that 10 percent of published photographs had been digitally altered in some way or another. The cover of an issue of *National Geographic*, for example, featured a photo of two of the pyramids in Giza, Egypt, that had been altered slightly to compress the space in between them. Editors debated whether this alteration was any different from a common analogue practice: waiting for just the right moment—say, when a camel train is in just the right spot—to shoot the photo you want.[24] Fred Ritchin observes that in 2008, concerns about political motives for and consequences of such practices emerged with particular potency. *Newsweek* was accused of political bias after it published an unretouched photograph of then–Republican vice presidential candidate Sarah Palin on its cover. The flaws visible in that photograph contrasted dramatically with the perfection of (allegedly retouched) cover photos of Democratic presidential candidate, Barack Obama.[25]

SEEING AND BELIEVING I: REFRAMING PHOTOGRAPHY

In *The Public Image: Photography and Civic Spectatorship*, renowned communications scholars Robert Hariman and John Louis Lucaites inquire into the impact and import of photojournalism for our communal and political lives. They seek to persuade their readers that despite these problems, photographs remain essential "resources for thinking what it means to see and be seen," a task we need to undertake if we are to "live well in a world connected by lines of sight."[26] Our new media landscape and the technologies that undergird it, including digital photography, only raise the stakes of that endeavor, they (rightly) claim, even as this new reality heightens skepticism about photography as a medium.[27]

Photography as a medium needs to be rethought, they argue, a task that will require a reboot of its scholarly discourse. We need a new paradigm, they say, for thinking about and with photography—one centered, I argue, on reframing the relationship between seeing and believing. At the heart of the old paradigm is a certain understanding of photographic truth as literal and unmediated, as nothing more (or less) than a representation of a certain "that-there-then." Photography's allegedly unmediated relationship to the real funded its use as a "modern recording technology" deployed in the service of "science, industry, advertising, art, and most notably the press."[28] Photojournalism put all its eggs in the literalist basket, if you will. It came to see its primary ethical obligation as simply to publish only photographs whose relationship to the real can be confirmed. (That said, editorial decisions about which photographs to publish are often considerably more complicated, especially where children are concerned. Until newspaper editors made the difficult decision to publish the iconic photograph from the Vietnam War now known as *Accidental Napalm*, journalistic convention placed photographs of naked children off-limits.[29])

According to the old paradigm, seeing *should* trump belief—or be enough to inspire belief (in the truth of what is put before your eyes). Yet it's precisely that confidence in photographic literalism that skeptics (Hariman and Lucaites call them "iconoclasts") reject. Documentarian Errol Morris argues in his 2011 book, *Believing Is Seeing*, that we see in photographs what we already believe to be true, Hariman and Lucaites report.[30] And Sontag, their exemplar of photographic iconoclasm, observes that despite the fact that we know photographs can be staged or altered, "everyone is a literalist when it comes to photographs."[31] And yet the very same photograph can serve the political interests of opposing sides. Both sides in the Bosnian conflict, for example, claimed the same photograph of Bosnian children killed by bombs as evidence of the other's war crimes, using it successfully to rally support. "No 'we' should be taken for granted when the subject is looking at other people's pain," Sontag observes.[32]

Hariman and Lucaites are hardly naïve when it comes to these realities, but they resist consigning photography to the dead end where literalism and iconoclasm meet. Significantly, they turn to a theo-logic of sorts to describe this dead end. They describe photographic literalism as a form of fundamentalism that flattens photography's relationship to reality. Photographs are more than mere mechanical reproductions of their that-there-then, they insist. Rather, they embody a complex relationship between "trace and artifact, reality and imagination."[33] As light writing, each photograph carries a literal trace of the artifact it represents (a constitutive element of its power to move us, per Roland Barthes). But the photograph is also an artifact itself and, as such, takes on a life of its own (potentially, an eternal one online).[34] But the biggest problem with photographic literalism is that it "sever[s] the most vital connections between the photograph and the world,"[35] which impoverishes our ability to have critical ethical discussions about what we see. Instead, Hariman and Lucaites urge us to think of photography as a "mode of extraordinary seeing,"[36] one that animates viewers' vision and imagination to expand their narrow understanding of reality. "A photograph is both image and optic: a picture of some part of reality and a way of seeing that reality more extensively."[37] This is what makes photography a crucial resource for our civic and political lives. Mining that resource requires cultivating a more nuanced understanding of photographic truth, one that can acknowledge and work with conflicts over the photograph itself as a representation of reality and over the reality it re-presents that (seemingly inevitably) arise. Reckoning with that complicated relationship between the real and the re-presented—and the re-presented as itself real—requires reconceiving the relationship between vision and imagination. We must resist in no uncertain terms a radical split between realism and imagination, a goal that will require a deeper dive into seeing and believing.

SEEING AND BELIEVING II: REFRAMING PHOTOGRAPHIC AFFECT

In *The Social Photograph*, Nathan Jurgenson offers a differently focused reboot of scholarship on photography that foregrounds the everyday digital images we shoot and share. That focus yields a different set of questions raised by the challenges and opportunities that the confluence of social media and digital photography opens up. That confluence has yielded a different form of photographic practice—what Jurgenson calls "social photography"—and a different genre, in a sense, of photography: the social photograph. *The Social Photograph* supplements and complements the analysis I've offered so far in several ways. For one thing, to the reframing of photographic truth it adds a reframing of photographic affect; that is, how photographs move us emotionally and to take action. For another, much about his analysis resonates with mine thus far in *Seeing and Believing*. As with digital photography, social photography is as much a cultural phenomenon as a technological one, a matter of evolution as much as revolution. All photographs—analogue or digital, professional or amateur—are social insofar as they are meant to be shared, Jurgenson acknowledges. But photographs these days are "units of communication," not "stand alone media objects."[38] We're less interested in how "good" they are than in what they communicate, less invested in the single image than in the image stream. Indeed, Jurgenson describes social photography as (riffing off Bauman) "liquid photography": created in an instant, infinitely shareable, even leakable; simultaneously ephemeral and potentially permanent. We have no control over where a given photograph, once shared on social media, ends up or how long it might stay there.

Social photography relies on the digital cell phone camera, to be sure, but the most critical technology may actually be the social platforms that inspire us to take and share.[39] Embedding the cell phone camera in a visually saturated digital ecosystem renders it a social camera. More software than hardware, the device itself is less important than the code that converts what the camera "sees" into shareable form. It's that conversion that makes social photography possible—a form of photography that is "more conversational, ephemeral, and expressive" than informational.[40]

Social photography may be enabled and sustained by technology, but it is fundamentally cultural: "a way of seeing, speaking and learning" that, like analogue photography did before it, is reshaping "time and space, privacy and visibility, truth and falsity"[41]—and, along the way, vision itself. In John Tomlinson's view, "information immediacy"—the speed at which we take, share, and scroll—both resembles and exceeds "machine speed"; that is, the much slower, panoramic experience of watching the landscape pass by while riding a train.[42] Not only do we "see the world as something to be recorded, measured, catalogued and shared" but we experience life "*in the service of*" documenting it for others to see. What Jurgenson calls our "documentary consciousness," in other words, has given rise to documentary vision.[43] Documentary vision is as much active as passive, constructive as observational.

Social photographs are what Sontag dubbed "photograph-trophies,"[44] Jurgenson writes, evidence that "I was there. I did that."[45] But whereas analogue photograph-trophies recorded primarily special occasions or tourist experiences, now any experience can become a digital photograph-trophy. Being always on the lookout for the photographable moment—even if only subconsciously—"yokes us" to picture taking, Jurgenson observes, which changes how we see ourselves and how we see and interact with each other and the larger world—and even who we are. The cell phone camera is no mere light pencil that we pick up and put down. Rather, it is functionally integrated into our sense of who we are. It exemplifies what Donna Haraway famously limned as cyborgian existence, one that generates "an augmented seeing that recodes how we look."[46]

A different residual theo-logic animates documentary vision, it turns out. The desire to document is a desire to know and thus to preserve, Jurgenson argues. It signals, in other words, that we fear death, a fear that is a function of increasing secularity, as fewer of us believe in life after death. "Documented, we feel eternal, relieving the modern anxiety over incomprehensible risk, omnipresent simulation, and personal inauthenticity," he writes.[47] At first glance, that desire seems at odds with social photography's ephemerality. Analogue photos (*mementos mori*, according to Roland Barthes) were material relics that preserved traces of those we've lost, but social photos are more like postcards: intended to reconnect us to someone at a distance and then be thrown away. And yet social photography's very speed and ephemerality render it a "protest against time" and death (50). Social photography "feels more like life and less like its collection" (49). Its very ephemerality allows us to believe that we are "leaving the present where it's found" (49).

That said, social photography comes with both affordances and limitations that create opportunities and challenges for us. Those who claim that our virtual lives can and, moreover, should be separated from our flesh-and-blood lives (Jurgenson calls them "disconnectionists") are both misguided and wrong. Disconnectionists subscribe to what he calls "digital dualism": the view that the only *real* world is offline. "The Web has everything to do with reality," he writes, as it is populated by "real people with real bodies, histories and politics" (68). For better or for worse, "we live in a mixed, augmented reality in which materiality and information, physicality and digitality, bodies and technology, atoms and bits, the offline and the online all intersect . . . The Internet *is* real life. It is the fetish objects of the offline and the disconnected that are not real" (68).

Jurgenson focuses his critique of digital dualism on the (exaggerated, he thinks) worry that social photography threatens self-authenticity. The concern for self-authenticity, he notes, is nothing new; it is, rather, the latest version of a long-standing modern worry that then-emergent media technologies threatened to replace "the real with something unnatural, thus prompting the death of absolute truth, of God" (71). The means of mediation have changed, but life has always been "mediated, augmented, documented," he argues (69). Moreover, postmodern theorists like Judith Butler—and Foucault, of course—"have long recognized the tension between the real and the pose" (71). In other words, "identity theatre is older than Mark Zuckerberg and doesn't end when you log off" (73).

Still, Jurgenson leaves plenty of room for critiquing the form and effects of social/digital mediation. Those critiques should focus less on concerns about the authenticity of our online selves and more on the all too real and widespread instances of "exploitation, hate, and harassment as they occur through our screens" (77). Jurgenson focuses on sexual harassment and exploitation, specifically. A teenage girl whose "sexts"—shared originally only with a boyfriend—find their way to pornographic websites may be subject to online harassment and, as an adult, may even lose her job over it while the person who circulated it goes unpunished, even remaining anonymous. Advocating digital disconnection—limiting, if not avoiding, social media altogether—as the solution is a nonstarter. First of all (as noted in the previous chapter), hate, exploitation, and harassment are hardly confined to the online world. That women whose sexts become what Jurgenson dubs "digital dirt" are judged more harshly than the men who most often circulate them reflects long-standing and deeply rooted sexist norms and expectations, he observes (61). Indeed, the asymmetrical systems that undergird and animate those norms and expectations originated offline and continue to flourish there. The occasional digital detox or permanent disconnection will do nothing to contest or resist these dynamics. Moreover, online engagement can provoke empathy, he observes; a possibility that disconnecting leaves unexplored. Instead, we need to attend to how we engage online.

While I agree with Jurgenson that our focus should be on *how* we engage rather than *whether*, I think he underplays the specific challenges that online life poses to us—especially those challenges documented by Sherry Turkle that I discussed in chapter 2. To Jurgenson, Turkle exemplifies digital dualism and disconnection. This is problematic on two fronts: not only does it misrepresent Turkle's actual position on disconnecting (she advocates *realteknik*, recall), but it also rejects out of hand the findings of her research. It's precisely the capacities required for cultivating empathy and offline connection that online life can cause to atrophy, she argues. That loss is even more problematic given another aspect of online life that Jurgenson mentions but doesn't fully investigate: the role of surveillance capitalism. Thanks to social photography, Foucault's panopticon has migrated from the prison to the street, Jurgenson observes, and, I'd add, from serving the interests of the state to serving those of surveillance capitalism. As I've argued, the agents of surveillance capitalism value clicks above all; thus, we tend to live online in filter bubbles made up of those who already think and believe as we do. Empathy—for anyone, but especially for those who are different from us—is not an automatic response online or off. Indeed, Jurgenson himself observes that physical, geographic proximity does not guarantee an empathetic response—or any particular affective response, for that matter— to those we encounter. How we might use generatively the opportunities for empathy and connection—limited though they may be—that social media provide will require more serious attention than Jurgenson gives them here. And that, in turn, will require acknowledging and wrestling more deeply with bio-disciplinary power's formative influence over what we believe we see.

That said, even if he doesn't walk all the way through them, Jurgenson's concept and analysis of social photography opens important doors for *Seeing and Believing*'s ultimate goal: to describe and resource what I'm calling "photographic insurrection." According to Jurgenson, that we look at social photographs via a "taxonomical gaze" reflects modern analogue photography's use to classify people and populations (25). And that, in turn, reflects the modern approach to knowledge: taking things apart to look inside them. Photography lends itself to this kind of reductionism by "atomizing" the complexities of what it sees into tiny, flat representations. In sum, "social photos are a 'technology of the self'" and a form of "mass self-regulation," Jurgenson writes (88). The more tightly self-expression is bound to the taxonomic boxes that contain and constrain us (online and offline), the more our capacity for "reinvention" of ourselves is limited (87). That's especially true, as the ever-present cell phone camera has rendered all of us photographic fodder for each other.

Yet, when it comes to self-regulation, "the social photo is both the disease and the cure," Jurgenson writes—specifically in the ways it remakes time and space (85). Echoes of the residual theo-logic of life and death embedded in social photography I limned earlier ground its curative potential. The social photograph medi-ates between the camera and its object, Jurgenson observes—a labor that requires physical and temporal distance. When we pause to snap a cell phone photo, we freeze that particular moment. Viewing the photo offers us "the opportunity to put the moment to work"; that is, "to think about the moment as a moment" by "involving yourself with it, immersing yourself in it" (79, 85). The geographical distance that (ironically) the "inti-macy of social media" requires provides the space for that immer-sion. Might this offer us the opportunity for reflection and resis-tance to bio-disciplined ways of seeing? If so, how do we make the most of it?

What we do with any distanced and frozen moment is, of course, up to us. But these moments offer us the opportunity to reflect on what we (believe we) see and why, as the photographic story line that is this book's touchstone reveals. The divergent responses to the visual images that constitute it reflect not so much disputes over their veracity, but over the meaning of what they show. Is the video of Philando Castile's fatal encounter with a police officer or of (now former officer and convicted murderer) Derek Chauvin kneeling on George Floyd's neck evidence of murder or just the officer doing his job (if poorly or overzeal-ously)?[48] Are the videos of deadly assaults on Asian Americans in broad daylight evidence of hate crimes or not? How a viewer responds to the photograph of young Trayvon Martin wearing his gray hoodie is likely unaffected by the fact that the photo-graph predates Martin's fatal encounter with George Zimmer-man. What a photograph indexes—its that-there-then—cannot really be separated from photographic affectivity (how a photo-graph "moves" us—emotionally and to take action). Whether digital or analogue, presented to us online or off, photographs can prompt affective responses that run the full gamut of our emo-tional repertoire: defensiveness; abject terror; righteous anger; sheer rage; deep sympathy; overwhelming sadness, joy, excitement; and more. Those responses can be fleeting or long-lasting, as can the impact of any actions that result.

Our responses to what we see are not uniform, however. The same photograph can compel not only different affects but also dramatically different actions: joining a #BlackLivesMatter pro-test, on the one hand, or plotting a mass murder, on the other, and everything in between. While our responses can track with the norms embedded in our bio-disciplinary formation, they don't always or necessarily do so. We are not utterly and thor-oughly determined by bio-disciplinary power; as Foucault observes, "Where there is power, there is resistance."[49] The real problem isn't with photography or any other medium but with those who use it and consume it; that is, with we the people and the society we inhabit, with what we expect from photography and from each other. How can we navigate the challenges and opportunities that social photography opens up and opens onto in ways that support living well together—online and off? What might religious ways of seeing contribute to that goal?

Jurgenson's concern, however, is primarily with the impact of this structure on self-presentation. It's certainly true that bio-disciplinary power's carrots and sticks are powerful motivators of docile self-policing, but they also deeply inform how we see each other. What we believe we see when we encounter a young Black man in a gray hoodie—online or off, in a photograph or in the flesh—is going to be shaped by those same carrots and sticks. That doesn't mean reinvention isn't possible. Dylann Roof's response to Martin's murder resulted in his self-reinvention as a white supremacist bent on violence—a cautionary tale if there ever was one about what online life makes possible. It is to these challenges and opportunities that I turn in the next chapter.

FIGURE 5.1 *Seeing Is Believing*, Layer 3.
Artist: Britt Stadig. Photographer: Amanda McCadams.
Printed with the permission of Vanderbilt University.

5

PHOTOGRAPHIC
INSURRECTION

U p to this point, my focus has primarily been on theorists of social media and visual culture who are not scholars of religion. That will change in this chapter, however, as I build toward proposing a visual repertoire that can support what I'm calling photographic insurrection; that is, ways of looking that, if cultivated, could resist the effects of our bio-disciplinary formation on what we (believe we) see in the photographs—still or moving—that we encounter online. I am not, of course, the first scholar of religion to address the challenges and opportunities of life online. Christian ethicist Kate Ott's 2019 book, *Christian Ethics for a Digital Society*, takes seriously the very real difficulties that this new media ecosystem poses to our real lives via our virtual lives.[1] She also argues that we possess capacities that, if nurtured and cultivated, can respond to those challenges in ways that mitigate potential harm. That aligns well with my aim of maximizing its affordances and minimizing its problems, as this new media ecosystem is not going anywhere. Moreover, while digital visual culture is not her primary concern, her articulation of the challenges and potential harms that confront us on our new public square accords closely with what I've traced so far. She affirms our need for a multipronged approach to them—one that requires the interventions not only of big government and big tech but of all of us, individually and collectively. (In her first chapter, for example, she attends particularly to the existence of a number of tech nonprofits created specifically to combat online bias and coding bias, an issue I discussed in chapter 3.) We share a focus on individual (re)formation seeking resources to support that goal in Christianity. Of particular benefit to *Seeing and Believing*, Ott roots her project in a theological perspective that counters the theo-logic that I've traced in the previous chapters. Instead of a traditional top-down theology of (divine) omniscience and omnipotence, Ott offers one that moves from the bottom up and is rooted in relationality. The fact that surveillance capitalism incorporates us into its networks accelerates, amplifies, and extends our networks of relationships exponentially, she argues. Being networked selves (re)makes us in the image of a relational (trinitarian) God, she suggests. Most important to her project, however, is liberation theology's close attention to the social and structural sins that marginalize some while concentrating power, wealth, and privilege in the hands of others. Doing the work of re-formation, on her read, requires attending to our formation by systems that privilege some over others, systems that originated long before but are now embedded in this new media landscape. The work of re-formation also requires acquiring the technological literacies necessary to engage productively, thoughtfully, and ethically with this ecosystem.[2]

Ott's ethics are grounded ultimately in liberation theology's focus on praxis; what we do is central to what we believe. Moreover, what we do doesn't just express what we believe; it also shapes it. Ott focuses primarily on identifying the "ethical responses" that can enable Christians to live faithfully in this digital/material world. She identifies four of these responses:

"expand diversity, cultivate attunement, practice metanoia, and responsibly co-create" (with God and with others).[3] Put into practice, they constitute a kind of theo-techno-logical hacktivism, one that repurposes digital technologies in order to disrupt the usual order of things in our virtual lives. That usual order of things keeps us bound to the asymmetrical systems that produce such systemic injustices like racism, heterosexism, cisgenderism, and so on—often without our awareness or conscious consent.

My proposal for photographic insurrection builds on two of the ethical values that Ott lays out: attunement and metanoia. Attunement in our virtual lives moves us "toward relationality and connection" in our real lives by providing an antidote to the isolation and distraction that, as we have seen, the attention economy encourages.[4] It is "an embodied and emotionally aware, even relational" approach to moral formation,[5] one that (in Christine Traina's words) "combines perception, imagination and experimentation."[6] While perception, imagination, and experimentation may "come naturally" to us, attunement must be cultivated, an important insight that aligns well with my goals in *Seeing and Believing*. Photographic insurrection moves us toward attuning ourselves to our formation by bio-disciplined ways of seeing, seriously wrestling with how conforming or resisting them has formed us and committing ourselves to practices (of looking, among other things) that resist that formation. The goal of attunement as photographic insurrection, then, is metanoia—conversion from and repentance for conforming to bio-disciplinary seeing.

In that spirit, I offer photographic insurrection as a form of ethical hacking, the topic of Ott's final chapter. Digital technologies target what and how we know and thus what, who, and how we are. Through determining what we see, they rewire our attention and thus what we desire in ways that we rarely consider. In Ott's view, hacking requires cultivating digital literacy, a version of which the previous chapters offer to my readers. But digital literacy alone will not suffice. Cultivating photographic insurrection requires us to become literate in how we've been trained to see—not just online but in the (so-called) real world. It also requires becoming literate in ways of seeing that we're likely already using, but if adopted more consciously and deliberately, could counteract that training and open us toward being moved—emotionally and to take action—in ways that resist biodisciplinary formation.

While my perspective as a Christian theologian aligns well with Ott's, there are some important differences between her book and *Seeing and Believing* (besides my obvious narrower focus). First, although both of us prioritize how individuals interact with the virtual world, she does a deeper dive into self-re-formation than I do here. I certainly hope and expect that photographic insurrection can prompt those who engage it to undertake the labor necessary to address the underlying causes of their visual formation, but laying out how that might unfold is beyond the scope of this project. Rather, consider photographic insurrection as a way to jump-start that process on those occasions when what we see prompts us to wrestle with how we see and why. Secondly, Ott addresses her work specifically, if not necessarily exclusively, to a Christian audience. The visual repertoire that I propose here, though resourced in Christian ways of seeing, is potentially available and accessible to viewers regardless of religious identification (or the lack thereof). Thus, it's important that this repertoire be found in the visual practices of other religious traditions and grounded in ways of seeing that "come naturally" to human beings. By "come naturally," I do not mean that these ways of seeing are merely biological or anatomical. The visual repertoire on offer here is, like all ways of seeing and sensing, as social as it is physical—as is fleshly embodiment itself.[7] Thanks in no small part to the vast expansion of digital technologies and social media, the visual challenges—and opportunities, let's not forget—that photographic insurrection faces are global as well as local, collective as well as individual.

FRAMING PHOTOGRAPHIC INSURRECTION: GLOBAL WITNESS CITIZENSHIP

In the sixth chapter of his book *Citizenship and Identity in the Age of Surveillance*, Indian postcolonial theorist Pramod Nayar argues that our globalized, digitized, mediatized world makes possible what he calls "global witness citizenship."[8] Global witness citizenship is, significantly, grounded in "dissident surveillance."[9] Unlike governmental surveillance (whose goal is control), dissident surveillance is a practice of self-surveillance that individual citizens undertake in order to protect civic structures that, in turn, protect and nurture us as civil citizens. Like Tufekci, Nayar recognizes that today's global virtual networks make possible the recognition, documentation, and response to often grievous harms that human beings suffer. Those harms may come at the hand of their governments (recent events like the Syrian civil war, Russia's war on Ukraine, and responses to civil unrest in Hong Kong and in Myanmar come to mind as I write), of nonstate actors (Islamic jihadists or white supremacists), or natural disasters (the destruction of the Fukushima nuclear plant, the devastation caused by Hurricane Maria in Puerto Rico, etc.).

Significantly, Nayar asserts that visual media lie at the heart of this potential.[10] Thanks to the global digital networks and social media platforms they support, eyewitnesses are able to share instantly videos or still photos of local instances of suffering/injustice/violence and reach a potentially global audience. (Yes, this violates privacy—an ethical dilemma, to be sure, he notes—but it also can mobilize humanitarian support.) Indeed, specific digital networks have been created for that very purpose (www.witness.org is one example).[11] Nayar's focus, though, is on the opportunity—and obligation—digital networks afford to those who see such visual documentation. Such encounters give viewers the opportunity to respond by embracing the role of global witness citizen, a role that, with governments weakened by neoliberalism, is particularly critical, Nayar argues. Taking up this opportunity requires more than simply looking. To become a global witness citizen requires looking deeply into what the visual image opens up and opens onto—to see in the image connections between self and other, between previous instances of violence or violation and this one, between one's own local context and the one to which you have only virtual and visual access.

Digital archivization—especially with new photographic technologies like virtual reality available to us—expands our access to evidence of atrocities (photographic and otherwise), which can potentially expedite and amplify activist responses to such evidence. The photographic affordances of digital connectivity offer the potential for creating "new transcultural and global regimes of memory" yielding a "counter-cosmopolitanism built around compassion and shared vulnerability."[12] Counter-cosmopolitanism, however, seems likely to default to what Nayar identifies as the "pity economy of compassionate cosmopolitanism," which he describes as "a whole new order of globalization."[13] At best, counter-cosmopolitanism recognizes that one's access to the resources human beings need to survive (if not thrive) is asymmetrically impacted by who one is and where one lives.

"Some bodies are deemed, in certain contexts, to *not* possess equal value," he writes.[14] Exposing the have's to the have not's prompts the have's to care about and for the have not's, to take pity on the have not's and actively contribute to their welfare.[15] A far cry from a "justice economy,"[16] the pity economy mines visual resources to move casual viewers to contribute to fund-raising campaigns that support others doing the real action.[17] And images of suffering are critical to the pity economy.[18]

As critical as compassionate cosmopolitanism may be in this neoliberal age, we'll need to do better if we are to make any progress toward a justice economy, Nayar argues. But attending to compassionate cosmopolitanism calls critical attention to the potential limits of global witness citizenship. Successfully navigating those limits, in my view, requires attending more thoughtfully and deliberately to the role that ways of seeing play in how we respond to what we see. Nayar takes some important steps in that direction. Viewing photographic evidence of genocide, say, "makes us bear witness" and even "visually *places* us in these zones of conflict," he observes, but becoming a global witness citizen is not a default response to that visual placement.[19] Photos of violated bodies may alert us to our shared humanity (and vulnerability), but how we see those who have been violated will be shaped by how we imagine those others. According to Nayar, becoming a global witness citizen requires a high degree of social literacy. The curators of the digital archives Nayar cites presumably possess the requisite level of social literacy that witnessing requires. But that will not necessarily be true for all of those who encounter the artifacts—particularly outside the archives—especially if the other presented to us is "the strange, primitive and hostile Other."[20] What will prompt those who lack the requisite social literacy to start down the path of global witness citizenship? What might closer attention to seeing itself and its role in our civic life—especially with reference to photography, given its ubiquity—offer to the pursuit of Nayar's justice economy?

FRAMING PHOTOGRAPHIC INSURRECTION II: THE CIVIL GAZE

Ariella Azoulay's work in *The Civil Contract of Photography* and, more recently, in *Civil Imagination: A Political Ontology of Photography* makes important strides in this regard.[21] Azoulay argues in *Civil Contract* that photography made possible a new and uniquely modern form of civic life, one that "modified the way in which individuals are governed and the extent of their participation in the forms of governance."[22] Photography is first and foremost neither a technology nor a form of seeing, she argues, but a tacit civil contract that binds viewers, photographed subjects and objects, and photographers together. To call this a "contract" bespeaks the social constitution of photographic practice that, for all practical purposes, though often without their conscious consent, obligates all of these parties. Especially given the ubiquity of the camera these days, any of us can (and most of us likely will) occupy any or all of those positions (photographer, photographed subject, viewer) at some point.[23] In taking up one or more of those positions, we effectively sign on to the photographic contract, thus becoming photographic citizen-subjects with all of the rights and responsibilities thereto appertaining, so to speak.[24]

Citizenship in a photographic body politic can constitute an important counterweight to politics as usual—or not. *Civil Contract* is anchored in and by Azoulay's own political situation as an Israeli citizen at odds with Israeli policy and practice regarding Palestine. That context makes her work particularly relevant to my project here. Of specific concern to Azoulay are the responses of (presumptively Jewish) Israeli citizen-spectators to photographs that document their government's mistreatment of Palestinians. Though excluded from (full, in the case of those who reside in Israel) Israeli citizenship, the photographic civil contract enables Palestinian photographed subjects to claim photographic citizenship with their Israeli spectators, a claim that registers as an ethical demand—that their suffering be seen, acknowledged, and, hopefully, addressed. That claim is honored by Israeli citizen-spectators as much in the breach as in the fulfillment. Photographs documenting mistreatment of Palestinians show up regularly in the Israeli news media, Azoulay observes.[25] Yet, for every Israeli citizen who responds to such photographs with outrage and compassion, there is another who responds with righteous triumph and yet another with a shrug—a phenomenon that trades on photographic ambivalence and reinforces the conventional relationship between seeing and believing. Not even the most arresting photograph can compel a given spectator to respond to it in a specific way. A viewer may pass over the photograph without blinking, they may question its truthfulness and dismiss it, or they may be moved to protest what they see.

For a time, Azoulay reports in *Civil Imagination*, she gave up on photography as a political resource. Turning reality into art seemed to render photographs ineffective in political advocacy. Photographs of suffering aestheticize it, thereby anaesthetizing spectators against the (all too real) pain that photographers aimed to capture. That is not the fault of photographers, Azoulay says, but of the mechanism at the center of the photographic contract: the camera. Unique among the various forms of documentation human beings employ, Azoulay argues, the photograph always contains more—and less—than the photographer intended. That this is so reflects the camera's stubborn independence. "Possess[ing] its own character and drives," Azoulay writes, the camera might seem "obedient, but it is also capable of being cunning, seductive, conciliatory, vengeful or friendly."[26] (Note that the camera has not only agency but also its own affective repertoire.) It is, moreover, "an opaque tool that does not expose anything of its inner workings" (16). What early adopters of the camera called the "pencil of nature," recall, is "an inscribing machine that transforms the encounter that comes into being around it, through it, and, by means of its mediation, into a special form of encounter," a "visual protocol" that confounds human visual sovereignty whether one is photographer, spectator, or photographed subject (17). Even when the camera is pointed at someone or something, those caught in its view cannot tell whether the camera is on or off or whether or what it's registering. This "creates conditions under which the mere possibility of the existence of a photograph of us taken without our knowledge might come to affect us with as much potency as if we had encountered the photograph itself," Azoulay writes (23). She offers the example of a Palestinian detainee threatened with the alleged existence of a photo that places the detainee in a problematic situation (one use to which the Abu Ghraib photographs were put by the U.S. military). The threat is effective without the photograph being shown (as is usually the case, she goes on to say); believing *is* (for all practical purposes) seeing, in such instances.

The camera-machine thus proves itself useful to the sovereign nation-state, itself "a kind of war machine" that promises its citizens safety via its security apparatus (8). The price for this promise of safety, Azoulay claims, is extracted primarily from those deemed threats, of course, but it also threatens democracy itself and thus the citizens the state aims to protect. The remedy to this problem is what she calls the "civil imagination" and the "civil gaze" that funds it. Together, they can generate a different form of being-with that cuts across the lines of "us" versus "them," of self versus other. Because it has the potential to animate the civil gaze, photography is uniquely able to jump-start the civil imagination. Photography's civil potential arises, she argues, from seismic shifts in political ontology generated by photography as a technology and a practice. Photography's advent inaugurates a change in human being-with, with one another and with visual images. By creating a public place/space that we share with everyone and everything, photography has created a visual culture that has transformed not only how people see images but how they see themselves and their surroundings as well: "Every gaze is always exposed to the gaze of the other and its sense changes in accordance with their reactions" (68).

The civil gaze, however, is anything but an automatic response to a given photograph. Our default response to our "culture of visual plenty" is what Azoulay calls the "leisurely gaze." Reminiscent in many ways of Walter Benjamin's flaneur (arguably a visual cosmopolite), the leisurely gaze wanders aimlessly through this visual landscape and its plethora of visual objects. In search of nothing in particular, it "skim[s] . . . the surface of the visible" largely undisturbed by what it sees (71). It is precisely this randomness, though, that gives rise to the civil potential in the leisurely gaze. Once animated, the civil gaze requires much more of spectators than does the leisurely gaze. Spectators must look more deeply into their visual landscapes and into themselves. In order to gaze civilly, the spectator must "transcend his or her own particular interests" to become "capable of judging in universal terms that which is on display" (44).

How well aligned are the civil gaze and the civil imagination with photographic insurrection? On the one hand, the attention

Azoulay gives to the specificities of photography adds some important insights to Nayar's analysis of global witness citizenship. First, she illuminates in more detail the challenges and opportunities that global witness citizenship confronts. The fact that the same photograph will move one person toward global witness citizenship but leave another unmoved is not just a matter of social literacy but also reflects an inherent ambiguity and ambivalence in the photographic relationship. Moreover, however important social literacy is to realizing the potential a given photograph holds to generate global witness citizenship, that goal also requires a particular way of looking, one defined by Azoulay as the civil gaze. Imagination—a civil imagination—likewise seems critical in motivating the pursuit of social literacy. Seeing is effectively the (metaphorical) horse needed to pull the (metaphorical) cart of the imagination toward global citizen-witnessing. That said, like global witness citizenship, the civil gaze requires one to transcend one's self-interest in favor of universality. Azoulay thus seems to yoke the civil gaze to the very modern invention that her account of the camera's agency called into question: the (allegedly) self-sovereign subject. Knowing and applying universal principles—especially instead of taking the easy route of self-gratification—is the very essence of self-mastery and thus self-sovereignty, as is (arguably) compassionate cosmopolitanism. However, a more Foucauldian genealogy of that subject, such as the one I'm carrying forward here from *Signs and Wonders*, would question whether the civil gaze is up to the task. Modern politico-visual culture and its sovereign subject are, in no small part, products of our modern bio-disciplinary regime. Man's status as sovereign is realized through achieving mastery over self and his others, a project that photography aided and abetted.

Azoulay's civil gaze, however, is not a product of self-sovereignty as self-mastery; it is, rather, a (quasi-Levinasian and explicitly Arendtian) response to the gaze of the photographed other.[27] The civil gaze is, of course, one response among others that our participation in the civil contract of photography can prompt. Nothing can guarantee that a given spectator—especially a white spectator—will respond to the video of George Floyd with outrage, much less join the movement to "Defund the Police." While one can invoke certain universal principles with the hope of evoking a sense of obligation, that desired result is far from guaranteed, as we've seen over and over again.[28] Still, Azoulay intends the civil gaze as a counterforce to visual capitulation to the sovereign nation-state that wants us to see things its way—no easy task, as she clearly recognizes. However, the analysis I've offered of photographic subjection—especially coupled with Nayar's analysis of global witness citizenship's relationship to compassionate cosmopolitanism—shows that the sovereign nation-state is not the only barrier to the civil imagination. And references to universal principles invoke liberal humanism (and its affective repertoire, liberal sentimentality), at whose center the modern sovereign subject resides, itself a product of bio-disciplinary power. That said, the path toward photographic insurrection can't go around liberal humanism any more than it can go around liberal sentimentality, as Nayar's pity economy also reminds us. It must go through both, I argue, and thus through their biopolitical milieu. We need a visual repertoire that is nimble and varied enough to provide multiple pathways for navigating the challenges and opportunities afforded to our civic life by our new public square.

While Azoulay's civil gaze is a start, it is insufficient on its own as a resource that can fund photographic insurrection and the visual repertoire needed to generate and sustain it. For one thing, this visual repertoire—two gazes, essentially; the leisurely and the civil—seems impoverished taxonomically and ethically.

The sets of photographs that anchor *Signs and Wonders* and the photographic story lines I've been referencing in *Seeing and Believing* open up and open onto seeing's role in multiple forms of othering present in our time and place that need specific attention. Furthermore, Azoulay's account of the civil gaze largely bypasses questions of photographic affect, how photographs move us—emotionally and to take action. Yet these are issues that are deeply connected to seeing and believing. Where might we begin to find resources for a visual repertoire that can meet these needs?

FRAMING PHOTOGRAPHIC INSURRECTION III: WHITE GAZES

Renowned philosopher George Yancy's *Black Bodies, White Gazes: The Continuing Significance of Race* provides a needed bridge between these accounts of seeing's political import and the visual repertoire I propose.[29] Like Nayar and Azoulay, Yancy foregrounds seeing's embeddedness in larger systems of injustice and its disruptive potential but in ways that address the diagnostic lacunae I have identified in their work. He focuses on anti-Black racism in the United States but with attention to its global context, including its connections to colonialism,[30] to the wider African diaspora and to other forms of racism (including, briefly, anti-Asian sentiment), and to (normative, at least) sexuality and gender.[31] As a result, Yancy helps us see Black bodies as a different form of the strange, primitive, and hostile other that Nayar references.

Central to (mis)perceptions of Black bodies—male and female—are their associations with sexual and gendered abnormality. Black men are basically configured as "walking penis[es]," their desire for sex insatiable and uncontrollable.[32] Whether Black women are truly women—either biologically or culturally—is also central to anti-Black racism, as the case of Sarah Baartman, the so-called Hottentot Venus (whom Yancy discusses in detail) demonstrates.[33] More recently, he notes the rumors that continue to circulate that former First Lady Michelle Obama is really a man and that the famous tennis players Serena and Venus Williams are actually brothers not sisters.[34]

Originally published in 2008, Yancy's updated and revised edition of *Black Bodies, White Gazes* (published in 2017) also connects particularly well to *Seeing and Believing*. For one thing, the photographic story line that anchors *Seeing and Believing* is central to the updates. For another, like me and like Morgan, Yancy understands seeing as embodied, affective, and deeply relational.[35] Indeed, he describes white gazes as a "species of attunement" and (per Judith Butler) a "visual field" that "is itself a racial formation, an episteme, hegemonic and forceful."[36] Rooted in "whiteness as the transcendental norm," white gazes are "the very expression of white embodied existence, orientation; modes of comportment, style, emotion, aesthetic responses, feelings of threat, neuronal activity; the activation of sweat glands, breathing patterns, heart rate, auditory and olfactory response."[37] Their primary affective mode is disgust, a persistent response to being in the presence of Black bodies that has historically manifested unbidden even in the bodies of white allies.[38] Doing full justice to Yancy's critically important effort here will have to wait for another day. For now, I'll lay out its central themes and approaches, highlighting their productive connections to my project here.

Black Bodies, White Gazes "explor[es] the Black body within the context of whiteness,"[39] which Yancy understands as a persistent and pernicious historical and social construct that entrains

white people—even "good white people"—in certain ways of seeing, feeling, knowing, doing, and, therefore, being. Though its
origins reach as far back as the earliest centuries of the Common Era, the fact that it is historical and social means that whiteness in all of its manifestations—including white gazes—can
and does change. Fostering positive change by disrupting normative ways of seeing is also a goal Yancy seeks to pursue, here
and elsewhere.[40]

"The twisted fate of the Black body" results from "white forms
of disciplinary control" and the racist bodily habits that conform
to them—both constitutive features of "epistemic white world-
making."[41] White gazing, the bodily habit at the heart of this
hegemonic system, serves as "an important site of power and control structured by white epistemic orders [of knowing, doing,
and being] and that perpetuates such orders in return" (xxxii).
It is no coincidence, from Yancy's perspective, that the killings
that prompted his update of *Black Bodies, White Gazes* involve
police or self-appointed vigilantes: "From the perspective of
whiteness, the Black body *is* criminality itself. It *is* the monstrous;
it is that which is to be feared and yet desired, sought out in for-
bidden white sexual adventures and fantasies; it is constructed
as a source of white despair and anguish, an anomaly of nature,
the essence of vulgarity and immorality" (xxx). By contrast,
"whiteness is deemed the transcendental norm, the good, the
innocent and the pure" (xxx). As a result, the white gaze (in the
words of Jean-Paul Sartre) embodies "the privilege of seeing
without being seen."[42]

Yancy refuses to cede the Black body entirely to totalizing white gazes, however. Indeed, the history of antiracist
activism—of which #BLM is the latest prominent instantiation—
has always pushed back against this way of seeing blackness.
Both sides of this history reveal the Black body as a "site of

contestation," as "less of a thing or a being than a shifting or changing historical meaning" (xxxvi). Contesting the meanings assigned to blackness requires seeking out and engaging "processes of interpretive fracture" and "moments of disarticulation" in our conformity to whiteness (xxxvii). *Black Bodies, White Gazes* offers a compelling and persuasive account of the impact of this hegemonic system on both white gazes and Black bodies with an eye toward locating such processes and moments. Yancy makes it clear that taking advantage of them will require serious labor from "good white people," work grounded in owning up to our own participation in and perpetuation of that system.

Yancy establishes seeing's centrality to the creation and sustenance of systemic racism by drawing on much of the canonical literature on experiences of Black men and women from W.E.B. Du Bois and Frantz Fanon to Audre Lorde and beyond. This approach enables him to establish the foundational role of *being seen* in the perpetuation of anti-Black racism. Reading this work alongside contemporary scholarship in philosophy and beyond, Yancy argues that this history has bound whiteness and blackness together in a "relational ontology."[43] While our default is to perpetuate its asymmetries, Yancy holds open the possibility that this relational ontology offers to reconfigure Black and white embodiment (xiv–xvi).

That relational ontology links Black and white embodiment in asymmetrical ways. If it "sutures" white bodies into a system that supports their existence, Black bodies are subject to "unsuturing" at the visceral, corporeal, and symbolic levels in ways that implicate the entire sensorium. As Judith Butler observes, being embodied exposes all human beings not only "to the gaze of others, but also to touch and to violence."[44] While this relational ontology shields white bodies from their vulnerability, it magnifies the vulnerability of Black bodies, as the recent police killings I've referred to demonstrate. Although Yancy's focus is on seeing, his analysis of what happened in the killing of Eric Garner in 2014 starts with speaking and hearing. The fact that white police officers failed to hear Garner's repeated cry, "I can't breathe!" (repeated more recently by George Floyd) is not due to auditory disfunction. Rather, it exemplifies the effects of the suturing of whiteness to certain embodied habits borne of, in the (modified) words of Frantz Fanon, "a thousand [white racist] details, anecdotes, [and] stories," Yancy writes.[45] Those embodied habits evidence the sedimentary buildup of associations of Black embodiment with abnormality, with impulsivity, savagery, and immorality. "Black bodies are shot in exchange not necessarily for what they do, but for what they *will* do," Yancy writes (6). Consider these words from white conservative columnist Ben Stein: Michael Brown, the unarmed Black teenager killed in Ferguson, Missouri, by a white policeman, may not have been carrying a gun when he was shot, but "he was armed with his incredibly strong, scary, self."[46]

The long history of experience living in and under this regime of whiteness shapes Black living as well as dying. Black becoming involves all too frequent wrestling with white expectations at every level: individual and social, cognitive and affective. (W.E.B. Du Bois expressed it well long ago: "How does it feel to be a problem?"[47]) But Yancy insists that neither Blacks nor whites are utterly determined by this regime and its effects. It is certainly possible for Black people to communicate to whites their experience and how they see the world. Indeed, another powerful aspect of Yancy's project builds on analyses of his own experiences and encounters that illustrate the embodied effects of this relational ontology and imagine a way out of it. But for that to be effective, white people must be willing to listen and

to hear and to begin to un-suture ourselves from our own formation, something that won't come easily.

It's significant, I think, that Yancy turns to hearing rather
than seeing as the possible route out of this destructive relational ontology. Though he doesn't say so explicitly, there is good
reason, given the evidence he presents here, to doubt seeing's
ability—on its own, at least—to disrupt this system. As his
analysis demonstrates time and again, and in multiple modalities
(including analyses of his own experiences), white gazes are an
immediate visceral reaction to being in the presence of Black
bodies. That doesn't mean vision is useless, of course. Reading,
itself a visual medium, is clearly a central mode of communication that Yancy engages. But reading deploys vision (or hearing
or touch, depending on the mode of reading) at a slower pace
and for a relatively longer duration. It requires reflection, something that seeing an image does not. Still, a visual image that
catches our eye or an actual encounter with a Black person can
prompt a reaction that disrupts white gazes. Such moments offer
white viewers an opportunity to start the deeper dive required to
un-suture themselves—if they are willing to act on it. Indeed,
Yancy observes that encountering Martin provided Zimmerman
with the opportunity "to look again, to wonder and to stand in
awe" of the humanity that they shared[48]—the very humanity, of
course, that white gazing and the hegemonic system behind it
denied to Martin. Of course, that opportunity was completely
lost on Zimmerman, costing Martin his life and his future and
leaving Zimmerman unrepentant. Asked if he had any regrets
about what he had done, Zimmerman responded emphatically,
"I feel that it was all God's plan."[49]

To be clear, Yancy is not at all sanguine about undoing white
gazes. Indeed, the great gift of his analysis is its exposure of the
substantial barriers to its undoing. Un-suturing ourselves from

habitually embodying white gazes will not happen overnight, much less in an instant.[50] Still, what I'm calling photographic insurrection can jump-start that process.

RELIGIOUS SEEING AND PHOTOGRAPHIC INSURRECTION

Thus far, this chapter has set the stage for the visual repertoire I will now offer of ways of looking that, if cultivated, can support and sustain photographic insurrection. These ways of looking can encourage viewers to take advantage of those moments of visual disruption to un-suture themselves from white gazes (which Yancy describes as a process of *"kenosis"* [13], or self-emptying, another term with religious resonance). That said, the visual repertoire I offer—grounded in religious seeing, as promised—does not directly engage white gazes or any other normative gazes. That is not an oversight on my part, but a deliberate choice. An indirect approach to challenging normative seeing, in my judgment—especially one grounded in religious ways of seeing— can achieve two things that a more direct approach likely would not. First, religious seeing disrupts a central feature of all forms of hegemonic seeing: the hierarchy they create that places seer over seen. Because religious ways of seeing focus on connecting the human to the divine, the immanent to the transcendent, the profane to the sacred, that hierarchy is reversed. The seer is subjected to the seen—and, in the case of the visual repertoire I describe below, in complex and varied ways. Second, while the object of these ways of seeing may be perceived as extraordinary, these religious gazes repurpose ordinary gazes, ways of seeing that "come naturally" to us. It's possible, then, for these gazes to provide a conceptual vocabulary for visual experiences that disrupt our conformity to normative seeing regardless of our faith commitments—or lack thereof.

I am not putting forward this repertoire as the only one; no doubt, there are many.[51] Remember, though, my focus here is on seeing and believing. And as I said at the outset, religions—including Christianity—have been wrestling with the relationship between them for eons. What resources might these ways of seeing hold, as a result, that could generate a visual repertoire that might build on the insights into seeing's importance for our collective life I have just described? That could generate Azoulay's civil gaze and animate a civil imagination? That could cultivate a form of global witness citizenship and thereby bring us a few steps closer to realizing Nayar's justice economy? That could disrupt white gazes and motivate "good white people" to unsuture themselves from systemic racism per Yancy? That could exemplify attunement that leads to practicing metanoia per Ott?

In this book's preface, I identified the work of historian and religious visual culture theorist David Morgan as particularly helpful—and for a variety of reasons. While his primary focus is on Christian visual cultures, he is also deeply attentive to religious seeing as it manifests in other traditions. The visual repertoire I will be working with here comes from his book *The Embodied Eye: Religious Visual Culture and the Social Life of Feeling*.[52] The ways of seeing he limns therein are found not only in Christian visual practice but in other religious traditions as well. Moreover, they are rooted in visual capacities and strategies that "come naturally" to us. Like Yancy, Morgan positions our visual capacities and strategies as embodied, social, affective, and cognitive. He, too, argues that one cannot disaggregate religious seeing from the full human sensorium, the full range of human feeling, and all that forms us. "Seeing . . . is driven by desire, conditioned by place, shaped by culture, memory, and history, and bodily engaged by the gaze of the other," he writes.[53] Whereas Yancy focuses on how we see other people, Morgan focuses here on how we see visual objects. However, like Yancy, he emphasizes that the act of seeing is interactive. "Whatever else it means, to see or be seen is to enter into a relationship," Morgan asserts (296). The visual object attracts a given seer by offering them access to an "other." The seer's response unites seer and seen via the seer's desire for an affective connection—love, fear, hate, or whatever—to which the seer anticipates the "other" will respond in and through being seen. The visual image is, in other words, a "material mediation" between the viewer and "what stands *in* the image" (297).

Particularly important, given my interests here, Morgan explicitly reframes the scholarly discourse on religious seeing in terms of its relationship to belief—reprising and expanding the definition of belief he articulated in *The Sacred Gaze*. That discourse understands visual images as symbols or signs that gain their meaning by reference to religious ideas—in other words, to theology. A painting of the crucified Christ, say, moves a given Christian because it presents to them in visual form their belief in Jesus Christ's death as salvific. This perspective overlooks a more fundamental relationship between religious seeing and believing, Morgan argues. When it comes to religious seeing, "belief," he writes (echoing *The Sacred Gaze*), "is more than an intellectual assent to doctrines"; it is primarily a form of "visual communion" between seer and seen, between individuals and communities, between "body and world" (317). The painting of the crucified Christ moves certain Christian viewers not because it *symbolizes* Christ's salvific death, but because these viewers (believe they) *encounter* Jesus Christ in and through the painting.

Morgan's understanding of seeing and believing in *The Embodied Eye* is informed by the influential French philosopher

Maurice Merleau-Ponty in how it positions the relationship between perception (the focus of Merleau-Ponty's early and most influential work) and thinking. (Merleau-Ponty was also an important influence on Frantz Fanon, whose work informs Yancy's *Black Bodies, White Gazes*.) Both arise out of the human situation as embodied and relational, en-fleshed and en-worlded. Perception and thinking are essentially two modes of being-in-relation. If thinking "operates at a distance from the world, contemplating it as a disembodied eye," Morgan writes, perceiving "discerns an organic continuity between body and world" (303). Merleau-Ponty (perhaps reflecting his Catholic upbringing) describes perception as "literally a form of communion" between our seeing bodies and the larger world.[54] Just as the elements of the Eucharist—provided we are "inwardly prepared" to receive it as such—simultaneously embody bread and wine and "the real presence of God," so perception is "an enfolding of organism and environment."[55] "Sight and movement are specific ways of entering into relationship with objects," which results in assembling the many different elements within an experience, "not by placing them all under the control of an 'I think,' but by guiding them toward the intersensory unity of a 'world.' "[56]

The specific practices of seeing and believing that Morgan goes on to describe are again, deeply embodied, enculturated, interactive, and affective. Religious seeing takes place in and on visual fields shaped as much by viewers' larger social context (family, nation, social location, etc.) as by their religious affiliation (or lack thereof). These visual fields generate multiple and multiform gazes, each of which inclines us toward our world and what transcends it in different ways. Recall that Morgan outlines eight religious gazes drawn primarily from Christian visual culture but evident in other religious visual cultures as well. This particular visual repertoire is intended to be invitational, not exhaustive—and necessarily so, given what they reveal about the nature of religious seeing. Some of these religious gazes are ephemeral while others endure. All come and go and shape-shift—even morph into one another—depending on the context. Notably, given my interests, Morgan has an expansive notion of what can be objects for these gazes. In addition to explicitly religious visual objects (religious icons, say), these gazes can be evoked by secular visual objects that invoke "a mythical past, a national destiny, a compelling narrative, a social order, a people, a totemic founder or hero, a place or a ritual enactment."[57] In other words, the visual objects that inspire religious seeing range from the mundane to the sublime, the ordinary to the extraordinary, the explicitly religious to the explicitly secular.

In what likely seems the most obviously religious way of seeing, the *devotional* gaze, believers submit themselves voluntarily to the visual object in a way that invites a kind of self-transcendence, "allowing the devotee to slip the bonds of pain, guilt, fear, or oppression," Morgan writes (74). Sometimes the devotional gaze morphs into the *reciprocal* gaze, in which a transformative exchange happens between the seer and the seen (73). (The Hindu concept of *darshan* is a prominent example. Similarly, apparitions of the Virgin Mary are often described this way.) Of course, both gazes risk idolatry, reducing the transcendent to the immanent, the infinite to the finite. A third gaze, the *aversive* gaze, avoids idolatry by "looking around" the visual object rather than directly at it, effectively rendering the visual object a veil that shields the divine from view (72).

Recall that ways of seeing are as much social as individual. The *communal* gaze evokes the influence of social settings—e.g., worship services, religious festivals, political rallies—on how we see. Social settings can be externally or internally focused; real or virtual (77). The *liminal* gaze "marks the edge of *us* and the beginning of *them*" often by trading in stereotypes of the religious "other"—Muslims or LGBTQIA+ people, say (79). Via the *virtual* gaze, we project ourselves into performative, interactive spaces that allow us to "vicariously participate" in ways of being very different from our everyday lives; Morgan gives Christian passion plays or online gaming as examples (76).

Religious seers are also visual objects themselves. To be caught in the *unilateral* gaze of an omnipotent and omniscient god or the "evil eye" renders one "powerless, subject to the manipulative, overwhelming, objectifying gaze of authority" (70). In response, one may take refuge in the *occlusive gaze* by putting up another visual object—an amulet, say—as a shield. The occlusive gaze is analogous to closing one's eyes in shame to avoid another's judgmental gaze (71).

This visual repertoire articulates seeing as "both a matter of agency and a medium of power" (69). Its gazes help us to understand how practices of seeing inform not only what we see but also how we feel about what we see—about ourselves and about others, "mortal and divine" (68). Gazes we've been schooled in by our social contexts dispose us to adopt certain attitudes toward what we see. Hence we tend to see what we believe (belief here understood as "a disposition to see, hear, feel or intuit" in alignment with the order of things we've accepted—consciously or unconsciously—as proper and real [69–70]). But religious seeing also pulls us beneath the surface and into what a given image opens up and opens onto. That can include challenges to our worldview and to its inevitable idolatries (more about that shortly). Those idolatries may close us off not only to the sacred or the transcendent in itself but also as it manifests in the profane and the immanent, including in one another and in the natural world that surrounds us.

PHOTOGRAPHIC INSURRECTION:
AN EXPERIMENT

So what makes me think that these gazes might fund a more productive relationship with our visually saturated new public square—especially for "good white people"? In the spring of 2021, I taught a course titled Theology, Visual Culture, and the New Media to a group of fifteen Vanderbilt Divinity School students, all of whom but one were white. Early in the semester, when we had barely begun the deep dive into the course readings, I showed the students the photographs of Trayvon Martin and Dylann Roof that are part of the photographic story line that anchors *Seeing and Believing* and that Britt Stadig incorporated into *Seeing Is Believing*, the art book that represents it. I asked them to write down their responses to whichever image(s) moved them and to keep those responses for further reflection later in the course. Toward the end of the semester, I shared with them the brief description above of Morgan's gazes and asked them to do two things. First I asked them to revisit what they wrote about their initial response to the images and identify which, if any, of the gazes might describe how they had seen them. Then I asked them to revisit one or both of the images and deliberately adopt one of the gazes (their choice) as a way of relooking—ideally, differently—and write a new brief reflection. I provided prompts crafted by my teaching assistant, Debbie Brubaker, to help. Of course, whether they used them or not I can't say.

I am not putting forward this experiment as conclusive evidence that this visual repertoire will work for everyone. For one thing, students who've chosen to pursue theological education at a progressive school embedded in an elite university are not broadly representative of the U.S. population, much less the global population. Not only are my students highly educated but, given the kind of students we attract and the kind of education we offer, I would also expect them to be more socially literate (to different degrees) in social justice issues like racism than many other folks. (That includes the "good white people" among them.) Furthermore, taking my course had probably increased their photographic (and digital) literacy as well. That said, their reflections made virtually no explicit reference to those *learned* literacies but focused instead on their affective responses and personal histories.[58]

Of Morgan's eight gazes, students referenced all but the unilateral gaze. Regardless of the gaze adopted (either intentionally or unintentionally), their responses were visceral and deeply affective. Several described feeling compelled—some at first viewing—to adopt the devotional gaze in response to Martin's photograph. Doing so prompted sobering reflections on the multiple layers of loss—of his future, to his parents, and more—that resulted from his murder. In addition, a personal connection to the incident prompted one student to reflect on the fear that Martin's murder provoked for a college friend of theirs, a neighbor of Martin's, and of the way their college community rallied around this friend to provide support. Using the reciprocal gaze established a relationship with Martin's image whose back-and-forth made one seer feel "heavy." One student reported trying to use the aversive gaze to look away from Martin's image—not to avoid idolatry but to avoid discomfort—but Martin's eyes simply wouldn't allow it. Adopting the communal gaze enabled students to connect Martin's killing (in a predominantly white neighborhood) to deeper reflections on the challenges that Black people face in navigating white spaces (a challenge that Yancy also analyzes). A student who chose the liminal gaze immediately encountered this reality in a visceral and personal way. Looking at Martin in his hoodie prompted this student to remember their own experience strolling through a white neighborhood. Because my student fit within its racial boundaries, they were able to do so without even a thought of fearing for their life.

Notably, looking at Dylann Roof's photograph provoked equally visceral responses and deep challenges to the white students who spent time with it. (Understandably, the only student of color in the class elected not to look at Roof but to focus solely on Martin.) For several, the aversive gaze aptly named how they initially looked—or avoided looking—at this image. They didn't want to look at Roof or at the Confederate flag in the photograph, given what it stands for. But they also recognized that to give in to the aversive gaze was to refuse ethical responsibility. Deliberately trying out another gaze (or other gazes) certainly brought ethical and affective challenges but also opportunities for deeper reflection on those challenges. Three students used the occlusive gaze for the second viewing of Roof, looking elsewhere and "contemplating the image from memory," as one put it, rather than looking at it. However, the feelings from the first viewing—"disgust, outrage, a deep distress at what human apathy is capable of," as that student went on to write—remained strong. It was as though Roof's photograph haunted these viewers even in its absence. Applying the communal gaze to his photograph prompted students to reflect on the likely similarities and differences in their upbringings—in the spaces and places (including faith communities) where they had grown up, in the ways those spaces and places had formed them. For one student, the liminal gaze morphed into the virtual gaze as they emplaced themselves in that scene, imagining additional details of it. For two students, adopting the communal and liminal gazes prompted a degree of compassion for Roof, given what he lost in giving himself over to violent white supremacist ideology (a view that disturbed some of their colleagues).

Motivated by the theological conviction that no human being is irredeemable, a conviction grounded in their work with formerly incarcerated men, a third student took the bold and very difficult step of adopting the devotional gaze to look at Roof's image. Continuing to look more deeply into the photo—especially into Roof's eyes—proved extremely trying, but the student persisted. Roof's eyes, which initially looked essentially "dead" to them (as to other students), took on something of the compelling power of a religious icon. Roof's gaze seemed to be calling out to viewers to join his cause and warning those who resisted it of the dangers of being "on the wrong side"—a look that the student realized some viewers would find compelling (the New Zealand mosque mass murderer, apparently, for one). The student's concluding reflections are worth quoting in full:

I ask him to see me as I am in front of him. I feel so sad, such despair, but I keep looking. "I'm not stopping," I tell him. "I'm with you as you are, but I would rather be with you as you might be. I will last as long as you do." He looks both large and small. I try to be with both sizes of him. He continues to refuse to connect with me. He is irredeemable on this plane. I leave, but I do not relent. But I feel so very sad, but perhaps more honestly so than after viewing the photo [the first time] in class.

CONCLUSION

My students' responses and reflections confirm my hope that this visual repertoire can indeed jump-start photographic insurrection. The ease with which the students engaged this visual repertoire—both to describe how they first looked at these images and to reengage them—confirms that its gazes do indeed "come naturally" even when used for visual encounters with nonreligious visual objects. The students' reflections also confirm that using religious gazes can disrupt the hierarchy of seer over seen that is so central to white and other normative gazes.

In every case, it was clear that the gazes were indeed generative for the students, that they opened up new ways of relating to the photographs that didn't occur to them at first glance—even when that first look (typically at Martin's photograph) was a lingering and reflective one. Their responses also confirm that these gazes can prompt seers toward deeper and often difficult reflections on what encountering a certain visual image opens up and opens onto—in themselves and in the larger world. Most importantly, these students weren't just moved emotionally; they were moved to be better and do better, to take action against systemic racism and its effects—or at least so they reported. What actions they will take and whether they will amount to more than compassionate cosmopolitanism, of course, remain to be seen—and likely not by me. And the degree to which they would credit this experience of deliberative seeing for those actions is unknown as well. Still, the promise is real.

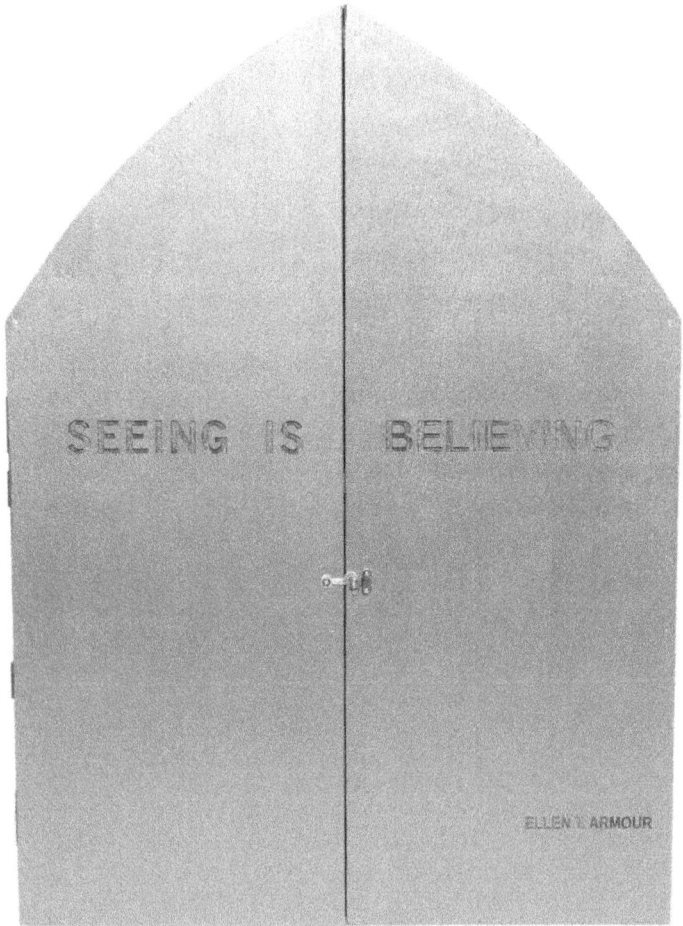

FIGURE E.1 *Seeing Is Believing*, art book cover.
Artist: Britt Stadig. Photographer: Amanda McCadams.
Printed with the permission of Vanderbilt University.

EPILOGUE

Hashtags don't build movements. People do. Now we have to learn how to build movements for the twenty-first century.

—Alicia Garza, cofounder of #BLM, *The Purpose of Power*

In these last few pages, I'll offer some final reflections on what *Seeing and Believing* has attempted to achieve and my hopes for what it can contribute to the struggle for social justice. I do so by placing the moves I've made toward jump-starting photographic insurrection within a larger framework drawn from the previous chapters of *Seeing and Believing* as well as from *Signs and Wonders*—supplemented, of course, with additional scholarly insights as needed. Some of the aspects of *Signs and Wonders* discussed herein will be familiar; others will be relatively new.

I begin by framing the experiment I conducted with my students in relationship to photographic askesis. "Askesis" is the etymological root of "asceticism," a disciplinary practice (or set of practices) undertaken in pursuit of self-(re)formation. While we may associate asceticism with religious devotees who are spiritual adepts (e.g., Christian or Buddhist monks), it can also take philosophical form (e.g., ancient Greek Stoicism). Toward the end of the introduction to *Signs and Wonders*, I position photographic askesis as a contemplative exercise designed to help readers understand photography's role in entraining us in ways of seeing, knowing, doing, and being that conform with bio-disciplinary power's demands (photographic subjection). The four sets of photographs that anchor *Signs and Wonders* open up and open onto that formation and its consequences in particularly powerful ways.

Seeing and Believing extends and expands photographic askesis first by updating our understanding of photographic subjection by attending to digital visual culture's impact on us. Its turn to photographic insurrection, however, goes further. It embodies photographic askesis as a contemplative practice that open us up to re-formation: to new ways of seeing and thus, potentially, knowing, doing, and being. We have at least some evidence that the visual repertoire sourced from Morgan works. My experiment with my students using Martin's and Roof's photographs demonstrates its ability to un-suture white people from white gazes, thereby potentially advancing the struggle for social justice. This repertoire invites the (re)attunement and metanoia that Ott deems necessary to individual and collective re-formation, thus moving us closer to realizing the promise of social justice. That augurs well, I think, for this repertoire's potential ability to animate the civil gaze (Azoulay) and create global citizen-witnesses (Nayar), though that would need to be tested on other photographs.

Of course, none of this will come easy. The barriers to realizing these goals are not just internal to us as individuals, but they also impact us through institutions—including those of surveillance capitalism. A contemplative practice of the sort I have proposed here may seem inadequate at best, given that reality, but it may be more powerful than it first appears. Recall that the attention economy created by surveillance capitalism seeks not only to get us to look but also (per Jonathan Crary) to "eliminate the *useless time of reflection and contemplation*"[1]—and quite successfully, it appears. We scroll through our social media feeds glancing from one digital artifact to another, then another and another. Digital viewing fragments our attention, thereby depriving us of the ability to "join visual discriminations with social and ethical valuations."[2] The time it takes to reflect or to contemplate may be useless to surveillance capitalism, but this experiment suggests that it is potentially vital to the struggle for social justice. And the photographic story line that anchors *Seeing and Believing* clearly indicates how important digital photographs are to that struggle. Indeed, of all the digital stuff we encounter on our new public square, still photographs—especially those that grab our attention because they disrupt normative ways of seeing—are particularly amenable to contemplative practices of the sort I'm suggesting. I make the case for why that is below.

> It is only when anti-Black racism becomes visible, it seems, that White folks can find a way to take it seriously. Mere verbal testimony never seems to suffice.
>
> —W.J.T. Mitchell, *Seeing Through Race*

The photographic story line that anchors *Seeing and Believing* confirms the epigraph above. What is it, though, about photographs—digital photographs, in particular—that makes this so? Recall that Hariman and Lucaites described photography as a "mode of extraordinary seeing" that can expand how we see the world.[3] Jurgenson describes digital photographs as social photographs; that is, "units of communication," not "stand alone media objects."[4] We prosumers are more invested in the photo stream than the individual photo and more in what that stream—or photographic story line—has to say to us (often in words as well as images) than the quality of a particular photograph, he argues. And yet, certain of Jurgenson's observations about individual photographs help explain why still digital photographs may be particularly potent objects for contemplation. Digital photographs freeze the photographic "moment" that prompted someone to click the shutter in the first place. Photographic askesis takes advantage of "the opportunity to put the moment to work" by "involving yourself with it, immersing yourself in it."[5]

Another of Jurgenson's insights—modified slightly—also pertains here. Certain photographs catch our eye and capture our attention not necessarily because they're good (though that may be a factor) but because of what they communicate; that is, what they open up and open onto—and it's likely those photographs that can best realize photography's potential to expand our worlds. "Iconic" photographs—photographs that evoke the import of certain events particularly effectively—emerged long before the advent of digital technologies. How might the concept of iconicity apply to the specific photographs I used in the experiment with my students?

In *On Racial Icons: Blackness and the Public Imagination*, Nicole Fleetwood defines and analyzes the role of racial icons, devoting her first chapter to Trayvon Martin. Racial icons are "public images that have come to represent, symbolize or substitute for a larger historical narrative of race and blackness in the US."[6] Their purpose is to *stand apart* and to *stand for*" the racialized other, Fleetwood writes (10). They "carry a . . . public burden in their attempt to transform the despised into the idolized" (4). Fleetwood presents racial icons—whether photographs

or people (Martin is arguably both)—as a category of cultural
icons, a concept that retains traces of the icon's religious origins.
Like their religious counterparts, cultural icons both "gesture
towards the sacred" and run the risk of accusations of idolatry
(8). Racial icons "can impact us with such emotional force that
we are compelled: to do, to feel, to see" (4), but not all in the
same ways or same directions, as we know all too well. Thanks
to racialized seeing, perceptions of racial icons oscillate between
veneration and denigration (literally, a blackening, Fleetwood
notes) that inhibits their ability to achieve secular sainthood.

Fleetwood's analysis illuminates where the power of Martin's
photograph lies in ways that align well with *Seeing and Believing*. Both in what they index and what they open up and open
onto, photographs like Martin's that become racial icons are
simultaneously exceptional and ordinary, she argues. That combination enables them to both conjure and overcome racist (mis)
perceptions. In Martin's case, the look (a young Black man in a
hoodie) that cost him his life becomes the very same look that so
many came to venerate—and for reasons that, according to Fleetwood, have everything to do with the iconic tropes that the photo
invokes, including religious tropes. The play of light and shadow
created around Martin's head by the hoodie and the cap beneath
it generates "a halo effect," she observes. The hood surrounds his
face, causing it to seem to "hover and levitate, as his eyes peer out"
beneath it. The photograph occupies a liminal space between life
and death, in a sense, as it simultaneously invokes Martin's presence at the time it was taken and seems to "speak to audiences
from the silence of [Martin's] death" (16).

That veneration showed up in socially mediated photographic
protests as well as in-person protests. Protesters (of varying
identities, racial and otherwise) took photos of themselves in
hoodies, posting them under "#I am Trayvon Martin." Such

images—including one featuring former President Obama— "symbolically demonstrate an identification with racial isolation, profiling and forms of abject suffering," Fleetwood writes (20). White people who undertook this form of protest were, like my white students, "able to recognize a young black male as a sympathetic character . . . and to see the machinations of structural and quotidian racism to portray him as other" (21). Still, Fleetwood worries about the limits of this form of (all-too-easy) protest. For one thing, photographic veneration threatens to obscure what's been truly and forever lost: Martin's future, his very real flesh-and-blood life cut short by his very real flesh-and-blood death. Contemplating Martin's photo, recall, prompted very similar reflections in my students—white and Black—which might assuage that concern somewhat. But Fleetwood's other concern homes in on the limits of photographic insurrection I noted in the previous chapter and calls to mind the critics of clicktivism I referenced in chapter 2. Photographic clicktivism like #IAmTrayvon may make those who engage in it feel better for the moment, but as Fleetwood says, it is no substitute for the pursuit of real, substantive change. The need for that change is evident, she notes, in the stark contrast between Zimmerman's acquittal and the conviction not long after of Marissa Alexander, a young Black woman who unsuccessfully invoked "Stand Your Ground" as her defense against the charge that she murdered her abusive husband (30–31). Addressing the systemic and structural causes of those inequities—not to mention Martin's murder— will require the hard work of social organizing. And, following the epigraph that headlines this chapter, that requires more than hashtags and social media postings, as its author knows and embodies very well.

Much about Fleetwood's analysis reinforces my own discussion of photographic iconicity in *Signs and Wonders*, helpfully extending it into our new public square. There, I drew on Hariman and Lucaites's aptly titled study of iconic analogue photos, *No Caption Needed* (which Fleetwood also cites). Recall that they describe iconic photographs as circuits of political affect that arise out of situations of social conflict or crisis. By "concentrat[ing] and direct[ing] emotions," iconic photographs serve as "aesthetic resources for the performative mediation of conflicts."[7] Of course, some will use them that way, while others will not, as Fleetwood's analysis shows. And how that mediation will turn out will always remain to be seen. Yet that, in turn, is likely to depend in part on what photographic story line(s) a given photograph may extend and embody. Martin's photograph is arguably *the* iconic photograph of the #BLM movement, thanks to both its own potency as a photograph and because of what it helped to engender and grow—including branches in this photographic story line that have fueled the movement (and resistance to it).

The iconic power in Martin's photograph comes in no small part from how it both invokes and resists the power that anti-Black racism continues to hold in our time and place, Fleetwood shows. Indeed, racism's power leads W.J.T. Mitchell in *Seeing Through Race* to define race itself as a "conceptual icon" created in the service of racism. As racism's creation, race has become a "medium" through which we see the world, one that takes multiple forms. As a cultural icon, race operates in three registers, Mitchell argues: as a fetish, a totem, and an idol (all three terms with religious valences). Of the three, the third is especially relevant to my concerns here. Mitchell identifies idolatry as "the most virulent form" of this conceptual icon's impact. As an idol, "race becomes a god term, the alibi for murder, slavery, and other forms of human sacrifice."[8]

Of course, as the conflict over religious icons that divided Eastern Christianity from Western Christianity many centuries ago illustrates, one person's (or tradition's) icon is another's idol. That's true for cultural and racial icons, as well, Mitchell argues. *Seeing Through Race* is informed by Mitchell's earlier book, *What Do Pictures Want*, where he deploys the concept of "iconoclash," a "war of images."[9] There, Mitchell notes that the architects of 9/11 targeted the World Trade Towers because of their iconic status (as the literal embodiment of the worship of global capital in the United States), rendering them idols in their eyes and thus worthy of destruction. (Of course, their ruins have since become the iconic representation for Americans of all that was lost that day and of American resilience.) Both sides in the global "War on Terror" that followed 9/11 positioned it as a religious war—a jihad, according to the members of Al Qaeda, or a "crusade . . . of good against evil," according to then-president George W. Bush, who helmed the U.S. response.[10] The United States, too, engaged in a war of images, Mitchell observes, especially in Iraq (remember "Shock and Awe"?), where American soldiers first toppled the statue of Saddam Hussein (thereby exposing him as an idol, not an icon), foreshadowing the "regime change" to come.

Mitchell's analysis of icons and idols coupled with the concept of iconoclash sheds light on the power of Roof's photograph and its place in the photographic story line that anchors *Seeing and Believing*. The story of Martin's killing and its aftermath started Roof down the digital rabbit hole that led to his radicalization. In the photograph, Roof poses holding a gun and sitting next to a Confederate flag—two cultural icons for the audience Roof likely hoped to reach in his goal of starting a race war. Roof's photograph renders those icons idols by Mitchell's definition; that is, "images to kill and die for" that "provide the objects in which holy war and race war converge."[11] Indeed, Roof carried out the first battle in that war on holy ground—Mother

Emmanuel A.M.E. Church—where he shot and killed nine Black Christians gathered there for Bible study. I would argue that my white students' (unconscious) use of the aversive gaze to *not* see precisely those elements in the photo implicitly recognizes them as idols: as the "god term[s]" that, in his mind, provided Roof with an "alibi for murder" (39–40).

In *What Do Pictures Want?* Mitchell puts forward "sounding the idols," a concept he gets from Friedrich Nietzsche, as an alternative to iconoclash and the all-too-real conflicts it can often generate (8).[12] Rather than smashing the idols (e.g., the World Trade Towers or Hussein's statue), sounding involves gently tapping the idol "with the hammer or 'tuning fork' of critical or philosophical language" in order to better hear—that is, understand—their power (8).[13] Mitchell returns to sounding the idols in *Seeing Through Race* as a strategy for reckoning with racism. That reckoning requires coming to terms with race's impact (as icon *cum* idol) not only on how we see but also on what we (think we) know, how we act, and thus who we are—individually and collectively—and on our institutions. This is essential to learning to see *through* race, not *with* it. To see through race, in Mitchell's view, is not to see beyond it but to see more deeply into how race as a viscous medium has formed us and our world (40).

Sounding the idols requires, in turn, attending to what pictures want. *What Do Pictures Want?* reframes how we engage with visual images via a new theo-logic, it turns out, that describes well how my students engaged with Roof's and Martin's photographs. That Mitchell speaks of "pictures" reminds us of just how ordinary and ubiquitous photographs—especially digital photographs—are, an especially important point today, given our visually saturated new public square. But even more importantly, asking what pictures *want* grants them a kind of agency and autonomy that calls to mind the transcendence of seen over seer characteristic of religious seeing in the visual repertoire I've sourced from Morgan. This characteristic of religious seeing, I argued, is key to its usefulness to photographic insurrection. Tellingly, Mitchell turns to another theo-logic to articulate pictures' agency and autonomy: animism, a form of iconicity associated with Indigenous religious traditions. Animism attributes to certain ordinary objects (rocks, trees, or animals, etc.) a real connection to the divine or the transcendent that exerts a visceral claim on those who encounter them.

How might our relationship to pictures change if we thought of photographs—digital photographs, in this case—as iconic in this way? Many Indigenous people already do, Mitchell notes, refusing to be photographed because they believe that the camera will literally steal their spirit. But Mitchell suggests that photographic animism isn't confined to Indigenous people. Rather, it aptly describes how many of us—regardless of ethnicity or religious tradition—respond to photographs, at least those that mean something to us. He points to an exercise that one of his colleagues routinely uses with students. The colleague asks each student to bring to class a photograph of their mother. In that class session, the colleague asks the students to cut the eyes out of their mothers' photographs. The colleague reports that the students inevitably refuse to do so.[14]

So what do the pictures of Martin and of Roof want? On the one hand, considered together, they embody a clash of icons: between a gray hoodie and a Confederate flag, for one thing.[15] Are these icons or idols? We're asked to decide: Does the gray hoodie signify coolness or criminality? Is the Confederate flag a relic of a noble "Lost Cause" or a harbinger of the evil of white supremacy? For many viewers, that will be all they choose to see before turning their attention away from the pictures and toward whatever else seeks or demands it. But these pictures want more from us than that. They invite us to look, really look, into them, to discern what they reveal about their subjects—the young Black man wearing the hoodie, the young white man holding the gun and sitting beside the Confederate flag—and, through them, about us and our world. It is up to us to decide how to respond to those mute requests. We can, of course, refuse to keep looking and move on. But we can also choose to open ourselves to what these pictures have to show and say. To approach responding to what they want as an opportunity to slow down and to look, really look, at what they open up and open onto. To engage in what I'm calling "photographic askesis" as a contemplative exercise.

Let me bring one more set of insights to these photographs that, I believe, speak to what these two pictures want. Both photographs are what we call "selfies" staged and taken by Roof and Martin themselves. No doubt, this is part of their power. They offer us access to both young men *as they want to be seen*—face-to-face, arguably, eye-to-eye. Given the experiment Mitchell's colleague uses with his students, it is perhaps no surprise that some of the most powerful moments my students described occurred when they looked into—or avoided looking into—Martin's or Roof's eyes. S. Brent Plate devotes a chapter of his book *Religion and Film* to the face—particularly, the role close-ups play in viewers' embodied responses to certain movies. Some of his insights—particularly those drawn from religion and neuroscience—apply here as well, adding to our understanding of the iconic power in Roof's and Martin's photographs.[16] Recall, for example, the importance of Martin's face and head to Fleetwood's analysis of his selfie's iconic power. Like religious icons, the power of the close-up lies in the visual relationship it establishes with its viewers. The close-up, like the icon, invites the viewer into a face-to-face, eye-to-eye exchange that allows the devotee to both see into the divine and be seen by it (what Morgan deems the reciprocal gaze).

The visual draw that icons and close-ups hold rests on the face's role in individual and social human development over time, Plate argues. Neuroscientists have shown that infants first connect with the world through face-to-face exchanges with their caregivers. They have also documented the centrality of looking into other people's eyes to our emotional and social growth as we mature. Learning to read others faces, though, also requires gaining social literacy, Plate notes, which studies have also shown encodes cultural biases for and against into how we see one another. He cites scholarship that shows that movies have both reinforced and eroded those biases, observing that "films can be transformational, but only as they lead beyond the self."[17] Nonetheless, he concludes, "By returning viewers to the faces and bodies of others through defamiliarization and refamiliarization, the cinematic rituals of film viewing offer the possibility for aesthetic, ethical, and religious re-creation."[18]

Plate's reference to "re-creation" brings us back, once again, to photographic askesis as a contemplative practice. Recall, once again, how taking up such a practice—consciously and intentionally using Morgan's gazes—impacted the ways my students responded to what the pictures of Martin and Roof want. First, it helped them identify and understand how they had responded to one or the other of those pictures well before they'd been coached in those gazes. But, more importantly, taking the time to deliberately adopt a different gaze to look at one or the other of the photographs allowed them to engage more fully with what those pictures wanted.

Adding Plate's insights regarding the visual importance of the face calls attention to the role Martin's and Roof's faces—their eyes in particular—played in my students' response to this exercise. Powerful insights resulted when my students either adopted the reciprocal gaze to look into Martin's or Roof's eyes or refused to by (unconsciously) using the aversive gaze. This suggests that both young men's faces are particularly critical access points to what these pictures want. It highlights the role that contemplating what those faces opened up and opened onto played in sounding what Mitchell calls the cultural idol of race. Adopting—and staying with—one or another of Morgan's gazes brought to my white students insights into how they had been attuned to see *with* race. Looking more deeply through the pictures and into their own formation opened up and onto ways of seeing not *beyond* race but *through* it.

Framing the visual repertoire used in this experiment through photographic askesis presents a way of thinking about those ways of seeing and what they might open up and open onto if taken up by a wider audience—particularly an audience, in the case of the photographic story line that concerns me here, of "good white people." Of course, the full experiment I conducted with my students embodies photographic askesis undertaken as a conscious practice, something that is unlikely to happen on a larger scale. However, because the ways of seeing that undergird this visual repertoire "come naturally" to all of us, it's quite likely that this larger audience is already using one or more of the gazes in this repertoire when they encounter online photographs that "move" them (emotionally and, sometimes, to take action). To unconsciously adopt one or more of these gazes—particularly on those occasions where the photographs they encounter challenge white gazing—could potentially jump-start or advance their progress on the complex journey of what Ibram Kendi calls becoming *anti*racist, one that requires other practices that will foster self-(re)formation (including, perhaps, reading Kendi's book).

Of course, there is no guarantee that this will happen. As I said in the previous chapter, I am not putting forward photographic insurrection as the panacea to all that ails us. The same holds true for this visual repertoire and, indeed, for any visual repertoire. However, I do think photographic insurrection can play a critically important role in disrupting normative ways of seeing, such as white gazes. That disruption can, in turn, disrupt normative ways of knowing, doing, and being. Recall that when I say "seeing," I do not mean with one's eyes only. As Yancy makes clear, every dimension of the human sensorium is involved in white gazes; every sense, then, can potentially contribute to its undoing. Indeed, thanks to digital visual culture, most of our interactions with visual images in our new media ecosystem are multisensory. We access them through touch, and the impact of cell phone videos on us comes as much from what we hear in them as what we see.

This will become only more important in the future, I suspect. Our socially mediated ecosystem enables photographic story lines to expand and diverge at unprecedented speed and in multiple directions, creating virtual visual cultures that pastoral theologian Sonia Waters describes as "fluid."[19] A Google search she conducted in July 2015 for "images of Michael Brown," the young Black man killed by police in Ferguson, Missouri, in 2014 (two years after Martin's murder) yielded 687 million results, Waters reports.[20] Tracking just some of the various trajectories of that photographic story line illustrates the challenges posed by this fluidity. For one thing, allegiances shift and change as new content emerges, she observes. That's important to remember, especially given the ease with which digital photographs can be altered or made up from whole (digital) cloth. For example, embedded in the Michael Brown photographic story line was a photograph that purported to show a Ferguson protester carrying a sign that read "No mother should have to fear for her son's life every time he robs a store." The image was a Photoshopped version of a photograph of protester Jermell Hasson, whose actual sign read, "No mother should have to fear for her son's life every time he *leaves the house*."[21] Images of Michael Brown became fodder for online iconoclash. Advocates for Brown posted positive images (such as Brown at his high school graduation), while detractors attempting to animate racist animus posted negative ones allegedly showing Brown embodying racist stereotypes: giving a gang salute or holding a gun in one hand and a bottle of alcohol in the other, for example.

As I have here, Waters calls attention to our responsibility as prosumers to engage our visually saturated media landscape with discretion and wisdom. Her reference to discretion and wisdom, though, calls to mind a deeper dimension to the phenomenological underpinnings of Morgan's religious gazes. Bringing the cognitive to the perceptive *and* the affective will help reattune how and what (we believe) we see, potentially prompting metanoia and leading to individual and social re-formation. But as scholars like Azoulay, Nayar, Yancy, and Ott have shown us, re-formation requires multiple literacies, not just visual ones. As Yancy indicates, every dimension of the human sensorium is involved in whiteness; every sense, then, can contribute to its undoing.

In addition to the multisensory and social literacies these scholars highlight, I join Ott in foregrounding digital literacy—in digital *visual* culture, in this case—such as that provided here. Becoming literate in the mechanisms of surveillance capitalism—of digital redlining, of digital photography as a technology and as social photography—and their impact on how and what we see online, will help us become smarter about how we engage online and, I hope, in real life. These literacies reinforce a critical insight embedded in these photographic story lines. The lines between the virtual and the real, between our online and our "real" lives and worlds are blurry at best. The virtual requires and reflects the real, and its impact on the real is itself very real—all *too* real sometimes. Even deepfakes require some (faked) presumptive real-world reference for their effect. The virtual, as we've seen, accelerates and expands systemic and structural challenges that predate the advent of digital technologies and our new media ecosystem. Wrestling with those realities requires cultivating those social literacies that Nayar and Yancy, in particular, advocate and how those, too, affect how and what we see, (think we) know and do, and thus who we are. That work will be enhanced, for those of us who pursue those literacies, by committing ourselves to learning and cultivating ways of seeing that can jump-start photographic insurrection and, through it, ways of knowing, doing, and being that exhibit metanoia.

It can't be said often enough: realizing that commitment will require that we adjust not just how we see but how we look. That said, not all of us will be moved in the same way by the same photographs; this is an important insight when it comes to my experiment with my students. Not just any photo of a young Black man would have the same impact on white viewers that Trayvon Martin's selfie did. The same is true for Roof's selfie. No doubt, this is due to what each photograph means to the photographic story line that contains them and to the larger discourse about race and racism in the United States in which that story line is embedded. But as we have seen, there is something about these photographs themselves that renders them particularly powerful.

When a picture grabs our attention, it's likely because it *is* particularly powerful. Paying attention to what that picture wants provides an opportunity to acknowledge its power, to explore where that power comes from and why it speaks to us—to use it as a teaching moment, if you will, as reconceived by W.J.T. Mitchell in *Seeing Through Race*. Instead of the typical "paternalistic and parental event" that provides "an occasion for inculcating elementary lessons in civilized behavior," he has in mind those moments when "normative assumptions and lesson plans are thrown into confusion and doubt and some form of 'newness.' . . . has a chance to 'enter the world.'"[22] Mitchell analyzes three specific "teaching moments" in *Seeing Through Race:* the Islamophobia sparked by 9/11, the "Semitic moment" that is the Israeli-Palestinian conflict, and the putative "post-racial" moment in the United States augured by the election of Barack Obama, the country's first Black president. Both "momentous" and "ephemeral," these teaching moments are turning points, of sorts, in the ongoing history of the racisms they manifest whose significance we are continuing to live into but that we don't yet fully comprehend. Indeed, we are experiencing "an epidemic of racialization, in which a variety of ethnicities and identities are mobilized to satisfy what looks like a structural need for an Other and an enemy."[23] This epidemic—one that also infects views of gender and sexuality—has only accelerated and expanded in the years since Mitchell wrote those words.

Not all of the photographs we encounter on our new public square will reference these teaching moments—or others that may come to readers' minds. However, some will. Instead of scrolling through our social media looking for the next high, I invite my readers to join me in committing ourselves to slow down and look—really look—at those photographs that grab our attention because they reference such moments. Looking at what they present to us, and what they open up and open onto, will be critical for every struggle for social justice now and into the future.

Appendix

WAYS OF SEEING PROMPTS

CREATED BY DEBBIE BRUBAKER
AND ELLEN T. ARMOUR

The prompts below are designed to help readers consciously try out one or more of the religious ways of seeing in the visual repertoire on offer in chapter 5. The gazes that make up that visual repertoire are described and defined by David Morgan in *The Embodied Eye: Religious Visual Culture and the Social Life of Feeling* (Berkeley: University of California Press, 2012).

Devotional: *voluntary submission to the visual object*

Approach the photograph as a devotional object; allow it to conjure in you something akin to worship, devotion, and submission. What does this feel like? How does this gaze affect you? Does devotional submission change how you understand or relate to the visual object? If so, how?

Reciprocal: *transformative exchange between the seer and the seen*

Consider the encounter happening between you and the photograph as a mutual and dynamic exchange. You encounter the photograph and are transformed. The photograph encounters you and is transformed. What is happening here? How does a reciprocal gaze change you, as the seer, and what you see in the photograph? What does this feel like? What do you learn about yourself and about the visual object?

Aversive: *"looking around" the visual object rather than directly at it*

Do not look directly at the photograph; look around it. What do you see? What does it feel like to gaze in this way? How does taking up the aversive gaze affect your relationship to the photograph? How does this gaze affect you?

Communal: *influence of social settings on how we see*

Consider your immediate social surroundings as you encounter the photograph. What social settings and relations shape where you are in this moment? What social surroundings show up in and through the photograph? How do these social settings impact how the photograph affects you? What effect does foregrounding these social settings have on how you relate to the photograph?

Liminal: *"marks the edge of us and the beginning of them"*

Reflect on the boundaries between you and the photograph. What social boundaries does your encounter with the object create or recreate? Where are you positioned in relation to these boundaries? How do these boundaries inform how you relate to the photograph?

Virtual: *"vicarious participation" via projecting yourself into unfamiliar ways of being*

Imagine you are in the photographed scene. What are you doing? What do you see, touch, taste, hear, or smell? How do you relate to the people or objects in the scene? Now imagine that the subject in the photograph is looking at the photograph with you. What do you imagine they see? What would they tell you about the photograph? How does that impact what you see?

Unilateral: *renders one "powerless, subject to the manipulative, overwhelming, objectifying gaze of authority"*

Consider the relationship between you and the photograph. Is there a dominant direction of viewing; are you or the object the dominant viewer? Which party has authority? Are you overwhelmed or powerless under the gaze of the visual object? Or is your gaze authoritative, objectifying, or manipulative? How does this feel? What are you experiencing?

Occlusive: *putting up another visual object as a shield; closing one's eyes to avoid another's judgmental gaze*

Close your eyes or use another object to block your view of the photograph. What happens? What do you see? What do you feel? Why did you block your view of the photograph? When you block your vision of the visual object, what feelings, relationships, histories, or memories do you become aware of? What feelings, relationships, histories, or memories are you avoiding? With your vision of the visual object blocked, what do you see? What does the visual object see in this moment?

NOTES

PREFACE

1. Christine Hauser, Derrick Bryson Taylor, and Neil Vigdor, "'I Can't Breathe': 4 Minneapolis Officers Fired after Black Man Dies in Custody," *New York Times*, May 26, 2020, sec. U.S., https://www.nytimes.com/2020/05/26/us/minneapolis-police-man-died.html/; Larry Buchanan, Quoctrung Bui, and Jugal K. Patel, "Black Lives Matter May Be the Largest Movement in U.S. History," *New York Times*, July 3, 2020, sec. U.S., https://www.nytimes.com/interactive/2020/07/03/us/george-floyd-protests-crowd-size.html/.

2. Alan Taylor, "Images from a Worldwide Protest Movement," *The Atlantic*, June 8, 2020, sec. In Focus, https://www.theatlantic.com/photo/2020/06/images-worldwide-protest-movement/612811/.

3. For a thorough look into Facebook's role in the insurrection, see Craig Timberg, Elizabeth Dwoskin, and Reed Albergotti, "Inside Facebook, Jan. 6 Violence Fueled Anger, Regret over Missed Warning Signs," *Washington Post*, October 20, 2021. https://www.washingtonpost.com/technology/2021/10/22/jan-6-capitol-riot-facebook/.

4. For a brief account of the killing and its aftermath, see "Trayvon Martin Fast Facts," CNN, February 14, 2022, https://www.cnn.com/2013/06/05/us/trayvon-martin-shooting-fast-facts/index.html/.

5. Ellen T. Armour, *Signs and Wonders: Theology after Modernity* (New York: Columbia University Press, 2016).

6. The photographs featured in *Signs and Wonders* were of the consecration of Rev. Gene Robinson as the first out gay bishop in the

Episcopal Church (chap. 3), the abuse of military detainees at Abu Ghraib (chap. 4), the aftermath of Hurricane Katrina (chap. 5), and two stills from the home movie circulated by the family of the late Terri Schiavo (chap. 6), who was (controversially) allowed to die after several years of living in a so-called vegetative state.

7. In addition to their works that informed *Signs and Wonders*, I engage here additional scholarship by Ariella Azoulay, Jonathan Crary, Robert Hariman and John Louis Lucaites, W.J.T. Mitchell, and Abigail Solomon-Godeau.

8. To cite just one example, the focus of much of the literature on religion and film appears to be on professionally produced films. There are profound differences between all that goes into producing professional films (as described briefly by S. Brent Plate in *Religion and Film: Cinema and the Re-creation of the World* [New York: Columbia University Press, 2017], 100–102) and cell phone videos. While both arguably impact viewers via the same bodily and social systems (as analyzed well by Plate), one would need to ask what role those differences in production might play in their reception.

9. They are hardly the first to draw on religious tropes when dealing with visual media. Take, for example, "iconic" photographs, a focal issue in *Signs and Wonders*. The term is rooted in a practice common to many religions (including but not limited to Christianity) centered on visual objects that are believed to connect the devout viewer to the divine or the transcendent. However, as several scholars of photography have observed, many photographs considered iconic (at least, in the United States) call to mind Christian theological motifs (Dorothea Lange's famous Dust Bowl photograph, *Migrant Mother*, recalls the *Pieta*, for example). I'll have more to say about photographic iconicity later.

10. Sonia Waters, "All Visual, All the Time: Towards a Theory of Visual Practices for Pastoral Theological Reflection," *Pastoral Psychology* 65, no. 6 (2016): 849–61, https://doi.org/DOI 10.1007/s11089-016-0711-7/. I engage Waters's essay more fully in the epilogue.

11. Britt Stadig, "Seeing Is Believing," http://tellingstoriesstoriesthattell .com/ellen-t-armour/. Photographs by Amanda McCadams.

12. Catherine C. Albanese, *America: Religions and Religion*, 3rd ed. (Belmont, CA: Wadsworth Press, 1999), 11. Quoted by David Morgan in *The Sacred Gaze: Religious Visual Culture in Theory and Practice* (Berkeley: University of California Press, 2005), 56. I discuss *The Sacred Gaze* in more detail in what follows.

13. Morgan observes, in his conclusion to *Sacred Gaze*, that each of these three dimensions includes a visual component (*Sacred Gaze*, 259). We can't really understand how these various components function—individually or collectively—without attending to seeing.

14. For my take on the instability of this distinction, see my invited contribution to a special issue of the *Journal of the American Academy of Religion*, "Theology in Modernity's Wake," *Journal of the American Academy of Religion* 74, no. 1 (March 2006): 1–16.

15. David Morgan, *The Embodied Eye: Religious Visual Culture and the Social Life of Feeling* (Berkeley: University of California Press, 2012).

16. I place "come naturally" in scare quotes for reasons that will become clear later and that align well with Plate's approach in *Religion and Film*. Like me, Plate also claims that insights from religious seeing are beneficial to visual culture studies—in his case, film studies. What Plate calls "religious cinematics" offers insights at multiple layers about movies' impact on viewers—including their "socio-ethical dimensions." As he writes, "Ideologies are always at play in viewing structures. By returning viewers to the faces and bodies of others through defamiliarization and refamiliarization, the cinematic rituals of film viewing offer the possibility for aesthetic, ethical, and religious recreation" (150).

17. Morgan, *Sacred Gaze*, 3. Morgan settles on the term "gaze," common to scholarship on visual culture, as best suited to capture seeing's multiple dimensions. "Gaze designates the visual field that relates seer, seen, the conventions of seeing, and the physical, ritual, and historical contexts of seeing," he writes (*Sacred Gaze*, Introduction, 5). There is, of course, a substantial lineage of scholarship on the power inherent in how we see that also uses the same terminology (see, e.g., Laura Mulvey's concept of the male gaze in "Visual Pleasure and Narrative Cinema," *Screen* 16, no. 3 (October 1, 1975): 6–18, https://doi.org/10.1093/screen/16.3.6/). In later chapters, I draw on the work of philosopher

George Yancy on "white gazes." Notably, Morgan resists associating conventional gazes only with reductive objectification—in part, due to his primary focus on religious seeing; another reason I find his work helpful. What Morgan dubs "the sacred gaze" promises to connect viewers to the holy, in part by resisting (its) objectification.

18. See Jonathan Crary, *Techniques of the Observer: On Vision and Modernity in the Nineteenth Century* (Cambridge, MA: MIT Press, 1990); and John Tagg, *The Burden of Representation: Essays on Photographies and Histories* (Minneapolis: University of Minnesota Press, 1993). I say more about both later.

19. Morgan, *Sacred Gaze*, 32.

20. Morgan, *Sacred Gaze*, 33.

21. The sets of photographs that anchor *Signs and Wonders* all circulated through legacy media. Some were taken by photojournalists, but most were taken by amateurs and picked up by the media, differences that I discuss therein.

22. See W.J.T. Mitchell, "There Are No Visual Media," *Journal of Visual Culture* 4, no. 2 (2005): 257–66. Isolating vision from the other senses is a common tendency in visual culture studies that Jonathan Crary also criticizes in *Suspensions of Perception: Attention, Spectacle, and Modern Culture* (Cambridge, MA: MIT Press, 2001). As will become clearer in later chapters, my perspective here (and in *Signs and Wonders*) aligns well with this insight.

23. Morgan, *Sacred Gaze*, 7.

24. Colin Koopman, *How We Became Our Data: A Genealogy of the Informational Person* (Chicago: University of Chicago Press, 2019).

25. Safiya Umoja Noble, *Algorithms of Oppression: How Search Engines Reinforce Racism* (New York: NYU Press, 2018). I have more to say about Noble's work later.

I. SETTING THE STAGE

1. Jim Zarroli and Avie Schneider, "Deluge Continues: 26 Million Jobs Lost in Just 5 Weeks," *Morning Edition*, National Public Radio, April 23, 2020, https://www.npr.org/sections/coronavirus-live-updates /2020/04/23/841876464/26-million-jobs-lost-in-just-5-weeks/.

2. Kim Parker, Rachel Minkin, and Jesse Bennett, "Economic Fallout from COVID-19 Continues to Hit Lower-Income Americans the Hardest," Pew Research Center, September 24, 2020, sec. Social and Demographic Trends, https://www.pewresearch.org/social-trends/2020/09/24/economic-fallout-from-covid-19-continues-to-hit-lower-income-americans-the-hardest/.

3. The charges against Amy Cooper were dismissed in early 2021. Sarah Maslin Nir, "How 2 Lives Collided in Central Park, Rattling the Nation," *New York Times*, June 14, 2020, sec. New York, https://www.nytimes.com/2020/06/14/nyregion/central-park-amy-cooper-christian-racism.html/; Jonah E. Bromwich, "Amy Cooper, Who Falsely Accused Black Bird-Watcher, Has Charge Dismissed," *New York Times*, February 16, 2021, sec. New York, https://www.nytimes.com/2021/02/16/nyregion/amy-cooper-charges-dismissed.html/.

4. Ibram X. Kendi, *How to Be an Antiracist* (New York: One World, 2019); Robin DiAngelo, *White Fragility: Why It's So Hard for White People to Talk about Racism* (Boston: Beacon Press, 2018).

5. Christianna Silva, "Mississippi Lawmakers Vote to Remove Confederate Emblem from State Flag," National Public Radio, June 27, 2020, sec. America Reckons with Racial Injustice, https://www.npr.org/2020/06/27/884306925/mississippi-lawmakers-clear-path-to-remove-confederate-emblem-from-state-flag/.

6. Neil MacFarquhar, "Many Claim Extremists Are Sparking Protest Violence. But Which Extremists?," *New York Times*, May 31, 2020, sec. U.S., https://www.nytimes.com/2020/05/31/us/george-floyd-protests-white-supremacists-antifa.html/.

7. Maegan Vazquez and Paul LeBlanc, "Proud Boys: Trump Refuses to Condemn White Supremacists at Presidential Debate," CNN, September 30, 2020, sec. Politics, https://www.cnn.com/2020/09/30/politics/proud-boys-trump-white-supremacists-debate/index.html/.

8. Katie Rogers, "Protesters Dispersed with Tear Gas So Trump Could Pose at Church," *New York Times*, June 2, 2020, https://www.nytimes.com/2020/06/01/us/politics/trump-st-johns-church-bible.html/.

9. In the wake of Trump's departure from the White House—notably, without issuing pardons to any of those charged by then in connection with the January 6 insurrection—the Proud Boys have begun to

distance themselves from Trump (and from national politics), expressing deep disillusionment and disappointment with him. Sheera Frenkel and Alan Feuer, "'A Total Failure': The Proud Boys Now Mock Trump," *New York Times*, January 20, 2021, sec. Technology, https://www.nytimes.com/2021/01/20/technology/proud-boys-trump.html/.

10. Azi Paybarah and Brent Lewis, "Stunning Images as a Mob Storms the U.S. Capitol," *New York Times*, January 7, 2021, sec. U.S., https://www.nytimes.com/2021/01/06/us/politics/trump-riot-dc-capitol -photos.html/; Benjamin Swasey, Alana Wise, and Elena Moore, "Congress Reconvenes after Pro-Trump Mob Brings Chaos to the Capitol," National Public Radio, January 6, 2021, sec. Capitol Insurrection Updates, https://www.npr.org/sections/congress-electoral-college-tally -live-updates/2021/01/06/954028436/u-s-capitol-locked-down-amid -escalating-far-right-protests/.

11. Chris Cameron, "These Are the People Who Died in Connection with Capitol Riot," *New York Times*, October 13, 2022, sec. Politics, https://www.nytimes.com/2022/01/05/us/politics/jan-6-capitol-deaths .html/.

12. Facebook subsequently referred its decision and its policy exempting world leaders from content restrictions to its independent oversight board for further review. Shira Ovide, "Facebook Invokes Its 'Supreme Court,'" *New York Times*, January 22, 2021, sec. Technology, https://www.nytimes.com/2021/01/22/technology/facebook-oversight-board -trump.html/. For more on the matter, see Craig Timberg, Elizabeth Dwoskin, and Reed Albergotti, "Inside Facebook, Jan. 6 Violence Fueled Anger, Regret over Missed Warning Signs," *Washington Post*, October 20, 2021, https://www.washingtonpost.com/technology/2021 /10/22/jan-6-capitol-riot-facebook/. In November 2022, Twitter's controversial new owner, Elon Musk, restored Trump's access to Twitter. Faiz Siddiqui, Drew Harwell, and Isaac Arnsdorff, "Elon Musk Restores Trump's Twitter Account," *Washington Post*, sec. Technology, https://www.washingtonpost.com/technology/2022/11/19/trump-musk -twitter/.

13. Bobby Allyn, "Judge Refuses to Reinstate Parler after Amazon Shut It Down," *All Things Considered*, National Public Radio, January 21, 2021, https://www.npr.org/2021/01/21/956486352/judge-refuses-to-reins

tate-parler-after-amazon-shut-it-down/. Parler returned online in early February 2021. Bobby Allyn and Rachel Treisman, "After Weeks of Being Offline, Parler Finds a New Web Host," National Public Radio, February 15, 2021, sec. Technology, https://www.npr.org /2021/02/15/968116346/after-weeks-of-being-off-line-parler-finds-a -new-web-host/. Google and Apple restored it to their app stores in the fall of 2022 after it agreed to moderate its content. Nico Grant, "Parler Returns to Google Play Store," *New York Times*, sec. Technology, September 9, 2022, https://www.nytimes.com/2022/09/02/tech nology/parler-google-play.html/.

14. See Tung-Hui Hu, *A Prehistory of the Cloud* (Cambridge, MA: MIT Press, 2015), for a particularly important take on this topic, its origins, and its consequences. Of particular interest, given the line of inquiry I'll pursue here, are the connections Hu exposes between the cloud and its infrastructure and the analogue systems and infrastructures that predate it. In subsequent chapters, I trace the impact between analogue social systems and our digital world.

15. German Lopez, "Pizzagate, the Fake News Conspiracy Theory That Led a Gunman to DC's Comet Ping Pong, Explained," *Vox*, December 8, 2016, sec. Policy and Politics, https://www.vox.com/policy-and -politics/2016/12/5/13842258/pizzagate-comet-ping-pong-fake-news/.

16. Sarah Mervosh, "Distorted Videos of Nancy Pelosi Spread on Facebook and Twitter, Helped by Trump," *New York Times*, May 24, 2019, sec. U.S., https://www.nytimes.com/2019/05/24/us/politics/pelosi-doc tored-video.html/.

17. Michael Calderone, "'It's Kind of the Wild West': Media Gears Up for Onslaught of Deepfakes," *Politico*, June 25, 2019, sec. Media, https:// politi.co/2YcRKzt/.

18. The following summary of *Signs and Wonders* and how *Seeing and Believing* connects with it is a revised and expanded version of that found in Ellen T. Armour, "Decolonizing Spectatorship: Photography, Theology, and the New Media," in *Beyond Man: Race, Coloniality, and Philosophy of Religion*, ed. An Yountae and Eleanor Craig (Durham, NC: Duke University Press, 2021), 128–35.

19. Pastoral theologian Sonia Waters also deploys a Foucauldian approach to these issues, but via Gary Shapiro's concept of visual regimes, which

she applies to the specific strands of the photographic story line aris-
ing out of Michael Brown's killing by police in Ferguson, Missouri.
See Sonia Waters, "All Visual, All the Time: Towards a Theory of
Visual Practices for Pastoral Theological Reflection," *Journal of Pastoral Psychology* 65 (2016): 849–61. While my use of Foucault is more
extensive, we share the goal of maximizing the potential in such story
lines for prompting change—individual and social—in and through
what I'll call "good white people." Appropriately, given the role of pastoral theology, Waters is particularly focused on white churchgoers.
As mentioned in the preface, my intended audience is broader.

20. Ladelle McWhorter, *Racism and Sexual Oppression in Anglo-America:
A Genealogy* (Bloomington: Indiana University Press, 2009).

21. To clarify, I am not claiming that only modern human beings divided
the world along these lines. However, the specifics of modern taxonomies are distinctive as are the resulting effects they produce.

22. In *Camera Lucida* Barthes speaks of the photograph's "that-has-been"
(*ça-a-été*). See Roland Barthes, *Camera Lucida: Reflections on Photography*, trans. Richard Howard (New York: Hill and Wang, 1981).

23. For more on this, see chapter 2 of Ellen T. Armour, *Signs and Wonders:
Theology after Modernity* (New York: Columbia University Press, 2016),
titled "Photography and/as Bio-discipline."

24. I also develop the concepts of photographic truth and *signifiance* in
chapter 2 of *Signs and Wonders*.

25. Robert Hariman and John Louis Lucaites, *No Caption Needed: Iconic
Photographs, Public Culture, and Liberal Democracy* (Chicago: University of Chicago Press, 2007), 36, 37.

26. See Julie Anne Lytle, "Virtual Incarnations: An Exploration of
Internet-Mediated Interaction as Manifestation of the Divine," *Religious Education* 105, no. 4 (2010): 395–412. Catholicism, too, was an early
adopter of virtual forms of connection. For a Catholic feminist's take
on that turn, Michele Stopera Freyhauf, "The Catholic Church and
Social Media: Embracing [Fighting] a Feminist Ideological Theo-
Ethical Discourse and Discursive Activism," in *Feminism and Religion in the 21st Century: Technology, Dialogue, and Expanding Borders*,
ed. Gina Messina-Dysert and Rosemary Radford Ruether, 57–68
(New York: Routledge, 2014). Second Life is a platform on which users

create the content including avatars for themselves. Much of the content replicates things people do (or wish we could do) IRL, thus allowing users to explore activities they might not have access to IRL.

27. I learned about Christian influencers from my students in the 2017 iteration of my Theology, Visual Culture, and New Media course. Christian evangelicals—cis men and women—are particularly prominent in this aspect of virtual religion, but so also LGBTQIA+ folks using social media to connect with their spiritual kin in search of spiritual sustenance. Thanks to my students in the course for alerting me to these phenomena.

28. See Clay Shirky, *Here Comes Everybody: The Power of Organizing without Organizations* (New York: Penguin, 2008).

29. See Sherry Turkle, *Alone Together: Why We Expect More from Technology and Less from Each Other* (New York: Basic Books, 2017).

30. See the essays in Pauline Hope Cheong, Peter Fischer-Nielsen, Stefan Gelfgren, and Charless Ess, eds., *Digital Religion, Social Media, and Culture: Perspectives, Practices, and Futures*, Digital Formations, v. 78 (New York: P. Lang, 2012). Communications scholar Heidi Campbell and theologian Stephen Garner sketch out some of the promise to be found in what they call "networked theology" by examining some of the more creative ways that institutional Christianity shows up online. Heidi A. Campbell and Stephen Garner, *Networked Theology: Negotiating Faith in Digital Culture* (Grand Rapids, MI: Baker Academic, 2016).

31. For example, the Anglican Cathedral of Second Life offers opportunities for worship and prayer on Epiphany Island (its online site) but does not offer any of the sacraments (baptism, Eucharist, or marriage) online on the grounds that they require and express "a real, physical and personal interaction" that simply isn't possible online. (See their statement at "Sacraments on Epiphany Island," *The Anglican Cathedral of Second Life* [blog], April 4, 2013, https://slangcath.wordpress.com/the -vision/sacraments-on-epiphany-island/.) Nonetheless, Julie Anne Lytle argues—using the work of theologians Catherine LaCugna and Karl Rahner—that online religion provides "virtual incarnations" of divine presence that can indeed foster genuinely faithful communal and personal devotion. See Lytle, "Virtual Incarnations."

32. As is the case with the research on social media in general, most of the scholarship on this topic is ethnographic and focuses on particular issues or particular communities and attends to photography as a dimension of social media. Jessie Daniels's, *Cyber Racism: White Supremacy Online and the New Attack on Civil Rights* (New York: Rowman & Littlefield Publishers, 2009), for example, explores briefly the role photographs play in how teenagers evaluate websites dealing with racial matters. Photographs get read as evidence; their presence enhances a website's credibility, and their absence calls it into question. An exception (in focus, though not in its sociological approach) is Edgar Gómez Cruz and Asko Lehmuskallio, eds., *Digital Photography and Everyday Life: Empirical Studies on Material Visual Practices* (New York: Routledge, 2016), which combines research in the role digital photography plays in various communities with research on photographic practices writ large.

33. Eli Pariser, *The Filter Bubble: How the New Personalized Web Is Changing What We Read and How We Think* (New York: Penguin Books, 2011), 9.

34. Darran Simon, "Trayvon Martin's Death Sparked a Movement That Lives on Five Years Later," CNN, February 26, 2017, https://www.cnn.com/2017/02/26/us/trayvon-martin-death-anniversary/. Appropriately, that photograph now adorns hoodies and T-shirts and other paraphernalia sold to support the Trayvon Martin Foundation, a testimony to its iconic power. Trayvon Martin Foundation, "SHOP," accessed March 1, 2021, https://www.trayvonmartinfoundation.org/shop/.

35. Kevin Sack and Alvin Blinder, "No Regrets from Dylann Roof in Jailhouse Manifesto," *New York Times*, January 5, 2017, https://www.nytimes.com/2017/01/05/us/no-regrets-from-dylann-roof-in-jailhouse-manifesto.html/; Rebecca Hersher, "What Happened When Dylann Roof Asked Google for Information about Race?" National Public Radio, *The Two Way*, sec. America, January 10, 2017, https://www.npr.org/sections/thetwo-way/2017/01/10/508363607/what-happened-when-dylann-roof-asked-google-for-information-about-race/.

36. Nathaniel Carey, "New Zealand Shooting: SC's Dylann Roof Inspired New Zealand Shooter, Manifesto Says," *Greenville News*, sec. South Carolina, March 15, 2019, https://www.greenvilleonline.com/story/news/local/south-carolina/2019/03/15/new-zealand-shooter-manifes

to/3172396002/; Patrick Kingsley, "New Zealand Massacre High-lights Global Reach of White Extremism," *New York Times*, March 15, 2019, sec. World, https://www.nytimes.com/2019/03/15/world/asia/chri stchurch-mass-shooting-extremism.html/

37. Ryan Mac, Kellen Browning, and Sheera Frankel, "The Enduring Afterlife of a Mass Shooting's Livestream Online," *New York Times*, May 19, 2022, https://www.nytimes.com/2022/05/19/technology/mass -shootings-livestream-online.html/.

38. I have in mind an expanded version of what disability theorists call "normates," the (temporarily) able-bodied and -minded; that is, those who, according to biopolitical standards, count as "normal" because of their race/ethnicity, gender or sexuality, and level of ability. For more, see the preface to the twentieth-anniversary edition of Rosemarie Garland-Thomson, *Extraordinary Bodies: Figuring Physical Disability in American Culture and Literature* (1997; New York: Columbia University Press, 2021), xii–xiii.

39. See, e.g., Adam Harris, "The GOP's Critical Race Theory Obsession," *The Atlantic*, May 7, 2021, https://www.theatlantic.com/politics/archive /2021/05/gops-critical-race-theory-fixation-explained/618828/.

40. For a trenchant analysis of the ways "good white people" (specifically, middle-class liberal whites) unintentionally perpetuate racism even when trying to resist it, see Shannon Sullivan, *Good White People: The Problem with Middle-Class White Anti-Racism* (Albany: SUNY Press, 2014).

41. See Saidiya V. Hartman, *Scenes of Subjection: Terror, Slavery, and Self-Making in Nineteenth-Century America* (New York: Oxford University Press, 1997). I'm grateful to Shannon Winnubst for pointing me toward Hartman's work and raising important critical questions about *Signs and Wonders'* truck with liberal sentimentality. Shannon Winnubst, "After Modernity: Whose? Which? When? And, Perhaps Most of All, How?," *Syndicate*, Symposium on *Signs and Wonders*, December 11, 2018, https:// syndicate.network/symposia/theology/signs-and-wonders/.

42. Birgit Meyer, "Religious Sensations: Why Media, Aesthetics, and Power Matter in the Study of Contemporary Religion," Inaugural Lecture, Free University, Amsterdam, October 6, 2006, https://www .researchgate.net/publication/241889837_Religious_Sensations_Why

_Media_Aesthetics_and_Power_Matter_in_the_Study_of_Contem porary_Religion/.

43. That Meyer uses ethnography to study media and their impact reminds us that all media are social media—even if put to use on occasion by an individual for their eyes only.

44. David Morgan, "Mediation or Mediatisation: The History of Media in the Study of Religion," *Culture and Religion* 12, no. 2 (2011): 137–52, https://doi.org/10.1080/14755610.2011.579716/. Morgan's larger aim is to contest perspectives on the relationship between religion and media distorted by presumptive narratives of modernity as the gradual triumph of secularism.

45. Of course, these cultures are not only visual. Morgan's account of the tract tracks along the way its imbrication not only in print culture but also in commerce, capitalism, and colonialism.

46. David Morgan, *The Embodied Eye: Religious Visual Culture and the Social Life of Feeling* (Berkeley: University of California Press, 2012), 73.

47. David Morgan, *Protestants & Pictures: Religion, Visual Culture, and the Age of American Mass Production* (New York: Oxford University Press, 1999). The allusion to Walter Benjamin's famous essay "The Work of Art in the Age of Mechanical Reproduction" (1936) is deliberate. Morgan endorses much of Benjamin's position but argues that mechanically reproduced religious images, at least, retain their (actual not simply metaphorical, as applied to art) sacred aura. Benjamin's essay can be found in a collection of his essays titled *Illuminations: Essays and Reflections*, ed. Hannah Arendt, trans. Harry Zohn (New York: Schocken Books, 1969), 166–95. I discuss Benjamin in my chapter on photography in *Signs and Wonders*.

48. See Jaco Hamman, *Growing Down: Theology and Human Nature in the Virtual Age* (Waco, TX: Baylor University Press, 2017); and Kate Ott, *Christian Ethics for a Digital Society* (Lanham, MD: Rowman & Littlefield, 2019).

2. LIFE ON THE NEW PUBLIC SQUARE

1. See Andrew Higgins, Mike McIntire, and Gabriel J. x. Dance, "Inside a Fake News Sausage Factory: 'This Is All about Income,'" *New York*

Times, November 25, 2016, sec. World, https://www.nytimes.com/2016/11/25/world/europe/fake-news-donald-trump-hillary-clinton-georgia.html/.

2. "Feed," *Merriam-Webster.com Dictionary*, https://www.merriam-webster.com/dictionary/feed. Accessed November 28, 2022.

3. Christine Hauser, "Delta Air Lines Bans Disruptive Donald Trump Supporter for Life," *New York Times*, November 28, 2016, sec. Business, https://www.nytimes.com/2016/11/28/business/delta-air-lines-bans-trump-supporter-for-life-after-rude-remarks.html/.

4. Howard Schultz and Rajiv Chandrasekaran, "Upstanders: The Mosque across the Street," Starbucks Stories & News, September 14, 2016, https://stories.starbucks.com/stories/2016/upstanders-the-mosque-across-the-street/.

5. Mark Sweney, "Amazon TV Ad Features Imam and Vicar Exchanging Gifts," *The Guardian*, November 16, 2016, sec. Media, http://www.theguardian.com/media/2016/nov/16/amazon-tv-ad-imam-vicar-exchanging-gifts/.

6. Jean Baudrillard, *Simulacra and Simulation*, trans. Sheila Faria Glaser (Ann Arbor: University of Michigan Press, 1994). A simulation of human-to-human (or animal-to-human) relationality has replaced the real thing, in other words.

7. Sherry Turkle, *Alone Together: Why We Expect More from Technology and Less from Each Other* (New York: Basic Books, 2017), 295.

8. Much of *Alone Together* focuses on research on interactions between prototypical robotic pets and children or senior citizens. They both demand our attention and respond to it in ways that change with our input. These "performances of relationality" (Turkle's term) are highly alluring to many of those who interact with the robots, including Turkle and her coresearchers. That is especially true when the robotic companions are meeting very real needs (e.g., for companionship). In *The Age of Surveillance Capitalism*, which I engage in more detail later, Shoshana Zuboff describes the Cayla doll, a robot that interacts both face-to-face and through our devices, including our smart phones, which embeds the Cayla doll in the dynamics of this new marketplace. In 2017 a German government agency determined that the doll was "an illegal surveillance device," banned any further sales of it, and

suggested previous purchasers of the doll destroy it. See Shoshana Zuboff, *The Age of Surveillance Capitalism: The Fight for a Human Future at the New Frontier of Power* (New York: PublicAffairs, 2019), 264–67.

9. Turkle, *Alone Together*, 295.

10. Drawing on the work of Nicholas Hudson, Safiya Umoja Noble discusses this in *Algorithms of Oppression: How Search Engines Reinforce Racism* (New York: NYU Press, 2018), 136–37. Also see Nicholas Hudson, "From 'Nation' to 'Race': The Origin of Racial Classification in Eighteenth-Century Thought," *Eighteenth-Century Studies* 29, no. 3 (1996): 247–64, http://www.jstor.org/stable/30053821/. I'll have more to say about Noble's work later.

11. Guy DeBord, *The Society of the Spectacle,* trans. Donald Nicholson-Smith (New York: Zone Books, 1994).

12. Clay Shirky, *Here Comes Everybody: The Power of Organizing without Organizations* (New York: Penguin, 2008).

13. See also Markus Schroer, "Visual Culture and the Fight for Visibility," *Journal for the Theory of Social Behaviour* 44, no. 2 (2014): 206–228; 207. The term "prosumers" originated in the 1980s to describe amateurs whose commitment to meeting professional standards for their hobby (as photographers, say) inspired them to purchase professional equipment. Schroer attaches the term to a desire for recognition/demand for self-presentation that's been present since at least the twentieth century but that digital photography, cell phones, YouTube, etc. have only amplified.

14. Shirky, *Here Comes Everybody*, 103.

15. Shirky, *Here Comes Everybody*, 35.

16. Shirky, *Here Comes Everybody*, 48.

17. Sheera Frenkel, "The Storming of Capitol Hill Was Organized on Social Media," *New York Times,* January 6, 2021, sec. U.S., https://www.nytimes.com/2021/01/06/us/politics/protesters-storm-capitol-hill-building.html/.

18. Zeynep Tufekci, *Twitter and Tear Gas: The Power and Fragility of Networked Protest* (New Haven, CT: Yale University Press, 2017).

19. Tufekci, *Twitter and Tear Gas*, 119, xxiv.

20. Tufekci, *Twitter and Tear Gas*, xv.

21. S. Brent Plate, *Religion and Film: Cinema and the Recreation of the World* (New York: Columbia University Press, 2017), 112–13.

22. For those unfamiliar with it, *Accidental Napalm* foregrounded an injured naked young Vietnamese girl screaming and running away from a napalm attack carried out by U.S. soldiers. Its publication and circulation increased opposition to the war, helping to bring about the U.S. withdrawal from Vietnam. Robert Hariman and John Louis Lucaites discuss it at length—and for good reason—in *No Caption Needed: Iconic Photographs, Public Culture, and Liberal Democracy* (Chicago: University of Chicago Press, 2007), chapter 6. I say more about this important book in chapter 4.

23. Zuboff, *Age of Surveillance Capitalism*. Shirky may be right that social communication has become "vanishingly cheap" (Shirky, *Here Comes Everybody*, 157), but the infrastructure that supports it—software and hardware—is anything but. Those costs are often hidden from your average consumer (and the financial models are different for Wikipedia than Facebook), but they are very real, as Hu notes. See Tung-Hui Hu, *A Prehistory of the Cloud* (Cambridge: MIT Press, 2015), xxvii.

24. Early in March 2019, Mark Zuckerberg announced what sounded like a sea change in Facebook's MO to focusing on facilitating private exchanges rather than public ones, thus becoming our online "living rooms." As the *New York Times* observed, this would seem to require a new business model for Facebook, perhaps one that more closely resembles China's WeChat, journalist Li Yuan suggested, but with its own cryptocurrency. See Li Yuan, "Mark Zuckerberg Wants Facebook to Emulate WeChat. Can It?," *New York Times*, March 8, 2019, sec. Technology, https://www.nytimes.com/2019/03/07/technology/facebook-zuckerberg-wechat.html/; and Jamie Condliffe, "The Week in Tech: Facebook's Privacy Pivot (Business Model Not Included)," *New York Times*, March 8, 2019, sec. Technology, https://www.nytimes.com/2019/03/08/technology/facebook-privacy-pivot.html/.

25. Zuboff, *Age of Surveillance Capitalism*, 17.

26. Zuboff, *Age of Surveillance Capitalism*, 17.

27. This means, of course, that vision isn't the only sense being surveilled. Speech and touch, too, are rendered into data via smart speakers,

Fitbits, and mattresses equipped with technologies that track our sleep patterns—when/whether we get up or toss and turn in the night, what our heart rate is, and so on. Wearables may expand from watches, bracelets, and rings to clothing and even skin in the near future. Zuboff mentions "smart skin," invented by engineers/scientists at Georgia Tech, that will enable unobtrusive monitoring of serious health conditions like Parkinson's disease, for example. Powered by a kind of osmosis (it draws energy from radio waves, eliminating the need for batteries), smart skin "can cognize, sense, analyze wirelessly, communicate, and 'modify parameters' [of treatment]" all without discomfiting the user. Zuboff, *Age of Surveillance Capitalism*, 240. We need a term bigger than Foucault's infamous "panopticon" to describe this network: "pansensorium," perhaps?

28. Zuboff, *Age of Surveillance Capitalism*, 238.

29. Zuboff cites a 2008 study that calculated it would take prosumers approximately seventy-six full workdays to read all of the online privacy policies one agrees to per year. The study's authors calculated the "national opportunity cost" of that labor to be $781 billion. Zuboff, *Age of Surveillance Capitalism*, 49.

30. Adam Satariano, "'Right to Be Forgotten' Privacy Rule Is Limited by Europe's Top Court," *New York Times*, September 24, 2019, sec. Technology, https://www.nytimes.com/2019/09/24/technology/europe-google -right-to-be-forgotten.html/.

31. Cecilia Kang, "The Man Deciding Facebook's Fate," *New York Times*, March 8, 2019, sec. Technology, https://www.nytimes.com/2019/03/08 /technology/ftc-facebook-joseph-simons.html/.

32. It remains to be seen whether the fallout from the Supreme Court's decision that overturned *Roe v. Wade* in June 2022 will call this right into question. But it has implications for data privacy where abortion is concerned. See Lauren Feiner, "*Roe v. Wade* Overturned: Here's How Tech Companies and Users Can Protect Privacy," CNBC, June 24, 2022, https://www.cnbc.com/2022/06/24/roe-v-wade-overturned-how -tech-companies-and-users-can-protect-privacy.html/.

33. For an analysis of the NSA scandal, see Roberto Simanowski, *Data Love: The Seduction and Betrayal of Digital Technologies* (New York: Columbia University Press, 2017), especially chapters 1–5.

34. In the same poll, 65 percent of respondents reported encountering what turned out to be "fake news." While respondents in total were split 44–46 percent on whether Facebook fostered division by creating self-referential bubbles (my language), generational differences were more pronounced with millennials, who were the most skeptical of what they saw online, and baby boomers, the most trusting. Chris Raymond, "So What Do You Think of Facebook Now?," *Consumer Reports*, March 15, 2019, https://www.consumerreports.org/social-media/what-do-you-think-of-facebook-now-survey/.

35. Stuart A. Thompson and Charlie Warzel, "Twelve Million Phones, One Dataset, Zero Privacy," *New York Times*, December 19, 2019, sec. Opinion, https://www.nytimes.com/interactive/2019/12/19/opinion/location-tracking-cell-phone.html/.

36. Dmitri Kaven, Haley Willis, Evan Hill, Natalie Reneau, et al., "Day of Rage: How Trump Supporters Took the U.S. Capitol," *New York Times,* June 30, 2021, https://www.nytimes.com/video/us/politics/100000007606996/capitol-riot-trump-supporters.html/.

37. Charlie Warzel and Stuart A. Thompson, "They Stormed the Capitol. Their Apps Tracked Them.," *New York Times*, February 5, 2021, sec. Opinion, https://www.nytimes.com/2021/02/05/opinion/capitol-attack-cellphone-data.html/.

38. Simanowski, *Data Love*, 19–23.

39. Noble, *Algorithms of Oppression*, 119–20.

40. In January 2020, Customs and Border Patrol agents turned away at least sixteen Iranian students with student visas, citing some bit of information (analogue or digital) as justification. Caleb Hampton and Caitlin Dickerson, "'Demeaned and Humiliated': What Happened to These Iranians at U.S. Airports," *New York Times*, January 25, 2020, sec. U.S., https://www.nytimes.com/2020/01/25/us/iran-students-deported-border.html/.

41. Colin Koopman, *How We Became Our Data: A Genealogy of the Informational Person* (Chicago: University of Chicago Press, 2019).

42. Jonathan Crary, *24/7: Late Capitalism and the Ends of Sleep* (London: Verso Books, 2013). Hereafter, citations to this source will be made parenthetically in the text.

43. Dominic Pettman, *Infinite Distraction* (Cambridge, UK: Polity Press, 2016), 30, 35.

44. Crary, *24/7*, 53.

45. Pettman, *Infinite Distraction*, 29.

46. Pettman, *Infinite Distraction*, 37.

47. Pettman, *Infinite Distraction*, 121.

3. (RE)MAKING US

1. Safiya Umoja Noble, *Algorithms of Oppression: How Search Engines Reinforce Racism* (New York: NYU Press, 2018), 1, 6.

2. Ta-Nehisi Coates, "The Case for Reparations," *The Atlantic*, June 2014, https://www.theatlantic.com/magazine/archive/2014/06/the-case-for -reparations/361631/.

3. Noble, *Algorithms of Oppression*, 111.

4. Jessie Daniels, *Cyber Racism: White Supremacy Online and the New Attack on Civil Rights* (New York: Rowman & Littlefield Publishers, 2009), 6; cited by Noble in *Algorithms of Oppression* (116). For much more on white supremacist cloaked websites and their impact, see especially chapter 7 of *Cyber Racism*.

5. Noble, *Algorithms of Oppression*, 163.

6. "Google Diversity Annual Report, 2022," https://static.googleusercontent .com/media/about.google/en//belonging/diversity-annual-report/2022 /static/pdfs/google_2022_diversity_annual_report.pdf?cachebust =1093852/. The Pew study reports that 7 percent of Science, Technology, Engineering, and Math (STEM) employees are Black and 8 percent are Hispanic, including (according to appendix A) "computer jobs." See Richard Fry, Brian Kennedy, and Cary Funk, "STEM Jobs See Uneven Progress in Increasing Gender, Racial and Ethnic Diversity," Pew Research Center, April 1, 2021, sec. Science, https://www.pewresearch .org/science/2021/04/01/stem-jobs-see-uneven-progress-in-increasing -gender-racial-and-ethnic-diversity/.

7. I conducted these searches several times between January of 2020 and January 2021.

8. Jeremy Kaplan, "Exclusive: Google Reveals 2,000-Person Diversity and Inclusion Product Team," *Digital Trends*, January 9, 2020, https:// www.digitaltrends.com/news/google-diversity-inclusion-champions -announcement-ces-2020/.

9. Paresh Dave and Jeffrey Dastin, "Google Fires Second AI Ethics Leader as Dispute Over Research, Diversity Grows," Reuters, February 19, 2021, *US News & World Report* edition, sec. Technology, //www.usnews.com/news/technology/articles/2021-02-19/second-google-ai-ethics-leader-fired-she-says-amid-staff-protest/.

10. For an in-depth inquiry into what happened and the larger dynamics at Google and the tech world in general, see Tom Simonite, "What Really Happened When Google Ousted Timnit Gebru | WIRED," *Wired*, June 8, 2021, sec. Backchannel, https://www.wired.com/story/google-timnit-gebru-ai-what-really-happened/, accessed July 24, 2021.

11. Noble, *Algorithms of Oppression*, 141.

12. See Noble, *Algorithms of Oppression*, chapter 4. For example, the vast majority (80 percent or more) of Dewey Decimal classifications under "religion" pertain specifically to Christianity, despite the fact that texts reflective of other religious traditions far outnumber those related to Christianity. Hope A. Olson, "Mapping beyond Dewey's Boundaries: Constructing Classificatory Space for Marginalized Knowledge Domains," *Library Trends* 47, no. 2 (1998): 233–54; 235; cited by Noble (140). Of note is the initially successful effort led by a Dartmouth student to get "illegal alien" replaced with less charged terms in the Library of Congress Subject Headings (LCHS). Congress later overturned that decision, thanks to efforts initiated by former representative Diane Black (of my home state of Tennessee), the first time it ever intervened in an LCHS decision of this sort. Alex Gangitano, "GOP Lawmaker Takes Aim at Library over 'Illegal Alien,'" *Roll Call*, April 18, 2016, sec. Heard on the Hill, https://www.rollcall.com/2016/04/18/gop-lawmaker-takes-aim-at-library-over-illegal-alien/.

13. Roberto Simanowski, *Data Love: The Seduction and Betrayal of Digital Technologies* (New York: Columbia University Press, 2017), xvii.

14. Simanowski, *Data Love*, 13; Colin Koopman, *How We Became Our Data: A Genealogy of the Informational Person* (Chicago: University of Chicago Press, 2019).

15. See Koopman, *How We Became Our Data*, chapter 3.

16. See Douglas Massey and Nancy A. Denton, *American Apartheid: Segregation and the Making of the Underclass* (Cambridge, MA: Harvard

University Press, 1993), cited in Koopman, *How We Became Our Data*, 117.

17. Koopman, *How We Became Our Data*, 137.
18. Jesse Meisenhelter, "How 1930s Discrimination Shaped Inequality in Today's Cities," *National Community Reinvestment Coalition* (blog), March 27, 2018, https://ncrc.org/how-1930s-discrimination-shaped-inequality-in-todays-cities/. COVID has only worsened economic inequality. See Kim Parker, Rachel Minkin, and Jesse Bennett, "Economic Fallout from COVID-19 Continues to Hit Lower-Income Americans the Hardest." Pew Research Center, September 24, 2020, sec. Social & Demographic Trends, https://www.pewresearch.org/social-trends/2020/09/24/economic-fallout-from-covid-19-continues-to-hit-lower-income-americans-the-hardest/.
19. "Mapping Prejudice," University of Minnesota Libraries, https://www.mappingprejudice.org/, accessed January 31, 2021. For an overview of the history of covenants in Minneapolis (including legal decisions), see Greta Caul, "With Covenants, Racism Was Written into Minneapolis Housing. The Scars Are Still Visible," *MinnPost*, February 22, 2019, sec. Metro News, https://www.minnpost.com/metro/2019/02/with-covenants-racism-was-written-into-minneapolis-housing-the-scars-are-still-visible/.
20. Delegard is cited in Olivia B. Waxman, "George Floyd's Death and the Long History of Racism in Minneapolis," *Time*, May 28, 2020, sec. History, Civil Rights, https://time.com/5844030/george-floyd-minneapolis-history/. Elsewhere, Delegard observes that in 2019, Minneapolis–St. Paul had "the lowest rate of African American home ownership in the country." See Kirsten Delegard, "Racial Housing Covenants in the Twin Cities," MNopedia (Minnesota Historical Society, September 18, 2019), https://www.mnopedia.org/thing/racial-housing-covenants-twin-cities/. Delegard also notes that although African Americans were the primary targets, others (including Asian Americans, Arab Americans, and Jews) were also sometimes subjected to this practice, especially in its early decades.
21. Waxman, "George Floyd's Death."

22. The account of Foucault's work I offer in the next few pages is distilled from chapter 1 in Ellen T. Armour, *Signs and Wonders: Theology after Modernity* (New York: Columbia University Press, 2016).

23. Koopman, *How We Became Our Data*, 172.

24. See part III.1, titled "Docile Bodies," in *Discipline and Punish* ["Les corps dociles" in *Surveiller et punir*]. Michel Foucault, *Discipline and Punish: The Birth of the Prison*, trans. A. M. Sheridan Smith (New York: Pantheon, 1978).

25. Jonathan Crary, *Techniques of the Observer: On Vision and Modernity in the Nineteenth Century* (Cambridge, MA: MIT Press, 1990). My account here of bio-disciplinary seeing and photography is based on my previous work in chapter 2 of *Signs and Wonders*.

26. John Tagg, *The Burden of Representation: Essays on Photographies and Histories* (Minneapolis: University of Minnesota Press, 1993), 92.

27. Tagg, *Burden of Representation*, 76.

28. Jonathan Crary, *24/7: Late Capitalism and the Ends of Sleep* (London: Verso Books, 2013), 52.

29. Crary, *24/7*, 53.

30. Crary, *24/7*, 42–43.

31. Crary, *24/7*, 47.

32. Zygmunt Bauman and David Lyon, *Liquid Surveillance: A Conversation* (Cambridge, UK: Polity Press, 2013), 73, 59; quoted by Simanowski in *Data Love*, 97.

33. Noble, *Algorithms of Oppression*, 25; Noble quotes Alexander Halavais, *Search Engine Society* (Cambridge, UK: Polity Press, 2009), 1–2.

34. Simanowski, *Data Love*, 99.

35. Simanowski, *Data Love*, 99.

36. Zuboff, *Age of Surveillance Capitalism*, 21.

37. See Zygmunt Bauman, *Liquid Modernity* (Cambridge, UK: Polity Press, 2000); and Bauman and Lyon, *Liquid Surveillance*.

38. In fact, it risks misconstruing how Foucault understands power per se by confusing what Foucault called "the terminal forms power takes" with the full network of dynamic ebbs and flows that actually constitute power. Cf. Michel Foucault, "Method," in *The History of Sexuality*, vol. 1: *An Introduction* (New York: Vintage Books, 1980); 92–97; 92.

39. Thomas Mathiesen, "The Viewer Society: Foucault's Panopticon Revisited," *Theoretical Criminology* 1, no. 2 (1997): 215–34; cited by Bauman and Lyon, *Liquid Surveillance*, 68.

40. As I've described it so far, the theo-logic present in surveillance capitalism resembles that of Ludwig Feuerbach, who (infamously) argued that "God" was actually a projection of human capacities onto a nonexistent singular being. Rather than perpetuating that projection, Feuerbach urged human beings to take it upon themselves as a species to realize it; that is, to fulfill the potential inherent in those capacities by expanding our sphere not only of knowledge but also of loving one another. See Ludwig Feuerbach, *The Essence of Christianity*, trans. George Eliot (Buffalo, NY: Prometheus Books, 1989).

41. For more on cosmopolitanism, seeing and believing, and refugees, see my "Justice for Alan Kurdi?: Philosophy, Photography, and the (Cosmo) Politics of Life and Death," *Philosophy Today* 63, no. 2 (October 1, 2019): 315–33, https://doi.org/10.5840/philtoday201981267/.

42. Didier Bigo, "Globalized (In)security: The Field and the Ban-Opticon," in *Traces 4: Translation, Biopolitics, Colonial Difference*, ed. Naoki Sakai and Jon Solomon, 109–156 (Hong Kong: Hong Kong University Press, 2006); cited in Bauman and Lyon, *Liquid Surveillance*, 62.

43. Notably, Noble concludes *Algorithms of Oppression* by describing an interview she conducted with a Black woman who owned her own hair salon in a college town. For most of the twenty-plus years she had been in business, the Black female population of the (mostly white) town found its way to her salon by word of mouth. One might think that apps like Yelp! would make it even easier, but the opposite turned out to be the case in her experience. Yelp!'s financial model rests on the number of reviews that meet their requirements (for authenticity, frequency, time frame, etc.). These requirements (an ever-moving goalpost in this woman's experience) proved difficult to meet—in part, because experiences with digital racism made her customers reluctant to post. Noble, "Conclusion: Algorithms of Oppression," 171–82.

44. Bauman and Lyon, *Liquid Surveillance*, 11.

45. Bauman and Lyon, *Liquid Surveillance*, 157.

46. Bauman and Lyon, *Liquid Surveillance*, 157.

4. REFRAMING PHOTOGRAPHY

1. Mary Meeker, "Internet Trends 2015" (Code Conference, KPCB, 2015); cited in Sonia Waters, "All Visual, All the Time: Towards a Theory of Visual Practices for Pastoral Theological Reflection," *Pastoral Psychology* 65, no. 6 (2016): 849–61, 3.

2. Mary Meeker, "Internet Trends 2019" (Code Conference, Recode by Vox, 2019), https://www.youtube.com/watch?v=G_dwZB5h56E/, accessed May 27, 2021. My thanks to Debbie Brubaker for pointing me toward this resource.

3. Abigail Solomon-Godeau, *Photography after Photography: Gender, Genre, History* (Durham, NC: Duke University Press, 2017), 4.

4. Solomon-Godeau, *Photography after Photography*, 4.

5. William J. Mitchell, *Reconfigured Eye: Visual Truth in the Post-Photographic Era* (Cambridge, MA: MIT Press, 1992). The author of *The Reconfigured Eye* is not to be confused with W.J.T. Mitchell, whose work I also discuss in *Seeing and Believing*. William J. Mitchell (now deceased) was the Alexander W. Dreyfoos Jr. Professor of Architecture and Media Arts and Sciences at MIT. W.J.T. Mitchell is the Gaylord Distinguished Service Professor at the University of Chicago, where he teaches in both the English and Art History departments.

6. Oliver Wendell Holmes, "The Stereoscope and the Stereograph," *Atlantic Monthly* (June 1859); quoted in Wm. J. Mitchell, *Reconfigured Eye*, 56.

7. Holmes, "The Stereoscope and the Stereograph"; quoted in Wm. J. Mitchell, *Reconfigured Eye*, 56.

8. Wm. J. Mitchell, *Reconfigured Eye*, 10.

9. Wm. J. Mitchell, *Reconfigured Eye*, 57. See https://www.usgs.gov/centers/eros for the EROS archive, which celebrated its fiftieth anniversary in 2022, and for further information about it.

10. Wm. J. Mitchell, *Reconfigured Eye*, 13.

11. Wm. J. Mitchell, *Reconfigured Eye*, 56.

12. Susan Sontag, *On Photography* (New York: Picador Books, 1977), 178; quoted in Wm. J. Mitchell, *Reconfigured Eye*, 56.

13. Analogue photographs were incorporated into other managerial and disciplinary techniques used in the nineteenth and twentieth centuries, including the codification of strategies for observing individuals

to the once-new science of statistical analysis. Supporting technologies similarly range from the monumental to the mundane, new forms of architecture to the vertical file cabinet. On this, see John Tagg, *The Disciplinary Frame: Photographic Truths and the Capture of Meaning* (Minneapolis: University of Minnesota Press, 2009), especially 20–21.

14. John Tagg, *The Burden of Representation: Essays on Photographies and Histories* (Minneapolis: University of Minnesota Press, 1993), 4–5.

15. For more on family photographs as channels of bio-disciplinary power, see Ellen T. Armour, *Signs and Wonders: Theology after Modernity* (New York: Columbia University Press, 2016), chapter 5, "Bio-Discipline and the Right to Life: Becoming Terri Schiavo."

16. Liz Wells, *Photography: A Critical Introduction* (London: Routledge, 2015), 26.

17. Wm. J. Mitchell, *Reconfigured Eye*, 27.

18. This raises all kinds of problems for copyright law and for the circulation of digital photographs, of course, as photojournalists (and art photographers) were quick to realize. The invention of the NFT (nonfungible token) uses blockchain technology (also a recent invention) to address this problem, but only for high-value digital objects (including digital artwork). Robin Conti and John Smith, "What Is an NFT? Non-Fungible Tokens Explained," *Forbes*, April 8, 2022, sec. Advisor Investing, https://www.forbes.com/advisor/investing/cryptocurrency /nft-non-fungible-token/.

19. Wm. J. Mitchell, *Reconfigured Eye*, 8.

20. Wm. J. Mitchell, *Reconfigured Eye*, 28.

21. Wm. J. Mitchell, *Reconfigured Eye*, 31.

22. Wm. J. Mitchell, *Reconfigured Eye*, 7. Here, Mitchell appears to be playing off of the French term *bricolage*, the creative use of whatever is at hand (by artists or others) and the artistic genre of collage.

23. Wm. J. Mitchell, *Reconfigured Eye*, 8.

24. A digital example of what Robert Sobieszek calls "photographic Orientalism," as I note in *Signs and Wonders*, 62–63. See Robert Sobieszek, "Historical Commentary," in Alfred Stieglitz Center, *French Primitive Photography* (New York: Aperture, 1970), 5.

25. Fred Ritchin, *Bending the Frame: Photojournalism, Documentary, and the Citizen* (New York: Aperture, 2013), 49.

26. Robert Hariman and John Louis Lucaites, *The Public Image: Photography and Civic Spectatorship* (Chicago: University of Chicago Press, 2016), 28. My discussion of this work is a slightly revised version of the one that appears in Ellen T. Armour, "Decolonizing Spectatorship: Photography, Theology, and the New Media," in *Beyond Man: Race, Coloniality, and Philosophy of Religion*, ed. An Yountae and Eleanor Craig, 135–37 (Durham, NC: Duke University Press, 2021).

27. Hariman and Lucaites remind us that photography is hardly the first (or the last, given critiques of social media) public medium to be accused of doing us more harm than good. Indeed, as I noted earlier, every media revolution has aroused concern about its deleterious effects on humanity—including writing. Nor is the most recent media revolution the first to enchant us. William Gibson, author of *Neuromancer*, the sci-fi novel that presciently envisioned our virtual reality today (and inventor of the term "cyberspace"), observed recently that TV's advent in the 1940s likely meant fewer people were hanging out on their front stoops in New York City, for example. That change went largely unremarked, he reports, perhaps because those who might note it were themselves inside watching TV. See Laura Sydell, "The Father of the Internet Sees His Invention Reflected Back through a 'Black Mirror,'" *Morning Edition*, National Public Radio, February 20, 2018, https://www.npr.org /sections/alltechconsidered/2018/02/20/583682937/the-father-of-the -internet-sees-his-invention-reflected-back-through-a-black-mir/.

28. Hariman and Lucaites, *Public Image*, 62.

29. See Hariman and Lucaites, *No Caption Needed*, chapter 6. I discuss *Accidental Napalm* in chapter 2 of Armour, *Signs and Wonders*, esp. 82– 84 and the associated endnotes. I take up another instance of a difficult editorial decision to publish a photograph of a child—this time, a dead Syrian refugee—in Ellen T. Armour, "Justice for Alan Kurdi?: Philosophy, Photography, and the (Cosmo)Politics of Life and Death," *Philosophy Today* 63, no. 2 (October 1, 2019): 315–33, https://doi.org/10 .5840/philtoday20198I267/.

30. See Errol Morris, *Believing Is Seeing: Observations on the Mysteries of Photography* (New York: Penguin, 2011).

31. Susan Sontag, *Regarding the Pain of Others* (New York: Farrar, Straus, and Giroux, 2003), 47. Sontag's work informs *Signs and Wonders*. This

book, in particular, is critical to my discussion of the Abu Ghraib photographs in chapter 4.

32. Sontag, *Regarding the Pain of Others*, 7.

33. Hariman and Lucaites, *Public Image*, 59. Canon, the camera company, sponsored an experiment that illustrates this point. They invited six professional photographers to shoot a portrait of the same person (an actor). Each photographer was told a different story about who the subject was. The results are striking. See Anna Gragert, "6 Photographers Invited to Photograph 1 Man Reveal the Power of Perspective," My Modern Met, November 5, 2015, https://mymodernmet.com/canon-decoy-experiment/?fbclid=IwAR1In8-t4bAhxpM2C1SjEToumQBUV3zhxoBhLNR8bFFqXUejaR-RKzm4X98/, accessed April 5, 2021.

34. In *Civil Imagination: A Political Ontology of Photography* (New York: Verso, 2015), Ariella Azoulay speaks of the photographic event: the ongoing call-and-response between a given photograph and the various publics who view it. I have more to say about this book (though not this topic) later.

35. Hariman and Lucaites, *Public Image*, 69.

36. Hariman and Lucaites, *Public Image*, 71.

37. Hariman and Lucaites, *Public Image*, 72.

38. Nathan Jurgenson, *The Social Photo: On Photography and Social Media* (New York: Verso Books, 2019), 9.

39. Jurgenson, *Social Photo*, 14.

40. Jurgenson, *Social Photo*, 21, 17.

41. Jurgenson, *Social Photo*, 10, 2.

42. John Tomlinson, *The Culture of Speed: The Coming of Immediacy* (Thousand Oaks, CA: Sage Publications, 2007), discussed in Jurgenson, *Social Photo*, 22.

43. Jurgenson, *Social Photo*, 34.

44. Jurgenson, *Social Photo*, 38.

45. Susan Sontag, *On Photography* (New York: Picador Books, 1977), 9; cited by Jurgenson, *Social Photo*, 40.

46. Here Jurgenson engages Joanna Zylinska's work on nonhuman photography. Jurgenson, *Social Photo*, 44. See Joanna Zylinska, *Nonhuman Photography* (Cambridge, MA: MIT Press, 2017). For more on the

cyborg, see Donna Haraway, *Simians, Cyborgs, and Women: The Reinvention of Nature* (New York: Routledge, 1991).

47. Jurgenson, *Social Photo*, 46. Hereafter, citations to this source will be made parenthetically in the text.

48. On April 20, 2021, a jury found former police officer Derek Chauvin guilty of murdering George Perry Floyd Jr. on three counts: second-degree murder, third-degree murder, and second-degree manslaughter. See Ashley Southall and Johanna Barr, "Derek Chauvin Trial: Chauvin Found Guilty of Murdering George Floyd," *New York Times*, April 20, 2021, sec. U.S., https://www.nytimes.com/live/2021/04/20/us/derek-chauvin-verdict-george-floyd/.

49. Foucault, *History of Sexuality*, vol. I, 95.

5. PHOTOGRAPHIC INSURRECTION

1. Kate Ott, *Christian Ethics for a Digital Society* (Lanham, MD: Rowman & Littlefield, 2019).

2. One doesn't need to be an adult to realize these possibilities. Michael Brandon McCormack analyzes the creative power Black youth have exercised in using digital technologies—including visual technologies—to respond creatively, courageously, and theo-ethically to the current epidemic of killings of Black people. See his "Left to Their Own Devices: Black Youth, Religion, and Technologies of Living," *Black Scholar: Journal of Black Studies and Research*, 52, no. 3 (2022): 52–62, DOI: 10.1080/00064246.2022.2079069/. Published online July 31, 2022.

3. Ott, *Christian Ethics for a Digital Society*, 129. Each of the approaches is focal to one of her chapters, each of which focuses on a specific challenge/opportunity posed to us by our digital world. So her chapter 1 focuses on the impact on diversity of predictive analytics, or algorithmic governance, of what we see. Chapter 2 takes a deep dive into how cultivating attunement can help us navigate the complex relationship between our networked self (the chapter's title) and our flesh-and-blood self. And her chapter 3, on metanoia, is a critical resource for navigating the results of dataveillance (the "eternal" record of our digital lives) and its larger impacts, including on those we encounter online and

IRL. Finally, chapter 4 takes up cocreation as a response to the way digital technologies "matter" IRL.

4. Ott, *Christian Ethics for a Digital Society*, 11.

5. Ott, *Christian Ethics for a Digital Society*, 42.

6. Cristina L. H. Traina, *Erotic Attunement: Parenthood and the Ethics of Sensuality between Unequals* (Chicago: University of Chicago Press, 2011), 217; quoted in Ott, *Christian Ethics for a Digital Society*, 47.

7. Fully explaining why this is the case is beyond the scope of this book. Regarding ways of seeing, I have in mind here the work of the French phenomenologist Maurice Merleau-Ponty on perception, which informs the scholarship I draw on to resource photographic insurrection later in this chapter. See Maurice Merleau-Ponty, *Phenomenology of Perception*, trans. Colin Smith (London: Routledge, 1962). I make a similar argument on different grounds in "Becoming Terri Schiavo," chapter 5 of Ellen T. Armour, *Signs and Wonders: Theology after Modernity* (New York: Columbia University Press, 2016).

8. Pramod K. Nayar, *Citizenship and Identity in the Age of Surveillance* (Delhi: Cambridge University Press, 2015). The concept of global witness citizenship calls to mind the work of my colleague, feminist philosopher Kelly Oliver, on witnessing in Kelly Oliver, *Witnessing: Beyond Recognition* (Minneapolis: University of Minnesota Press, 2001) and elsewhere. Exploring those connections will have to wait for another time and place.

9. Nayar, *Citizenship and Identity*, 10. For more, see especially his chapter 5.

10. To make his case, Nayar draws on several concepts and figures central to *Signs and Wonders* and to my essay "Justice for Alan Kurdi?" referenced earlier.

11. "WITNESS: Documenting Human Rights with Video," WITNESS, https://www.witness.org/, accessed July 23, 2021.

12. Nayar, *Citizenship and Identity*, 191. Nayar points to Judith Butler's recent work on precarity—work I also draw on in *Signs and Wonders* and that I return to briefly later in this chapter—as defining the sense of shared vulnerability needed to cultivate counter-cosmopolitanism. See Judith Butler, *Precarious Life: The Powers of Mourning and Violence* (New York: Verso, 2006).

13. Nayar, *Citizenship and Identity*, 197, 198.

14. Nayar, *Citizenship and Identity*, 197.

15. Lilie Chouliaraki dubs this the "humanitarian imaginary" in *The Ironic Spectator: Solidarity in the Age of Post-Humanitarianism* (Cambridge, UK: Polity Press, 2013), 45; quoted in Nayar, *Citizenship and Identity*, 197.

16. Luc Boltanski, *Distant Suffering: Morality, Media, and Politics* (Cambridge, UK: Cambridge University Press, 1999); cited by Nayar, *Citizenship and Identity*, 198.

17. When counter-cosmopolitanism veers into compassionate cosmopolitanism, it risks reinforcing an amplified and sped-up version of the humanitarian that is the quintessential modern cosmopolite, itself a creation of modern notions of subjectivity: "To be 'modern—to be fully human—is to have the responsibility to aid and uplift an Other who is not (yet) modern.'" David Jefferess, "Benevolence, Global Citizenship and Post-Racial Politics," *Topia*, no. 25 (2013): 77–95, 78; quoted in Nayar, *Citizenship and Identity*, 195. For my own critique of cosmopolitanism, see Ellen T. Armour, "Justice for Alan Kurdi?: Philosophy, Photography, and the (Cosmo)Politics of Life and Death," *Philosophy Today* 63, no. 2 (October 1, 2019): 315–33, https://doi.org/10.5840/philtoday201981267/.

18. Some refer to the use of such images in this way—including the videos of police killings of Black people—as "trauma porn." See Alisha Ebrahimji, "Some Say Sharing Videos of Police Brutality against Black People Is Just 'Trauma Porn,'" CNN, August 25, 2020, https://www.cnn.com/2020/08/25/us/police-brutality-videos-trauma-porn-trnd/index.html/.

19. Nayar, *Citizenship and Identity*, 180.

20. Nayar, *Citizenship and Identity*, 179. Here, Nayar is referencing Edward W. Said, *Orientalism* (London: Routledge & Kegan Paul, 1978), a source I draw on as well in *Signs and Wonders*, in the chapter on Abu Ghraib.

21. Ariella Azoulay, *The Civil Contract of Photography* (New York: Zone Books, 2008); and Ariella Azoulay, *Civil Imagination: A Political Ontology of Photography*, trans. Louise Bethlehem (New York: Verso Books, 2015). *The Civil Contract* is central to *Signs and Wonders*, especially chapter 2 (see pp. 90–91). The account I offer of it and of *Civil Imagination*

here is a slightly modified version of Ellen T. Armour, "Decolonizing Spectatorship: Photography, Theology, and the New Media," in *Beyond Man: Race, Coloniality, and Philosophy of Religion*, ed. An Yountae and Eleanor Craig, 127–50 (Durham, NC: Duke University Press, 2021). I offer a different but related take on the social contract's relevance to spectatorial responsibility in Armour, "Justice for Alan Kurdi?"

22. Azoulay, *Civil Contract*, 89.

23. Though Azoulay notes that the disenfranchised and those at the bottommost rungs of the social ladder are more often photographed than photographer.

24. For much more on this in relationship to what I call "spectatorial responsibility," see chapter 2 of *Signs and Wonders*.

25. Some of the photographs Azoulay considers are arguably acts of photographic insurrection in a different mode. They were taken by Israeli photographers who share Azoulay's political perspective with the goal of moving their fellow citizen-viewers toward sympathy with and action in solidarity with Palestinians.

26. Azoulay, *Civil Imagination*, 15. Hereafter, page numbers for this source are given in the text.

27. Azoulay, *Civil Imagination*, 44. I refer here to the philosophers Hannah Arendt and Emmanuel Levinas. See further Hannah Arendt, *The Origins of Totalitarianism*, (New York: Harcourt Brace Jovanovich, 1973); Emmanuel Levinas, *Humanism of the Other*, trans. Nidra Poller (Chicago: University of Illinois Press, 2003); and Emmanuel Levinas, *Totality and Infinity*, trans. Alphonso Lingis (Pittsburgh: Duquesne University Press, 1969).

28. This connects the civil gaze and civil imagination yet more deeply with cosmopolitanism, which has its own conflicted relationship with sovereignty. For more, see Armour, "Justice for Alan Kurdi?"

29. George Yancy, *Black Bodies, White Gazes: The Continuing Significance of Race in America*, 2nd ed. (Lanham, MD: Rowman & Littlefield, 2016).

30. Yancy quotes Sara Ahmed on this point: "Colonialism makes the world 'white,' which is of course a world 'ready' for certain kinds of bodies, as a world that puts certain objects within their reach." Sara Ahmed, "A Phenomenology of Whiteness," *Feminist Theory* 8, no. 2 (2007): 149–68; quoted in Yancy, *Black Bodies, White Gazes*, 10.

31. The absence of attention to nonnormative gender and sexuality in *Black Bodies, White Gazes* feels particularly acute given the recent killings of trans folk of color—especially trans women. While those killings are rarely explicitly connected to the story lines that anchor *Seeing and Believing*, they *are* deeply linked. This lacuna may reflect the fact that those killings—like those of Sandra Bland (to which Yancy does attend) and, more recently, Breonna Taylor—were not photographed. Shatema Threadcraft observes that is often the case when cis women and trans women are the victims. She worries that this reality will allow #BLM activists to set them aside, even though (as she acknowledges, I think) #BLM's founders clearly see the need to address them. See further Shatema Threadcraft, "North American Necropolitics and Gender: On #BlackLivesMatter and Black Femicide," *South Atlantic Quarterly* 116, no. 3 (July 2017): 553–79, https://doi.org/10.1215/00382876-3961483/.

32. Yancy, *Black Bodies, White Gazes*, 90. Hence the threat they allegedly pose to white women that justified many lynchings and was one justification that Roof gave for his actions. See Lisa Wade, "How 'Benevolent Sexism' Drove Dylann Roof's Racist Massacre," *Washington Post*, June 21, 2015, https://www.washingtonpost.com/posteverything/wp/2015/06/21/how-benevolent-sexism-drove-dylann-roofs-racist-massacre/. Yancy references lynchings briefly (*Black Bodies, White Gazes*, 83), a topic I take up at some length in chapter 4 of *Signs and Wonders*.

33. I also discuss Sarah Baartman's case in *Signs and Wonders*. As Yancy notes, that perception is rooted in what scholars call the Cult of True Womanhood—to which Black women were denied membership. For more on that, see Ellen T. Armour, *Deconstruction, Feminist Theology, and the Problem of Difference: Subverting the Race/Gender Divide* (Chicago: University of Chicago Press, 1999).

34. Yancy, *Black Bodies, White Gazes*, 6.

35. For those familiar with the various genres of continental philosophy, Yancy's approach to these important questions and issues is grounded in part in phenomenology—as is Morgan's work. I'll say more about that later.

36. Yancy, *Black Bodies, White Gazes*, 244; Judith Butler, "Endangered/Endangering: Schematic Racism and White Paranoia," in *Reading*

Rodney King / Reading Urban Uprising, ed. Robert Gooding-Williams (New York: Routledge, 1993), 17; cited by Yancy, *Black Bodies, White Gazes*, 4, 251. The language of *episteme* appears throughout *Black Bodies, White Gazes*. Readers who know Foucault will recognize in Yancy's reference to *episteme* a nod, at least, to Foucault—and not the only one. In the chapter on Baartman, Yancy takes note of the "European power/knowledge position of spectatorship" that created "the epistemic conditions under which Ba(a)rtman(n)[*sic*] 'appeared'" (91). He describes the police officer who stopped Sandra Bland as having "exercised white panoptic surveillance and state power/violence" (251), and he references white "discursive regimes" (253) in one list of all of the different forms whiteness takes. Together these create very productive connections to *Signs and Wonders*.

37. Yancy, *Black Bodies, White Gazes*, 245.
38. Yancy references two white women who were activists in the civil rights movement in the 1960s. Both tried to sit down and eat with Black people and experienced, to their shame, such visceral revulsion that one simply couldn't eat; the other managed to eat but couldn't keep her food down. Yancy, *Black Bodies, White Gazes*, 245–46.
39. Yancy, *Black Bodies, White Gazes*, xxx.
40. Yancy regularly gives presentations about whiteness to white audiences. He attempts to get his audiences to "linger with the gravitas of their own whiteness and the history of whiteness. I want them to feel the weight of their responsibility for the perpetuation of white power, hegemony, and privilege." Yancy, *Black Bodies, White Gazes*, 120. He also wrote an op ed for the *New York Times* on the subject in 2015, a project he described as a "love letter" to white people but that instead (no surprise) garnered all kinds of online racist hatred and vitriol. See George Yancy, "Dear White America," *New York Times*, December 24, 2015, sec. Opinionator, https://opinionator.blogs.nytimes.com/2015/12/24/dear-white-america/.
41. Yancy, *Black Bodies, White Gazes*, xxx. Hereafter, page numbers for this source are given in the text.
42. Jean-Paul Sartre, "Black Orpheus," in *Race*, ed. Robert Bernasconi (Malden, MA: Blackwell, 2001), 115; cited in Yancy, *Black Bodies, White Gazes*, xxxiii. The roots of white gazes are much older than the modern

era of bio-disciplinary power. Yancy traces anti-Blackness back to the fifth century CE—significantly in the work of the Christian monastic John Cassian, which was widely circulated by Benedict of Nursia, the founder of the Order of St. Benedict. Yancy, *Black Bodies, White Gazes*, xxxiv.

43. For example, Yancy engages scholarship in whiteness studies by philosophers such as Shannon Sullivan (whose work I cited earlier) and Linda Martín Alcoff, among others, and calls attention to an essay by Du Bois, "The Souls of White Folk," that scholarship on whiteness often overlooks (Yancy, *Black Bodies, White Gazes*, 81ff.).

44. Judith Butler, *Precarious Life: The Powers of Mourning and Violence* (New York: Verso, 2006), 26; quoted in Yancy, *Black Bodies, White Gazes*, 2.

45. Frantz Fanon, *Black Skin, White Masks*, trans. Charles Lam Markmann (New York: Grove Press, 1967), 111; quoted by Yancy, *Black Bodies, White Gazes*, 4, bracketed modifications made by Yancy.

46. Miranda Blue, "Ben Stein: Michael Brown 'Wasn't Unarmed. He Was Armed with His Incredibly Strong, Scary Self,'" *Right Wing Watch*, August 27, 2014, https://www.rightwingwatch.org/post/ben-stein-mic hael-brown-wasnt-unarmed-he-was-armed-with-his-incredibly-str ong-scary-self/; quoted in Yancy, *Black Bodies, White Gazes*, 5.

47. W.E.B. DuBois, *The Souls of Black Folk*, ed. Brent Hayes Edwards (New York: Oxford University Press, 2007), 7.

48. Yancy, *Black Bodies, White Gazes*, 12.

49. Yancy, *Black Bodies, White Gazes*, 250. Yancy cites George Zimmerman's interview on Fox TV with Sean Hannity. See further ABC News, *George Zimmerman FOX Interview: Says Shooting Was "God's Plan" to Sean Hannity (2012)*, accessed July 26, 2021, https://www.youtube.com /watch?v=CjhxXwbt8E8/.

50. Nor, by extension, will its counterparts like the male gaze (Laura Mulvey) or ableist staring (Rosemarie Garland-Thomson). See Rosemarie Garland-Thomson, *Staring: How We Look* (Oxford, UK: Oxford University Press, 2009), which I discuss in *Signs and Wonders*.

51. That I turn to religious seeing is not an indication that resources exist *only* here. There are resources to be found in other scholarly disciplines (and interdisciplines) as well. Attending to the full range of that body of literature, however, is beyond the scope of this project.

52. David Morgan, *The Embodied Eye: Religious Visual Culture and the Social Life of Feeling* (Berkeley: University of California Press, 2012). I first sketched very briefly some of the relevant central insights of *The Embodied Eye* in Armour, "Decolonizing Spectatorship," 142–43. I expand substantially on those brief comments in what follows.

53. David Morgan, "The Look of the Sacred," in *The Cambridge Companion to Religious Studies*, ed. Robert A. Orsi (New York: Cambridge University Press, 2012), 296–318; 302. I start my engagement with Morgan here because this essay provides an excellent summary of his approach. Hereafter, page numbers for this source are given in the text.

54. Maurice Merleau-Ponty, *Phenomenology of Perception*, trans. Colin Smith (London: Routledge, 1962), 246; quoted in Morgan, "Look of the Sacred," 304.

55. Morgan, "Look of the Sacred," 304.

56. Merleau-Ponty, *Phenomenology of Perception*, 159, 169; quoted in Morgan, "Look of the Sacred," 304.

57. Morgan, *Embodied Eye*, 69. Hereafter, page numbers for this source are given in the text.

58. The responses to this exercise that I share below are anonymized and used with permission.

EPILOGUE

1. Jonathan Crary, *24/7: Late Capitalism and the Ends of Sleep* (London: Verso Books, 2013), 40; emphasis mine.

2. Crary, *24/7*, 33.

3. Robert Hariman and John Louis Lucaites, *The Public Image: Photography and Civic Spectatorship* (Chicago: University of Chicago Press, 2016), 71.

4. Nathan Jurgenson, *The Social Photo: On Photography and Social Media* (New York: Verso Books, 2019), 9.

5. Jurgenson, *Social Photo*, 79, 85.

6. Nicole R. Fleetwood, *On Racial Icons: Blackness and the Public Imagination* (New Brunswick, NJ: Rutgers University Press, 2015), 4. Hereafter, page numbers for this source are given parenthetically in the text.

7. Robert Hariman and John Louis Lucaites, *No Caption Needed: Iconic Photographs, Public Culture, and Liberal Democracy* (Chicago: University of Chicago Press, 2007), 36, 37. For more on how I understand iconicity, see

esp. chapter 2 of Ellen T. Armour, *Signs and Wonders: Theology after Modernity* (New York: Columbia University Press, 2016).

8. W.J.T. Mitchell, *Seeing Through Race* (Cambridge, MA: Harvard University Press, 2012), 39–40.

9. W.J.T. Mitchell, *What Do Pictures Want? The Lives and Loves of Images* (Chicago: University of Chicago Press, 2005), 11. *What Do Pictures Want?* informs *Signs and Wonders* as well.

10. W.J.T. Mitchell, *What Do Pictures Want?*, 209n2.

11. W.J.T. Mitchell, *Seeing Through Race*, 149. Hereafter, page numbers for this source are given parenthetically in the text.

12. Friedrich Nietzsche, *Twilight of the Idols*, (orig. pub. 1889; London: Penguin Books, 1999), 31, quoted in W.J.T. Mitchell, *What Do Pictures Want?*, 8.

13. Nietzsche, *Twilight of the Idols*, 32, quoted in W.J.T. Mitchell, *What Do Pictures Want?*, 8.

14. W.J.T. Mitchell, *What Do Pictures Want?*, 9

15. That Stadig frames Martin's photograph in a carefully folded actual gray hoodie and Roof's photo in a carefully folded actual Confederate flag highlights these artifacts' iconicity—along with the shape she chose for the artbook's wooden frames (fig. 1.6; also available in color at http://tellingstoriesstoriesthattell.com/ellen-t-armour/).

16. Plate also draws briefly on contemporary philosophy, including the work of Emmanuel Levinas, whose work also informs Azoulay's. The concept of the face is central to Levinas's focus on the ethical demand that the other makes on us, something that photographs also channel, per Morgan (as I discussed previously). See Emmanuel Levinas, *Totality and Infinity*, trans. Alphonso Lingis (Pittsburgh: Duquesne University Press, 1969).

17. Plate, *Religion and Film*, 149.

18. Plate, *Religion and Film*, 150.

19. Sonia Waters, "All Visual, All the Time: Towards a Theory of Visual Practices for Pastoral Theological Reflection," *Pastoral Psychology* 65, no. 6 (2016): 849–61; 852.

20. Waters, "All Visual, All the Time," 857.

21. Waters, "All Visual, All the Time," 857.

22. W.J.T. Mitchell, *Seeing Through Race*, 9–10.

23. W.J.T. Mitchell, *Seeing Through Race*, 31.

BIBLIOGRAPHY

ABC News. *George Zimmerman FOX Interview: Says Shooting Was "God's Plan" to Sean Hannity (2012).* https://www.youtube.com/watch?v=Cjhx Xwbt8E8/. Accessed July 26, 2021.

Ahmed, Sara. "A Phenomenology of Whiteness." *Feminist Theory* 8, no. 2 (2007): 149–68.

Albanese, Catherine C. *America: Religions and Religion,* 3rd ed. Belmont, CA: Wadsworth Publishing, 1999.

Allyn, Bobby. "Judge Refuses to Reinstate Parler after Amazon Shut It Down." *All Things Considered.* National Public Radio, January 21, 2021. https://www.npr.org/2021/01/21/956486352/judge-refuses-to-reinstate -parler-after-amazon-shut-it-down/.

Allyn, Bobby, and Rachel Treisman. "After Weeks of Being Offline, Parler Finds a New Web Host." National Public Radio, February 15, 2021, sec. Technology. https://www.npr.org/2021/02/15/968116346/after-weeks-of -being-off-line-parler-finds-a-new-web-host/.

Arendt, Hannah. *The Origins of Totalitarianism.* New York: Harcourt Brace Jovanovich, 1973.

Armour, Ellen T. "Decolonizing Spectatorship: Photography, Theology, and the New Media." In *Beyond Man: Race, Coloniality, and Philosophy of Religion,* ed. An Yountae and Eleanor Craig, 127–50. Durham, NC: Duke University Press, 2021.

———. *Deconstruction, Feminist Theology, and the Problem of Difference: Subverting the Race/Gender Divide.* Chicago: University of Chicago Press, 1999.

————. "Justice for Alan Kurdi?: Philosophy, Photography, and the (Cosmo) Politics of Life and Death." *Philosophy Today* 63, no. 2 (October 1, 2019): 315–33. https://doi.org/10.5840/philtoday201981267/.

————. *Signs and Wonders: Theology after Modernity*. New York: Columbia University Press, 2016.

————. "Theology in Modernity's Wake." *Journal of the American Academy of Religion* 74, no. 1 (March 2006): 1–16.

Azoulay, Ariella. *The Civil Contract of Photography*. New York: Zone Books, 2008.

————. *Civil Imagination: A Political Ontology of Photography*. Trans. Louise Bethlehem. New York: Verso Books, 2015.

Barthes, Roland. *Camera Lucida: Reflections on Photography*. Trans. Richard Howard. New York: Hill and Wang, 1981.

Bauman, Zygmunt. *Liquid Modernity*. Cambridge, UK: Polity Press, 2000.

Bauman, Zygmunt, and David Lyon. *Liquid Surveillance: A Conversation*. Cambridge, UK: Polity Press, 2013.

Benjamin, Walter. "The Work of Art in the Age of Mechanical Reproduction." In *Illuminations: Essays and Reflections*. Ed. Hannah Arendt. Trans. Harry Zohn, 166–95. New York: Schocken Books, 1969.

Bigo, Didier. "Globalized (In)Security: The Field and the Ban-Opticon." In *Traces 4: Translation, Biopolitics, Colonial Difference*, ed. Naoki Sakai and Jon Solomon, 109–156. Hong Kong: Hong Kong University Press, HKU, 2006. https://muse.jhu.edu/book/19858/.

Blue, Miranda. "Ben Stein: Michael Brown 'Wasn't Unarmed. He Was Armed with His Incredibly Strong, Scary Self.'" *Right Wing Watch*, August 27, 2014. https://www.rightwingwatch.org/post/ben-stein-mich ael-brown-wasnt-unarmed-he-was-armed-with-his-incredibly-strong -scary-self/.

Boltanski, Luc. *Distant Suffering: Morality, Media, and Politics*. Cambridge, UK: Cambridge University Press, 1999.

Bromwich, Jonah E. "Amy Cooper, Who Falsely Accused Black Bird-Watcher, Has Charge Dismissed." *New York Times*, February 16, 2021, sec. New York. https://www.nytimes.com/2021/02/16/nyregion/amy-cooper -charges-dismissed.html/.

Buchanan, Larry, Quoctrung Bui, and Jugal K. Patel. "Black Lives Matter May Be the Largest Movement in U.S. History." *New York Times*, July 3,

2020, sec. U.S. https://www.nytimes.com/interactive/2020/07/03/us /george-floyd-protests-crowd-size.html/.

Butler, Judith. "Endangered/Endangering: Schematic Racism and White Paranoia." In *Reading Rodney King / Reading Urban Uprising*, ed. Robert Gooding-Williams, 15–22. New York: Routledge, 1993.

———. *Precarious Life: The Powers of Mourning and Violence*. New York: Verso, 2006.

Calderone, Michael. "'It's Kind of the Wild West:' Media Gears Up for Onslaught of Deepfakes." *Politico*, June 25, 2019, sec. Media. https://politi .co/2YcRKzt/.

Calvin, John. *Institutes of the Christian Religion*. Trans. Henry Beveridge. Grand Rapids, MI: W. B. Eerdmans, 1989.

Calvino, Italo. *Six Memos for the Next Millennium*. Trans. Patrick Creagh. Cambridge, MA: Harvard University Press, 1988.

Campbell, Heidi A., and Stephen Garner. *Networked Theology: Negotiating Faith in Digital Culture*. Grand Rapids, MI: Baker Academic, 2016.

Carey, Nathaniel. "New Zealand Shooting: SC's Dylann Roof Inspired New Zealand Shooter, Manifesto Says." *Greenville News*, sec. South Carolina, March 15, 2019. https://www.greenvilleonline.com/story/news/local /south-carolina/2019/03/15/new-zealand-shooter-manifesto/3172396o 02/.

Caul, Greta. "With Covenants, Racism Was Written into Minneapolis Housing. The Scars Are Still Visible." *MinnPost*, February 22, 2019, sec. Metro News. https://www.minnpost.com/metro/2019/02/with-covenants -racism-was-written-into-minneapolis-housing-the-scars-are-still -visible/.

Cheong, Pauline Hope, Peter Fischer-Nielsen, Stefan Gelfgren, and Charles Ess, eds. *Digital Religion, Social Media, and Culture: Perspectives, Practices, and Futures*. Digital Formations, v. 78. New York: P. Lang, 2012.

Chouliaraki, Lilie. *The Ironic Spectator: Solidarity in the Age of Post-Humanitarianism*. Cambridge, UK: Polity Press, 2013.

CNN. "Trayvon Martin Fast Facts." February 14,2022. https://www.cnn .com/2013/06/05/us/trayvon-martin-shooting-fast-facts/index.html/.

Coates, Ta-Nehisi. "The Case for Reparations." *The Atlantic*, June 2014. https://www.theatlantic.com/magazine/archive/2014/06/the-case-for -reparations/361631/.

Condliffe, Jamie. "The Week in Tech: Facebook's Privacy Pivot (Business Model Not Included)." *New York Times*, March 8, 2019, sec. Technology. https://www.nytimes.com/2019/03/08/technology/facebook-privacy -pivot.html/.

Conti, Robin, and John Smith. "What Is an NFT? Non-Fungible Tokens Explained." *Forbes*, April 8, 2022, sec. Advisor Investing. https://www .forbes.com/advisor/investing/cryptocurrency/nft-non-fungible-token/.

Crary, Jonathan. *24/7: Late Capitalism and the Ends of Sleep*. London: Verso Books, 2013.

———. *Suspensions of Perception: Attention, Spectacle, and Modern Culture*. Cambridge, MA: MIT Press, 2001.

———. *Techniques of the Observer: On Vision and Modernity in the Nineteenth Century*. Cambridge, MA: MIT Press, 1990.

Cruz, Edgar Gómez, and Asko Lehmuskallio, eds. *Digital Photography and Everyday Life: Empirical Studies on Material Visual Practices*. New York: Routledge, 2016.

Daniels, Jessie. *Cyber Racism: White Supremacy Online and the New Attack on Civil Rights*. New York: Rowman & Littlefield, 2009.

Dave, Paresh, and Jeffrey Dastin. "Google Fires Second AI Ethics Leader as Dispute over Research, Diversity Grows." Reuters, February 19, 2021, *US News & World Report* edition, sec. Technology. //www.usnews.com /news/technology/articles/2021-02-19/second-google-ai-ethics-leader -fired-she-says-amid-staff-protest/.

DeBord, Guy. *The Society of the Spectacle*. Trans. Donald Nicholson-Smith. New York: Zone Books, 1994.

Delegard, Kirsten. "Racial Housing Covenants in the Twin Cities." MNo-pedia. Minnesota Historical Society, September 18, 2019. https://www .mnopedia.org/thing/racial-housing-covenants-twin-cities/.

DiAngelo, Robin. *White Fragility: Why It's So Hard for White People to Talk about Racism*. Boston: Beacon Press, 2018.

DuBois, W.E.B. *The Souls of Black Folk*. Ed. Brent Hayes Edwards. New York: Oxford University Press, 2007.

Earth Resources Observation and Science (EROS) Data Center. https:// www.usgs.gov/centers/eros.

Ebrahimji, Alisha. "Some Say Sharing Videos of Police Brutality against Black People Is Just 'Trauma Porn.'" CNN, August 25, 2020. https://www

.cnn.com/2020/08/25/us/police-brutality-videos-trauma-porn-trnd/index
.html/.

Fanon, Frantz. *Black Skin, White Masks*. Trans. Charles Lam Markmann.
New York: Grove Press, 1967.

Feiner, Lauren. "*Roe v. Wade* Overturned: Here's How Tech Companies and
Users Can Protect Privacy." CNBC. June 24, 2022. https://www.cnbc
.com/2022/06/24/roe-v-wade-overturned-how-tech-companies-and
-users-can-protect-privacy.html/.

Feuerbach, Ludwig. *The Essence of Christianity*. Trans. George Eliot. Buffalo, NY: Prometheus Books, 1989.

Fleetwood, Nicole R. *On Racial Icons: Blackness and the Public Imagination*.
New Brunswick, NJ: Rutgers University Press, 2015.

Foucault, Michel. *Discipline and Punish: The Birth of the Prison*. Trans. A. M.
Sheridan Smith. New York: Pantheon, 1978.

———. *The History of Sexuality: An Introduction*. New York: Vintage Books,
1980.

Frenkel, Sheera. "The Storming of Capitol Hill Was Organized on Social
Media." *New York Times*, January 6, 2021, sec. U.S. https://www.nytimes
.com/2021/01/06/us/politics/protesters-storm-capitol-hill-building
.html/.

Frenkel, Sheera, and Alan Feuer. "'A Total Failure': The Proud Boys Now
Mock Trump." *New York Times*, January 20, 2021, sec. Technology.
https://www.nytimes.com/2021/01/20/technology/proud-boys-trump
.html/.

Freyhauf, Michele Stopera. "The Catholic Church and Social Media:
Embracing [Fighting] a Feminist Ideological Theo-Ethical Discourse
and Discursive Activism." In *Feminism and Religion in the 21st Century:
Technology, Dialogue, and Expanding Borders*, ed. Gina Messina-Dysert
and Rosemary Radford Ruether, 57–68. New York: Routledge, 2014.

Fry, Richard, Brian Kennedy, and Cary Funk. "STEM Jobs See Uneven
Progress in Increasing Gender, Racial, and Ethnic Diversity." Pew
Research Center, April 1, 2021, sec. Science. https://www.pewresearch
.org/science/2021/04/01/stem-jobs-see-uneven-progress-in-increasing
-gender-racial-and-ethnic-diversity/.

Gangitano, Alex. "GOP Lawmaker Takes Aim at Library over 'Illegal
Alien.'" *Roll Call*, April 18, 2016, sec. Heard on the Hill. https://www

.rollcall.com/2016/04/18/gop-lawmaker-takes-aim-at-library-over
-illegal-alien/.

Garland-Thomson, Rosemarie. *Extraordinary Bodies: Figuring Physical Disability in American Culture and Literature.* New York: Columbia University Press, 2021. First published 1997.

———. *Staring: How We Look.* Oxford, UK: Oxford University Press, 2009.

Garza, Alicia. *The Purpose of Power: How We Come Together When We Fall Apart.* New York: Random House Publishing Group, 2020.

"Google Diversity Annual Report, 2022." https://static.googleusercontent
.com/media/about.google/en//belonging/diversity-annual-report/2022
/static/pdfs/google_2022_diversity_annual_report.pdf?cachebust=109
3852/.

Gragert, Anna. "6 Photographers Invited to Photograph 1 Man Reveal the Power of Perspective." My Modern Met, November 5, 2015. https://mymod
ernmet.com/canon-decoy-experiment/?fbclid=IwAR1In8-t4bAhxpM2C
1SjEToumQBUV3zhxoBhLNR8bFFqXUejaR-RKzm4X98/.

Halavais, Alexander. *Search Engine Society.* Cambridge, UK: Polity Press, 2009.

Hamman, Jaco. *Growing Down: Theology and Human Nature in the Virtual Age.* Waco, TX: Baylor University Press, 2017.

Hampton, Caleb, and Caitlin Dickerson. "'Demeaned and Humiliated': What Happened to These Iranians at U.S. Airports." *New York Times,* January 25, 2020, sec. U.S. https://www.nytimes.com/2020/01/25/us/iran
-students-deported-border.html/.

Haraway, Donna. *Simians, Cyborgs, and Women: The Reinvention of Nature.* New York: Routledge, 1991.

Hariman, Robert, and John Louis Lucaites. *No Caption Needed: Iconic Photographs, Public Culture, and Liberal Democracy.* Chicago: University of Chicago Press, 2007.

———. *The Public Image: Photography and Civic Spectatorship.* Chicago: University of Chicago Press, 2016.

Harris, Adam. "The GOP's Critical Race Theory Obsession." *The Atlantic,* May 7, 2021. https://www.theatlantic.com/politics/archive/2021/05/gops
-critical-race-theory-fixation-explained/618828/.

Hartman, Saidiya V. *Scenes of Subjection: Terror, Slavery, and Self-Making in Nineteenth-Century America.* New York: Oxford University Press, 1997.

Hauser, Christine. "Delta Air Lines Bans Disruptive Donald Trump Supporter for Life." *New York Times*, November 28, 2016, sec. Business. https://www.nytimes.com/2016/11/28/business/delta-air-lines-bans-trump-supporter-for-life-after-rude-remarks.html/.

Hauser, Christine, Derrick Bryson Taylor, and Neil Vigdor. "'I Can't Breathe:' 4 Minneapolis Officers Fired after Black Man Dies in Custody." *New York Times*, May 26, 2020, sec. U.S. https://www.nytimes.com/2020/05/26/us/minneapolis-police-man-died.html/.

Hersher, Rebecca. "What Happened When Dylann Roof Asked Google for Information about Race?" National Public Radio, January 10, 2017, The Two Way, sec. America. https://www.npr.org/sections/thetwo-way/2017/01/10/508363607/what-happened-when-dylann-roof-asked-google-for-information-about-race/.

Higgins, Andrew, Mike McIntire, and Gabriel J. x. Dance. "Inside a Fake News Sausage Factory: 'This Is All About Income.'" *New York Times*, November 25, 2016, sec. World. https://www.nytimes.com/2016/11/25/world/europe/fake-news-donald-trump-hillary-clinton-georgia.html/.

Holmes, Oliver Wendell. "The Stereoscope and the Stereograph." *Atlantic Monthly* (June 1859). https://www.theatlantic.com/magazine/archive/1859/06/the-stereoscope-and-the-stereograph/303361/.

Hu, Tung-Hui. *A Prehistory of the Cloud*. Cambridge, MA: MIT Press, 2015.

Hudson, Nicholas. "From 'Nation' to 'Race': The Origin of Racial Classification in Eighteenth-Century Thought." *Eighteenth-Century Studies* 29, no. 3 (1996): 247–64. http://www.jstor.org/stable/30053821/.

Jefferess, David. "Benevolence, Global Citizenship, and Post-Racial Politics." *Topia*, no. 25 (2013): 77–95.

Jurgenson, Nathan. *The Social Photo: On Photography and Social Media*. New York: Verso Books, 2019.

Kang, Cecilia. "The Man Deciding Facebook's Fate." *New York Times*, March 8, 2019, sec. Technology. https://www.nytimes.com/2019/03/08/technology/ftc-facebook-joseph-simons.html/.

Kaplan, Jeremy. "Exclusive: Google Reveals 2,000-Person Diversity and Inclusion Product Team." *Digital Trends*, January 9, 2020. https://www.digitaltrends.com/news/google-diversity-inclusion-champions-announcement-ces-2020/.

Kaven, Dmitri, Haley Willis, Evan Hill, Natalie Reneau, et al. "Day of Rage: How Trump Supporters Took the U.S. Capitol." *New York Times*, June 30, 2021. https://www.nytimes.com/video/us/politics/100000007606996/capitol -riot-trump-supporters.html/.

Kendi, Ibram X. *How to Be an Antiracist*. New York: One World, 2019.

Kingsley, Patrick. "New Zealand Massacre Highlights Global Reach of White Extremism." *New York Times*, March 15, 2019, sec. World. https:// www.nytimes.com/2019/03/15/world/asia/christchurch-mass-shooting -extremism.html/.

Koopman, Colin. *How We Became Our Data: A Genealogy of the Informational Person*. Chicago: University of Chicago Press, 2019.

Levinas, Emmanuel. *Humanism of the Other*. Trans. Nidra Poller. Chicago: University of Illinois Press, 2003.

———. *Totality and Infinity*. Trans. Alphonso Lingis. Pittsburgh: Duquesne University Press, 1969.

Lopez, German. "Pizzagate, the Fake News Conspiracy Theory That Led a Gunman to DC's Comet Ping Pong, Explained." *Vox*, December 8, 2016, sec. Policy and Politics. https://www.vox.com/policy-and-politics/2016/12 /5/13842258/pizzagate-comet-ping-pong-fake-news/.

Lytle, Julie Anne. "Virtual Incarnations: An Exploration of Internet-Mediated Interaction as Manifestation of the Divine." *Religious Education* 105, no. 4 (2010): 395–412.

Mac, Ryan, Kellen Browning, and Sheera Frankel. "The Enduring After-life of a Mass Shooting's Livestream Online." *New York Times*, May 19, 2022. https://www.nytimes.com/2022/05/19/technology/mass-shootings -livestream-online.html/.

MacFarquhar, Neil. "Many Claim Extremists Are Sparking Protest Vio-lence. But Which Extremists?" *New York Times*, May 31, 2020, sec. U.S. https://www.nytimes.com/2020/05/31/us/george-floyd-protests-white -supremacists-antifa.html/.

"Mapping Prejudice." University of Minnesota Libraries. https://www .mappingprejudice.org/. Accessed January 31, 2021.

Massey, Douglas, and Nancy A. Denton. *American Apartheid: Segregation and the Making of the Underclass*. Cambridge, MA: Harvard University Press, 1993.

Mathiesen, Thomas. "The Viewer Society: Foucault's Panopticon Revisited." *Theoretical Criminology* 1, no. 2 (1997): 215–34.

McCormack, Michael Brandon. "Left to Their Own Devices: Black Youth, Religion, and Technologies of Living." *Black Scholar: Journal of Black Studies and Research* 52, no. 3 (2022): 52–62. DOI: 10.1080/00064246.2022.2079069. Published online July 31, 2022.

McWhorter, Ladelle. *Racism and Sexual Oppression in Anglo-America: A Genealogy*. Bloomington: Indiana University Press, 2009.

Meeker, Mary. "Internet Trends 2015." Presented at the Code Conference, KPCB, 2015.

——. "Internet Trends 2019." Presented at the Recode by Vox's 2019 Code Conference, June 11, 2019. https://www.youtube.com/watch?v=G_dwZB5h56E/.

Meisenhelter, Jesse. "How 1930s Discrimination Shaped Inequality in Today's Cities." *National Community Reinvestment Coalition* (blog), March 27, 2018. https://ncrc.org/how-1930s-discrimination-shaped-inequality-in-todays-cities/.

Merleau-Ponty, Maurice. *Phenomenology of Perception*. Trans. Colin Smith. London: Routledge, 1962.

Mervosh, Sarah. "Distorted Videos of Nancy Pelosi Spread on Facebook and Twitter, Helped by Trump." *New York Times*, May 24, 2019, sec. U.S. https://www.nytimes.com/2019/05/24/us/politics/pelosi-doctored-video.html/.

Meyer, Birgit. "Religious Sensations: Why Media, Aesthetics, and Power Matter in the Study of Contemporary Religion." Inaugural Lecture, Free University, Amsterdam, October 6, 2006. https://www.researchgate.net/publication/241889837_Religious_Sensations_Why_Media_Aesthetics_and_Power_Matter_in_the_Study_of_Contemporary_Religion/.

Mitchell, W.J.T. *Seeing Through Race*. Cambridge, MA: Harvard University Press, 2012.

——. "There Are No Visual Media." *Journal of Visual Culture* 4, no. 2 (2005): 257–66.

——. *What Do Pictures Want? The Lives and Loves of Images*. Chicago: University of Chicago Press, 2005.

Mitchell, William J. *The Reconfigured Eye: Visual Truth in the Post-Photographic Era*. Cambridge, MA: MIT Press, 1992.

Morgan, David. *The Embodied Eye: Religious Visual Culture and the Social Life of Feeling*. Berkeley: University of California Press, 2012.

———. "The Look of the Sacred." In *The Cambridge Companion to Religious Studies*, ed. Robert A. Orsi, 296–318. New York: Cambridge University Press, 2012.

———. "Mediation or Mediatisation: The History of Media in the Study of Religion." *Culture and Religion* 12, no. 2 (2011): 137–52. https://doi.org/10.1080/14755610.2011.579716/.

———. *Protestants & Pictures: Religion, Visual Culture, and the Age of American Mass Production*. New York: Oxford University Press, 1999.

———. *The Sacred Gaze: Religious Visual Culture in Theory and Practice*. Berkeley: University of California Press, 2005.

Morris, Errol. *Believing Is Seeing: Observations on the Mysteries of Photography*. New York: Penguin, 2011.

Mulvey, Laura. "Visual Pleasure and Narrative Cinema." *Screen* 16, no. 3 (October 1, 1975): 6–18. https://doi.org/10.1093/screen/16.3.6/.

Nayar, Pramod K. *Citizenship and Identity in the Age of Surveillance*. Delhi: Cambridge University Press, 2015.

Nir, Sarah Maslin. "How 2 Lives Collided in Central Park, Rattling the Nation." *New York Times*, June 14, 2020, sec. New York. https://www.nytimes.com/2020/06/14/nyregion/central-park-amy-cooper-christian-racism.html/.

Noble, Safiya Umoja. *Algorithms of Oppression: How Search Engines Reinforce Racism*. New York: NYU Press, 2018.

Oliver, Kelly. *Witnessing: Beyond Recognition*. Minneapolis: University of Minnesota Press, 2001.

Olson, Hope A. "Mapping beyond Dewey's Boundaries: Constructing Classificatory Space for Marginalized Knowledge Domains." *Library Trends* 47, no. 2 (1998): 233–54.

O'Shea, Keith, Darran Simon, and Holly Yan. "Dylann Roof's Racist Rants Read in Court." CNN, December 14, 2016, sec. US. https://www.cnn.com/2016/12/13/us/dylann-roof-murder-trial/index.html/.

Ott, Kate. *Christian Ethics for a Digital Society*. Lanham, MD: Rowman & Littlefield, 2019.

Ovide, Shira. "Facebook Invokes Its 'Supreme Court.'" *New York Times*, January 22, 2021, sec. Technology. https://www.nytimes.com/2021/01/22/technology/facebook-oversight-board-trump.html/.

Pariser, Eli. *The Filter Bubble: How the New Personalized Web Is Changing What We Read and How We Think.* New York: Penguin Books, 2011.

Parker, Kim, Rachel Minkin, and Jesse Bennett. "Economic Fallout from COVID-19 Continues to Hit Lower-Income Americans the Hardest." Pew Research Center, September 24, 2020, sec. Social & Demographic Trends. https://www.pewresearch.org/social-trends/2020/09/24/economic-fallout -from-covid-19-continues-to-hit-lower-income-americans-the-hardest/.

Paybarah, Azi, and Brent Lewis. "Stunning Images as a Mob Storms the U.S. Capitol." *New York Times*, January 7, 2021, sec. U.S. https://www .nytimes.com/2021/01/06/us/politics/trump-riot-dc-capitol-photos .html/.

Pettman, Dominic. *Infinite Distraction.* Cambridge, UK: Polity Press, 2016.

Plate, S. Brent. *Religion and Film: Cinema and the Re-creation of the World.* New York: Columbia University Press, 2017.

Raymond, Chris. "So What Do You Think of Facebook Now?" *Consumer Reports*, March 15, 2019. https://www.consumerreports.org/social-media /what-do-you-think-of-facebook-now-survey/.

Ritchin, Fred. *Bending the Frame: Photojournalism, Documentary, and the Citizen.* New York: Aperture, 2013.

Rogers, Katie. "Protesters Dispersed with Tear Gas So Trump Could Pose at Church." *New York Times*, June 2, 2020, sec. U.S. https://www.nytimes .com/2020/06/01/us/politics/trump-st-johns-church-bible.html/.

Sack, Kevin, and Alvin Blinder. "No Regrets from Dylann Roof in Jailhouse Manifesto." *New York Times*, January 5, 2017. https://www.nytimes.com /2017/01/05/us/no-regrets-from-dylann-roof-in-jailhouse-manifesto .html/.

Said, Edward W. *Orientalism.* London: Routledge & Kegan Paul, 1978.

Sartre, Jean-Paul. "Black Orpheus." In *Race*, ed. Robert Bernasconi, 115–42. Malden, MA: Blackwell, 2001.

Satariano, Adam. "'Right to Be Forgotten' Privacy Rule Is Limited by Europe's Top Court." *New York Times*, September 24, 2019, sec. Technology. https://www.nytimes.com/2019/09/24/technology/europe-google -right-to-be-forgotten.html/.

Schroer, Markus. "Visual Culture and the Fight for Visibility." *Journal for the Theory of Social Behaviour* 44, no. 2 (2014): 206–228. https://doi.org/10 .1111/jtsb.12038/.

Schultz, Howard, and Rajiv Chandrasekaran. "Upstanders: The Mosque across the Street." Starbucks Stories & News, September 14, 2016. https://stories.starbucks.com/stories/2016/upstanders-the-mosque-across-the-street/.

Shirky, Clay. *Here Comes Everybody: The Power of Organizing without Organizations.* New York: Penguin, 2008.

Silva, Christianna. "Mississippi Lawmakers Vote to Remove Confederate Emblem from State Flag." National Public Radio, June 27, 2020, sec. America Reckons with Racial Injustice. https://www.npr.org/2020/06/27/884306925/mississippi-lawmakers-clear-path-to-remove-confederate-emblem-from-state-flag/.

Simanowski, Roberto. *Data Love: The Seduction and Betrayal of Digital Technologies.* New York: Columbia University Press, 2017.

Simon, Darran. "Trayvon Martin's Death Sparked a Movement That Lives On Five Years Later." CNN, February 26, 2017. https://www.cnn.com/2017/02/26/us/trayvon-martin-death-anniversary/.

Simonite, Tom. "What Really Happened When Google Ousted Timnit Gebru | WIRED." *Wired*, June 8, 2021, sec. Backchannel. https://www.wired.com/story/google-timnit-gebru-ai-what-really-happened/.

Sobieszek, Robert. "Historical Commentary." In Alfred Stieglitz Center, *French Primitive Photography.* New York: Aperture, 1970.

Solomon-Godeau, Abigail. *Photography after Photography: Gender, Genre, History.* Durham, NC: Duke University Press, 2017.

Sontag, Susan. *On Photography.* New York: Picador Books, 1977.

——. *Regarding the Pain of Others.* New York: Farrar, Straus, and Giroux, 2003.

Southall, Ashley, and Johanna Barr. "Derek Chauvin Trial: Chauvin Found Guilty of Murdering George Floyd." *New York Times*, April 20, 2021, sec. U.S. https://www.nytimes.com/live/2021/04/20/us/derek-chauvin-verdict-george-floyd/.

Stadig, Britt. *Telling Stories / Stories That Tell.* http://tellingstoriesstoriesthattell.com/. Vanderbilt University, 2018. Photographs by Amanda McCadams.

Sullivan, Shannon. *Good White People: The Problem with Middle-Class White Anti-Racism.* Albany: SUNY Press, 2014.

Swasey, Benjamin, Alana Wise, and Elena Moore. "Congress Reconvenes after Pro-Trump Mob Brings Chaos to the Capitol." National Public

Radio, January 6, 2021, sec. Capitol Insurrection Updates. https://www
.npr.org/sections/congress-electoral-college-tally-live-updates/2021/01/06
/954028436/u-s-capitol-locked-down-amid-escalating-far-right-protests/.

Sweney, Mark. "Amazon TV Ad Features Imam and Vicar Exchanging
Gifts." *The Guardian*, November 16, 2016, sec. Media. http://www
.theguardian.com/media/2016/nov/16/amazon-tv-ad-imam-vicar
-exchanging-gifts/.

Sydell, Laura. "The Father of the Internet Sees His Invention Reflected Back
through a 'Black Mirror.'" *Morning Edition*, National Public Radio, February 20, 2018. https://www.npr.org/sections/alltechconsidered/2018/02
/20/583682937/the-father-of-the-internet-sees-his-invention-reflected
-back-through-a-black-mir/.

Tagg, John. *The Burden of Representation: Essays on Photographies and Histories*. Minneapolis: University of Minnesota Press, 1993.

——. *The Disciplinary Frame: Photographic Truths and the Capture of Meaning*. Minneapolis: University of Minnesota Press, 2009.

Taylor, Alan. "Images from a Worldwide Protest Movement." *The Atlantic*,
June 8, 2020, sec. In Focus. https://www.theatlantic.com/photo/2020/06
/images-worldwide-protest-movement/612811/.

Thompson, Stuart A., and Charlie Warzel. "Twelve Million Phones, One
Dataset, Zero Privacy." *New York Times*, December 19, 2019, sec. Opinion. https://www.nytimes.com/interactive/2019/12/19/opinion/location
-tracking-cell-phone.html/.

Threadcraft, Shatema. "North American Necropolitics and Gender: On
#BlackLivesMatter and Black Femicide." *South Atlantic Quarterly* 116,
no. 3 (July 2017): 553–79. https://doi.org/10.1215/00382876-3961483/.

Timberg, Craig, Elizabeth Dwoskin, and Reed Albergotti, "Inside Facebook, Jan. 6 Violence Fueled Anger, Regret over Missed Warning Signs."
Washington Post, October 20, 2021. https://www.washingtonpost.com
/technology/2021/10/22/jan-6-capitol-riot-facebook/.

Tomlinson, John. *The Culture of Speed: The Coming of Immediacy*. Thousand
Oaks, CA: Sage Publications, 2007.

Traina, Cristina L. H. *Erotic Attunement: Parenthood and the Ethics of Sensuality between Unequals*. Chicago: University of Chicago Press, 2011.

Trayvon Martin Foundation. "SHOP." Accessed March 1, 2021. https://www
.trayvonmartinfoundation.org/shop/.

Tufekci, Zeynep. *Twitter and Tear Gas: The Power and Fragility of Networked Protest*. New Haven, CT: Yale University Press, 2017.

Turkle, Sherry. *Alone Together: Why We Expect More from Technology and Less from Each Other*. New York: Basic Books, 2017.

Vazquez, Maegan, and Paul LeBlanc. "Proud Boys: Trump Refuses to Condemn White Supremacists at Presidential Debate." CNN, September 30, 2020, sec. Politics. https://www.cnn.com/2020/09/30/politics/proud-boys-trump-white-supremacists-debate/index.html/.

Wade, Lisa. "How 'Benevolent Sexism' Drove Dylann Roof's Racist Massacre." *Washington Post*, June 21, 2015. https://www.washingtonpost.com/posteverything/wp/2015/06/21/how-benevolent-sexism-drove-dylann-roofs-racist-massacre/.

Warzel, Charlie, and Stuart A. Thompson. "They Stormed the Capitol. Their Apps Tracked Them." *New York Times*, February 5, 2021, sec. Opinion. https://www.nytimes.com/2021/02/05/opinion/capitol-attack-cellphone-data.html/.

Waters, Sonia. "All Visual, All the Time: Towards a Theory of Visual Practices for Pastoral Theological Reflection." *Pastoral Psychology* 65, no. 6 (2016): 849–61. https://doi.org/DOI 10.1007/s11089-016-0711-7/.

Waxman, Olivia B. "George Floyd's Death and the Long History of Racism in Minneapolis." *Time*, May 28, 2020, sec. History, Civil Rights. https://time.com/5844030/george-floyd-minneapolis-history/.

Wells, Liz. *Photography: A Critical Introduction*. London: Routledge, 2015.

Winnubst, Shannon. "After Modernity: Whose? Which? When? And, Perhaps Most of All, How?" *Syndicate*, Symposium on Signs and Wonders, December 11, 2018. https://syndicate.network/symposia/theology/signs-and-wonders/.

WITNESS. "WITNESS: Documenting Human Rights with Video." https://www.witness.org/. Accessed July 23, 2021.

Yancy, George. *Black Bodies, White Gazes: The Continuing Significance of Race in America*. 2nd ed. Lanham, MD: Rowman & Littlefield, 2016.

———. "Dear White America." *New York Times*, December 24, 2015, sec. Opinionator. https://opinionator.blogs.nytimes.com/2015/12/24/dear-white-america/.

Yuan, Li. "Mark Zuckerberg Wants Facebook to Emulate WeChat. Can It?" *New York Times*, March 8, 2019, sec. Technology. https://www

.nytimes.com/2019/03/07/technology/facebook-zuckerberg-wechat
.html/.

Zarroli, Jim, and Avie Schneider. "Deluge Continues: 26 Million Jobs Lost in Just 5 Weeks." *Morning Edition*, National Public Radio, April 23, 2020. https://www.npr.org/sections/coronavirus-live-updates/2020/04/23/841876464/26-million-jobs-lost-in-just-5-weeks/.

Zuboff, Shoshana. *The Age of Surveillance Capitalism: The Fight for a Human Future at the New Frontier of Power*. New York: PublicAffairs, 2019.

Zylinska, Joanna. *Nonhuman Photography*. Cambridge, MA: MIT Press, 2017.

INDEX

Illustrations are indicated by page numbers in *italics*.

GPSR Authorized Representative: Easy Access System Europe, Mustamäe tee 50, 10621 Tallinn, Estonia, gpsr.requests@easproject.com

www.ingramcontent.com/pod-product-compliance
Lightning Source LLC
Chambersburg PA
CBHW032129020426
42334CB00016B/1097